EXPLORATIONS IN SOCIOLOGY

British Sociological Association conference volume series

*Published by Macmillan

Families and Households

Divisions and Change

Edited by

Catherine Marsh
sometime Professor of Quantitative Methods
University of Manchester

and

Sara Arber
Professor of Sociology
University of Surrey

MACMILLAN

First published 1992 by
MACMILLAN PRESS LTD
Houndmills, Basingstoke, Hampshire RG21 2XS
and London
Companies and representatives
throughout the world

ISBN 0–333–56533–9 hardcover
ISBN 0–333–63353–9 paperback

A catalogue record for this book is available
from the British Library.

10   9   8   7   6   5   4   3   2
03   02   01   00   99   98   97   96   95

Printed and bound in Great Britain by
Antony Rowe Ltd
Chippenham, Wiltshire

Contents

List of Figures

List of Tables

vii

Preface to the 1995 Reprint

The paperback edition of *Families and Households: Divisions and Change* is dedicated to Catherine Marsh, who tragically died of breast cancer on 1 January 1993.

The chapters in this book are based on presentations at the British Sociological Association annual conference held at the University of Surrey in April 1990 on the theme of *Social Divisions and Social Change*. The conference was organised by Sara Arber, Roger Burrows, Nigel Gilbert and Catherine Marsh. Three other volumes of conference papers have been published by Macmillan: *Women and Working Lives: Divisions and Change* (edited by Sara Arber and Nigel Gilbert), *Consumption and Class: Divisions and Change* (edited by Roger Burrows and Catherine Marsh), and *Fordism and Flexibility: Divisions and Change* (edited by Nigel Gilbert, Roger Burrows and Anna Pollert).

I would like to thank the contributors to this volume, Anne Dix and Sheila Tremlett of the British Sociological Association, and Tim Farmiloe of Macmillan, for all their encouragement and support.

Sara Arber
May 1994

Notes on the Contributors

Sara Arber is Professor in the Department of Sociology at the University of Surrey. She is co-author (with Jay Ginn) of *Gender and Later Life* (1991) and (with Maria Evandrou) of *Ageing, Independence and the Life Course* (1993), and has published widely on inequalities in women's health, social stratification, informal care and gender issues in later life.

Walter Bien is Head of the Department for Social Reporting at the German Youth Institute. He received a degree in computer science in 1971 (Fachhochschule Niederrhein), a master's degree in education in 1976 (RWTH Aachen) and a PhD in psychology in 1981 (RWTH Aachen). His main research interests are network theory, network methods, social relations and the family.

Alan Carling trained in mathematics and teaches sociology in the Department of Interdisciplinary Human Studies at the University of Bradford. He has been busy applying rational-choice theory to a variety of cases of social division. This research effort is reported most fully in *Social Division* (1991).

Wai-yee Cheung works in the Postgraduate School of Medicine and Health care at the University of Swansea. She graduated in sociology in the Chinese University of Hong Kong in 1984, and obtained a PhD from the Department of Sociology and Anthropology at University College, Swansea.

Rosemary Collins is a research associate at the Socio-Legal Centre for Family Studies at the University of Bristol and tutor with the Open University. Her PhD was on the conjugal division of domestic labour and she has worked on various court-based research projects. Her current research is on unmarried parents and the law. She is co-editor (with Paul Close) of *Family and Economy in Modern Society* (1985).

Graham Crow is a Lecturer in Sociology at the University of Southampton. He read PPE at Oxford and then did a PhD in sociology at Essex. He is co-editor (with Graham Allan) of *Home and Family* (1989) and author of various papers on sociological theory, family farming and community studies. He is also co-editor (with Michael Hardey) of a volume on *Lone Parenthood* (1991).

Jay Ginn is researching the careers of social services staff at the National Institute of Social Work. She was previously a researcher at the Sociology Department, University of Surrey, focusing first on gender differences in the resources of older people and their carers, and more recently on the employment of mid-life women. She is co-author (with Sara Arber) of *Gender and Later Life* (1991).

Michael Hardey is a Lecturer in the Department of Sociology and Social Policy, University of Southampton. He previously worked as a sociologist in a Department of Health research unit at the University of Surrey. He is co-author (with Graham Crow) of *Lone Parenthood* (1991) and (with Anne Mulhall) of *Nursing Research: Theory and Practice* (1994), and has conducted research on lone-parent families, social policy and organisational aspects of health care.

Susan Hutson is a contract researcher in the Department of Sociology and Anthropology at University College, Swansea. Her recent research has centred on youth issues. She has taken a particular interest in unemployment, juvenile justice and youth homelessness.

Gill Jones is a Senior Research Fellow at the Centre for Educational Sociology at the University of Edinburgh. Her research has centred on the influence of family and other institutions on young people's transition to adulthood. She is co-author (with Claire Wallace) of a book on the effects of recent social policy on young people's relationships with their families of origin.

Jan Marbach is a member of the Department for Social Reporting at the German Youth Institute. He received his master of arts in sociology from the University of Munich (FRG) in 1976. His research interests and recent publications deal with social networks of families.

Catherine Marsh (1951–93) was Professor of Quantitative Methods at the University of Manchester, a post held jointly in the Department of Sociology and the Department of Econometrics and Social Statistics. She was the author of two books and several articles on research methods, and she published widely on issues such as hours of work, the family and unemployment. She had a long-term interest in the population census, was the first Director of the Census Microdata Unit, University of Manchester, and was co-author (with Angela Dale) of *The 1991 Census User's Guide* (1993).

Volker Schmidt is a Research Fellow at the Centre for Social Policy research at the University of Bremen. His research interests include the effects of social change on the stability (or fragility) of major social security institutions. Recently he has begun work on an international project on 'local justice' which investigates how institutions allocate scarce resources. He is co-author of *Neue Technologien –verschenkte Gelegenheiten?* (1991).

Robert Templeton received his bachelor's and master's in sociology from the University of California, Riverside, in 1987 and 1989 respectively. He is currently employed at the German Youth Institute (DJI) as a research assistant. His research interests are computer simulation of sociological theory, artificial intelligence and networking.

Richard Wall is a Senior Research Associate with the Cambridge Group for the History of Population and Social Structure. He has published many books and articles about population history, including *Household and Family in Past Time* (with Peter Laslett) and *The Upheaval of War* (with Jay Winter). His current research includes the study of the incidence of illness and malnutrition among English schoolchildren in the twentieth century.

1 Research on Families and Households in Modern Britain: An Introductory Essay[1]

Catherine Marsh and Sara Arber

FAMILIES AND SOCIAL DIVISIONS

Each generation imbues family life with myths about the golden era of the past and the breakdown of norms in the present. The explanation for this continued sense of social decay is probably a very basic confusion between processes of history and those of personal biography. But whatever the cause, this strong sense that people have of the changes that are taking place to the family, irrespective of any social reality, makes it especially hard for researchers to assemble and interpret the facts about social change in family composition and structure, and in values and attitudes towards the family. The ease with which explanations can slip into 'common sense knowledge' makes it particularly important to support statements about change with empirical evidence collected across time rather than with data collected in the present and contrasted with an assumption about the past.

The aim of this volume is to present a conspectus of recent research into the changing structure of the family and of living arrangements. The contributions address both the folk myths and social constructions themselves (the category 'lone parent' for example) and the real behavioural patterns which lie behind the ideological curtains (who gives money to whom inside the household, for example).

The volume is subtitled 'Divisions and Change'. Most of the papers were first presented at the 1990 British Sociological Association Annual Conference, whose principal theme was the changing bases of social division. Conference contributors, whether writing about the family or the workplace, about ill health or leisure, tended to interpret 'divisions' as conflictual divisions of interest. Many sociologists believe that the old bases for social division, the class system in particular, are giving way to new bases for social conflict and social inequality.

1

These new divisions arise because of the profound changes taking place as manufacturing economies restructure and promote differences based on consumption and lifestyle; two of the companion volumes to this book deal precisely with these themes (Gilbert, Burrows and Pollert, 1991; Burrows and Marsh, 1991). Furthermore, gender as a basis for stratification and division was widely discussed, and formed the basis of a third volume (Arber and Gilbert, 1991).

But 'division' in the sense of differentiation and demarcation of varying roles for individuals within an institution need not imply conflict. For a long time, it was in this sense that divisions were perceived in the family. For Parsonian sociologists, the family was a social institution which had a special role to play in the development of capitalism, and it became more specialised and differentiated as industrialisation proceeded (for example Smelser, 1967). Parsons himself (1949) believed that external specialisation rested on divisions of function *within* the family, especially between instrumental and expressive roles. Principal among the instrumental functions was the participation in the formal economy, the production of goods and services for exchange; principal among the expressive functions were having and bringing up children, problem-solving and emotion and tension management. These different roles tended in practice to be mapped on to differences between breadwinner and housewife, or men and women.

This specialisation of function within allowed the family to function as a unit with respect to the outside world, according to Parsonian sociologists. Others, not so strongly committed to the teleology of such a view, nonetheless agreed that the family acted as the basic building block of social stratification (Goldthorpe, 1983) or as the emotional shelter where the working class could take refuge from the struggle between classes being waged at work (Humphries, 1977).

Differentiation, however, always contains the potential for conflictual social division. There has been widespread criticism of this view of the family, much of it, ironically, pointing to tensions and problems within the family of which Parsons himself was well aware. These alternative views have concentrated on divisions in the conflictual sense within the family. First, there have been those who have sought to show the family, far from being the harmonious haven of emotional calm, as the epicentre of violent battles between personalities. From the 'anti-psychiatrists' (Laing and Esterson 1964; Laing and Cooper, 1964), who saw in family interactions the roots of mental illness, to radical feminists uncovering the degree of physical violence that occurs within marriage (Dobash and Dobash, 1980; Finkelhor, 1983), one persistent theme has been the family as a site of power games in which the subordinate can lose vital parts of their self-identity.

Some of the critiques of the Parsonian view of the family stepped into the discarded functionalist framework but merely reversed some of the labels. Instead of viewing the family as the principal glue sticking industrial capitalism together, some feminists prefer to see it as the principal institution propping up patriarchy (for example, Delphy, 1977). They would deny the mutual supportive performance of expressivity within the family, seeing rather a conflict between the sexes: emotional and sexual 'servicing' is demeaning, with undertones of prostitution, done by women for men. Theorists of patriarchy tend to view the domination of women by men as a cross-historical truth (Millett, 1969), and have had a relatively hard time accounting for major processes of change in family forms and the treatment of women in different types of society (Acker, 1989). Ironically, such theories tend to be particularly weak in accounting for the very change of which they are a core part, namely the surge of egalitarian ideology particularly since the Second World War. Work has begun to broaden the concept to rise to such criticisms (Walby, 1989; Waters, 1989), but in so doing, such theorising seems to have robbed the term of its conceptual clarity.

A second strand of research and criticism has accused sociologists of paying insufficient attention to the more routine aspects of day-to-day living which occur inside families. One important strand of this materialist critique has been mounted by economists. On the one hand, Marxist economists during the 1970s began to outline a vocabulary to describe and quantify the nature of unequal domestic exchange (for example Seccombe, 1974; Gardiner, 1976). On the other hand, a group of American economists began asking somewhat similar questions about the organisation of housework, child-care and meal preparation; the New Home Economics, as this approach is termed (Berk and Berk, 1983), injected the conventional theoretical apparatus of microeconomics into discussions of the family. Becker, its ideological leader, accepts the idea of the family as a unit performing functions for all members in it, but sees the needs of members in more materialistic terms than did the Parsonians (Becker, 1981). The simplifying assumptions that people might be expected to act in their own calculative self-interest in forming families and exchanging labour has proved a fruitful generator of research hypotheses, and has provoked lively and stimulating debate.

But sociologists have also had a significant part to play in this shift towards a more materialist conception of the family. One of their major contributions to the study of domestic life has been to turn the attention away from the family and focus it instead on the household. There has been an important research effort into the actual behaviour and cooperation between the people who co-reside, much of it aimed at establishing empirically whether the people who lived together engaged in behaviour which could be described as 'strategic', indeed implicitly testing the assumptive basis of much of the New Home Economics (Gershuny, 1982; R. E. Pahl, 1984; Morris, 1990). This empirical approach to documenting the divisions of labour within and between households has eschewed functionalist claims about what the family or household is 'for', and has concentrated on the more humble task of documenting what each member actually 'does'.

This spirit is reflected in many of the chapters in this volume. Jones considers transitions in board payments of young people without getting drawn into whether the family as an institution actually encourages this process of independence; Wall documents changes in patterns of support of elderly people without declaring the family either to be succeeding or failing in some metaphysical function; Bien and colleagues document whom people eat with or borrow money from, and whether they regard them as family members or not.

Yet the question of whether there are underlying conflicts of interest among these co-residing individuals lurks not far beneath the surface. One chapter in this volume addresses the issue directly.

Carling attempts to take the economists' principal theoretical tool – rational choice theory – and see how far it illuminates the decision by married women to participate in the labour market, and to what extent it still leaves room for traditional sociological explanations in terms of roles and values. It takes seriously the idea that people may make narrowly economic calculations about how much they need to be paid before it is worth their while going out to work in the formal economy. He constructs two formal models of how individuals band together in households. An Exchange model, adapted from Roemer's neo-Marxist theory of exploitation, predicts a division of labour and domestic exploitation of women without recourse to the notion of role. By contrast, a Chicken model assumes the public character of the goods provided in the household, and predicts an outcome in which gender ideology helps to determine the existence of a conventional division of labour in the household. Couples where the wives earn more than the husbands form a critical test for these theories, and Carling concludes that on balance the Chicken model outperforms the Exchange model.

The idea that women in fact lose out in many family and household relationships is a theme that other contributors to the volume take up. Arber and Ginn, for example, show that elderly women are particularly disadvantaged when it comes to arrangements that are made to care for frail elderly people. And Collins makes it abundantly clear how little most unmarried women get from taking the fathers of their children to court to try to extract maintenance payment from them. But no contributor argues that exploitation of women is the *raison d'etre* of the prevalent family forms, nor that improvement in women's situation would be advanced by their breakdown.

DEFINING KEY TERMS

Before outlining the major changes in family and household composition in recent years, we must address some difficult definitional and measurement issues.

The twin concepts of 'family' and 'household' are often treated as interchangeable; the Pocket Oxford Dictionary, for example, defines a family as 'parents, children, servants etc. forming a household'. But social science has made an important conceptual contribution (yet to be recognised by the Pocket Oxford!) in distinguishing between them.

One of the reasons for this lack of conceptual clarity must be because, in many instances, the two empirically coincide. There are, however, interesting and important questions to ask about the non-overlapping areas: those who live in the household but who are not family on any social or legal definition, and those considered as bound by the obligations of family in popular regard or in law but who do not co-reside. As several contributors to this volume argue, if the two are not defined separately, important areas of social reality and social change become impossible to identify. Crow and Hardey in particular show that official thinking on parenthood has been muddled precisely because it has not clarified whether the objects of policy were families or households.

We next outline some of the problems researchers face when trying to operationalise these fundamental concepts.

Household

It is easiest to start with the concept of a 'household'. On the face of it, the term is descriptive (compared to the normative and legal load carried by the term 'family'). However, the word always denotes something more than the people who happen to be together in a particular house at a particular time. Household membership denotes communal activity; on censuses, the benchmark for much research, this activity was traditionally eating. Although census schedules are not subject to a high degree of control over the operation of definitions, the household was explicitly defined in the 1971 British census, to group together people who ate at least one meal a day together (or who shared common catering). However, there was widespread feeling during the 1970s that this definition missed an important group of people, often young, single people sharing a flat, who had a real identity in common; they may not have found it convenient to eat together, but they took part in leisure activities together (Todd, 1987). Since the 1981 census, the definition of a household has been extended to bring in people who shared a living room. Having changed the census definition, the household surveys like the General Household Survey, the Family Expenditure Survey and the Labour Force Survey were brought into line.

The change had an important effect on the household surveys. Todd (1987) followed up a sample of complex family units in the Employment Department's regular Labour Force Survey to investigate the effect of the change. She estimates the result was an apparent small decline in the total number of households of 0.6 per cent, and a corresponding small rise in the average size of a household. However, the number of households in the privately rented sector fell by 17 per cent. The change also had an important effect on a large number of basic housing indicators. It reduced the number of people who appeared to be sharing amenities, for example; under the new definition, individuals previously classed as sharing kitchens were more likely to be classified in the same household. Perhaps most interesting of all was the very unstable nature of the group investigated: households which were not coterminous with families changed very frequently, forming and reforming much faster than other households.

Head of Household

Traditionally, one person within the household, however defined, is identified as the 'head'. While eating and watching television are the key activities defining the existence of households, the concept of a household head in official surveys turns upon property, gender and age relationships. The head of household is not the person who decides what to eat or which TV channel to watch; it is the person in whose name the accommodation is owned or rented. In government surveys, however, whenever this person is a married women, if her husband is present, he takes precedence (see Atkinson, 1971, pp. 116–7; OPCS, 1989b, p. 248). The justification for such a procedure has never been fully spelled out, and has been criticised as sexist by feminist sociologists (Oakley and Oakley, 1979); the charge of 'ageist' might also be added in our increasingly sensitive times, since when two people have equal claim the older takes precedence.

The historical evolution of the definition of household head is probably linked to the empirical overlap between family and household. This might explain both use of a term such as 'head' with its strong normative overtones, and the outrage expressed by those who suspect a covert reference to a 'pater familias' figure. But, sexism aside, there are still two important reasons for social researchers wanting to identify a 'head of household'. The first relates to inferring characteristics about the whole household from information about an indicator person in it; the income and occupation of such household heads have routinely been used to indicate the social position and likely life chances of other people in the household. This procedure is easy to justify when only one household member has access to a job or income. When there are two or more earners, and when we cannot justify collecting indicative information on more than one household member, we need empirical evidence to tell us who has most influence on the life chances of other household members. We should note, however, that there is good reason to think that the income or occupation of the husband may have more influence even on the wife's own life chances for some research topics (Marsh, 1986; Arber, 1990; 1991). The feminist critique of 'heads of household' has tended in effect to push for an overly individualistic position, in which the most important influence on someone's current position is assumed to be that person's own past experience.

The second reason for needing the concept of a household head is to identify relationships between household members. In theory, it should be possible to define a household and then discover the relationship between every pair of persons in that household. In fact, an attempt was made to redesign the 1991 census form to collect household relationship information in precisely that way: respondents were asked to list all household members and then identify the relationship of each member to each other. However, around one quarter found the task impossible, and the experiment was abandoned. Even with skilled interviewers, no major survey collects full relational information in this way. The use of a head of household as a relational reference point therefore continues for its operational ease. However, there are well-recognised problems with this approach. The most important is the propensity of the method for concealing secondary family units within the household: one does not know, for example, whether, when one finds two lodgers in a household, one male and one female, if they are married to each other.

The concern expressed by some members of the public at the use of the term 'head of household' on the census form led to census authorities diplomatically deciding from 1981 onwards to allow adult householders freedom to put anyone they wished to as the head of household first on the census form (or to nominate two joint heads), and then to relate every other person to the first-named person; only if the first-named person was under sixteen or a visitor would the census office move further down the list to identify someone as a head of household. It is striking that the overwhelming majority of husband and wife pairs still nominated the husband as the first person on the form; 98 per cent of men with spouses were placed first on the census form, and virtually nobody insisted on being described as a 'joint head of household'[2]. Allowing respondents to decide who is the householder is a somewhat arbitrary solution to the problem. A sociologically preferable alternative might be to select the partner who is deemed 'occupationally dominant' (Erickson, 1984), which is usually taken to be the one with the higher status job.

Marital Status

Another area bedevilled by conceptual and definitional issues is marital status. This variable is collected as an indicator of the respondent's current status on many surveys, yet it should more properly be treated as a variable summarising marital history. The categories 'single, married, cohabiting, separated, divorced, widowed' are used in most surveys, but they do not imply a unidirectional scale. We do not know from the state a person is currently in which states they have been in before (except that they have all been through the 'single' state). The classification miserably fails the logical test of a good coding scheme, whereby categories should be mutually exclusive and exhaustive. An individual can be married and separated; divorced and widowed (by different partners); cohabiting and any of the others. Those who live with a partner of the same sex are not readily catered for by the scheme.

The standard census categories are single, married (first marriage), remarried, divorced and widowed. Until the 1991 Census, there was no way of explicitly identifying people cohabiting with partners. However, information on the relationship to head of household in 1981 revealed that people who were described as single were often also the 'husband/wife' of the head of household, and sometimes people explicitly said they were 'lovers' or similar. In all 2.4 per cent of people with partners described themselves in this apparently contradictory way, and were recoded by the census offices as *de facto* spouses. However, this was not a satisfactory arrangement, as many common-law spouses coded their relationship with the head of household simply as 'other unrelated'. The unreliability of the procedure was revealed in the quality checks done on the 1981 census; in the 1981 Post-Enumeration Survey, the level of agreement between the follow-up survey and the census return for *de facto* spouse was 85 per cent, and 'other unrelated' was only 64 per cent (cited in Penhale, 1990). Furthermore, the census produced a very high estimate of the number of lone parents, especially the number of men who seemed to have sole responsibility for looking after their children. As a result of pressure, the census wording changed in 1991 to allow a category of 'living together as a couple' on the question about relationship to head of household. However, it will be hard to make clear statements about between-census trends as a result, because an unknown amount of cohabitation was hidden in the 1981 census. It is likely that the results of the 1991 census will show the official cohabitation rate rising and the number of lone parent households dropping dramatically!

Economic activity Status

Adults in the population are traditionally subdivided into those who are economically active in the labour force, whether employed or unemployed, and those, such as students, housewives, the permanently sick and the retired who are 'economically inactive'. The distinction is fundamentally subjective, as the boundary between unemployment and non-employment relates to the individual's intention and desire for work. Moreover, people often resist social researchers' binary classification urges, often moving into and out of considering themselves as retired (for example White, 1983). Indeed, as Schmidt argues in his chapter, one of the key features of recent economic change has been a dissolving of some of the formal definitions of employment status, and a loosening of employment contracts, not always to the benefit of the employees. The norm, certainly as far as women are concerned, is multiple economic activities, being both housewife and paid worker.

Once again, it is instructive to consider how the variable is collected and coded on the census. On the census schedule, the form-filler is explicitly permitted to multiple code the question about economic activity status. Yet the census offices make hardly any use of this potentially interesting data; they have a computer algorithm which assigns priority for various statuses. The category of student in full-time education, for example, takes priority over being a part-time worker. In this way, the extent of the involvement of students in casual and Saturday employment is disguised – a theme which Hutson and Cheung discuss in this volume.

Family

Finally we must consider the meaning of the more complex term 'family'. Almost all societies recognise such primary kinship groups whose members are related either genetically or by marriage. Unlike the household, the family is a unit which has a formal, legal definition in most societies: laws specify who may marry whom, and lay down rights of inheritance to property and titles. However, although families may be universally found, societies differ widely in the content of their laws – about relations who are forbidden to marry, or the line of descent through which property should pass. The discipline of social anthropology has put the most work into defining the vast array of ways in which different societies organise such ties of blood, marriage and descent, and has supplied us with a host of somewhat legalistic terms to define the biological and legal ties very precisely.

But as well as involving biological or legal ties, family relationships are fundamentally social, prescribing norms of behaviour for members. The core unifying notion is probably the idea of obligation (Finch, 1989): to say that someone is a family member is to accept social rules defining the obligations which different family members owe to each other.

This theme runs through many of the chapters of this book, as different authors examine its reality in family and household practices, and try to assess the sort of obligations that kin and householders impose on each other, and how these may have been changing. Wall's challenging argument is that the obligation to care for elderly people within families has actually grown, at least inasmuch as the number being cared for in this way has grown; Carling considers the extent to which the exchange represented by the domestic division of labour in house-holds is reciprocal or characterised by features of exploitation; Jones' analysis of young people living at home casts doubt on the traditional idea of long-term reciprocity of exchange within families.

Insight can be gained into the relative importance of biological, legal and social components of the family by considering the case of men who are biological fathers but who have not adopted the legal ties of marriage. Collins, in her chapter, reports on a study in Nottingham and Bristol of unmarried mothers who had attempted to use the legal apparatus to make a claim against the child's natural father for main-tenance. These men may have been fathers in a biological sense, but only half had shown any commitment to fatherhood in the social sense. She shows that many of the mothers based the presentation of their cases on the nuclear family model, but that magistrates and judges alike relied on the model even more than the mothers, often offering rights of access to fathers who had not applied for them, and approving the mother's and children's claims to financial support in all cases, at least in principal. The law, it would appear, continues to regulate and prescribe about norms of behaviour even for those who have not entered into a formal legal contract of marriage.

Despite the everyday definition of a family which extends beyond the household group, most official definitions are much more restricted, and based on the family as a co-resident group. The standard census definition of a family revolves centrally around the existence of chil-dren, although no limit is put on the age of the children, so long as they are co-resident. A census family consists of either a married couple and any co-resident never-married children, a lone parent together with his or her never-married children, or grandparents with grandchil-dren if no parents are present. Many other official definitions of 'family' have been propounded for various purposes; there are, for example, two alternative definitions commonly used with census data (Penhale, 1990). A further popular definition of a family is the unit entitled to means-tested Income Support from the Department of Social Secur-ity.

The choice of family or household as the unit of analysis can have dramatic effects on research findings. In 1988, for example, the official British poverty series changed from family-as-benefit-unit to a house-hold unit. The result was a reduction of the number of the poor (those with incomes of below half the average) from around 5.5 million to less than 4.5 million. Single adults, both with and without children, were more likely to be in poor family units but rich households

(Johnson and Webb, 1989). Until more is known about income sharing within these different units, the choice of unit for studies such as these is arbitrary, and thus open to the charge of political manipulation.

Cohabiting couples cannot on the standard census definition form families, and neither can single people. But even modifying the strict census definition to recognise unmarried couples, 15 per cent of people in the 1981 census were still classified as 'not in a family'. This percentage was larger among people aged 60 or more (22 per cent) but it was also quite substantial among those under the age of sixty (11 per cent). However, these percentages represented a *reduction* on the equivalent numbers not living in conventional families in the 1971 census: 16 per cent overall, 25 per cent among people aged 60 or more and 12 per cent among the rest.[3]

The stress on couples and dependent children as the focal points of a family has encouraged a relative neglect of those who do not fall neatly into families so defined. Two major groups in this respect – elderly people and lone person householders – are of growing numerical importance, and receive central attention in this volume. The authors have also taken care not to view the people officially classified as 'not in families' as if they were pathological. In much past writing about elderly people, for example, their dependent status has been stressed, and the focal point of discussion has been the problems of elaborating systems of social support for them. Similarly, lone householders are often treated as objects of social concern, as people lacking important sources of social support. The reality of both stereotypes will be called into question in this volume.

There is a tension in all social research between changing definitions to keep up to date with real social change, and keeping the definitions sufficiently constant to document the changes that do occur. Our discussion of these definitional difficulties has highlighted the extent to which our knowledge about the family and households is constrained by our ability to conceptualise clearly and measure accurately these fundamental social relationships.

SUMMARY OF TRENDS IN FAMILY AND HOUSEHOLD CHARACTERISTICS

We can now turn to considering some of the major changes in families, households and living arrangements that have taken place in recent decades.[4] We concentrate principally on changes that have taken place in Britain, but it is striking how very similar changes have affected most industrialised countries since the end of the Second World War.

Demographic Changes

Changes in the age structure of the population since the Second World War must be the starting point for changes affecting the family. The size of particular birth cohorts varies widely; the number of people born in 1965 in Britain, for example, was 50 per cent higher than the number of people born in 1977. These fluctuations are relatively new arrivals on the social stage (Easterlin, 1987), compared to a past in which family size was more influenced by mortality than fertility rates (Werner, 1987); Figure 1.1 shows these fluctuations over the past 150 years.

Whether the oscillations will get wider or not is still an open matter which demographers debate hotly, but there is no doubt that they are self-reproducing across generations; providing that the age of child-bearing and the desired numbers of children remain fairly constant, a large birth cohort now will produce a large cohort 25–30 years on. The influence of size of peer group on various social outcomes can be very great, affecting competition for housing, education and jobs. (Trends in fertility rates are considered separately below.)

By contrast, the number of elderly people in the British population has risen rapidly over the last thirty years, with the fastest growth among the very elderly. The relative rise of the elderly as a proportion of the total population is in part due to the cumulative effects of declining fertility rates. But it is also a welcome result of rising life expectancy, and as such is a social achievement of rising standards of living and of health care. The rate of growth of the elderly population is not projected to rise as fast in the next twenty years; between 1987 and 2011, the numbers aged 65-84 are only expected to rise between 3 and 4 per cent (CSO, 1989, Table 1.2), although the rate of growth of those aged 85 or over will continue to be more rapid.

The implications of any growth in the numbers of very elderly people for the cost of health and welfare services will depend on whether longer life means improved or worsening health. There are two conflicting schools of thought about this. Some believe that incapacity is delayed to a later age as life expectancy increases, and is compressed into fewer years before death (for example Fries 1980, 1989). The explanation given for this 'compression of morbidity' thesis is usually

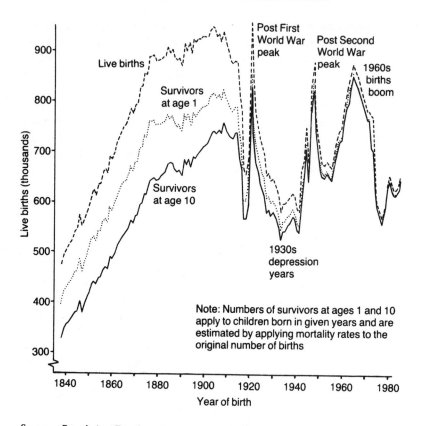

Source   *Population Trends*, vol. 48, Summer 1987 (HMSO) p. 6; Crown Copyright

Figure 1.1   Live births and numbers of survivors at ages 1 and 10, 1838–1985,
England and Wales

improved material conditions and lifestyles. On the other hand, others
suggest that the major determinant of increasing longevity is medical
intervention, and that increased life expectancy has been accompanied
by an extension of the period of illness and disability (for example
Verbrugge 1984a, 1989b). Surey evidence certainly documents rising
morbidity rates, but this may just reflect greater awareness of chronic
diseases and thus higher reporting of such conditions in surveys
(1989b).

    Whatever the cause, Arber and Ginn explore an important and hith-
erto unnoticed consequence of these trends in Chapter 5. Women have

the advantage over men of living longer, but they are more likely to be frail and disabled, and are more likely than men to have to rely on care from adult children rather than their spouses. Most elderly people prefer to be cared for in their own home. There is a big difference between care as of right under the normative structure of reciprocity that they might expect from a spouse and the care from adult children and other providers. The title of Arber and Ginn's paper is 'In Sickness and in Health', yet they show that there is a wide gap between the percentage of elderly disabled men and women who can rely on this ideal sort of care.

Economic Changes

The percentage of women participating in the formal economy has grown steadily in all industrialised countries this century. The change has been greatest among married women, 10 per cent of whom worked in 1931, increasing to 30 per cent in 1951 and to around two thirds at the end of the 1980s. The average amount of time which women spend out of the labour market has declined correspondingly, to the point where both sexes can be expected to spend most of their middle four decades of life active in the labour market. This is taken by some to indicate a long-run trend towards women having similar working patterns to men (for example Kiernan and Wicks, 1990). However, if we take a longer time perspective we may find that the unusual period was in fact the early twentieth century, the nadir of the female participation rate when compared either with mid-twentieth or the mid-nineteenth century (Hakim, 1980). Secondly, few women have continuous labour market experience; only five per cent of mothers remain continuously employed throughout their working lives (Walters and Dex, 1991). Third, although the percentage working continues to increase, most of the increase is in part-time work, and the hours which part-timers (overwhelmingly females) work have been dropping at the same time as men's hours have been rising (Marsh, 1991).

The extent to which Britain is typical of other European countries here is a matter for debate. On the one hand, Britain seems exceptional in some respects; it lies near the extreme (second only to Holland) in the proportion of women engaged in part-time work, and at the extreme in the long hours worked by men (Marsh, 1991). Yet it shares with most countries in Europe an increasing tendency towards 'flexibility' in employment practices. One important aspect of this has been a growing differentiation in working time arrangements. The cause of this trend has often been put down to the need of firms for greater adaptability of labour in order to respond to modern product markets, but there is a reciprocal relationship between changes in working time and changes in household forms and needs. The growth of single person households and the rise in female participation rates in particular, as well as the general decline of work as the single dominating sphere in people's lives, leads to varied working time demands by different people and those at different stages of their life course. On the basis of German experience, which has already gone a lot further in changing conventional working time policies than has Britain, Schmidt argues for a new and more equitable working time policy which would be more responsive to these changed household arrangements.

Second, the end of the long post-war economic boom and the rise of unemployment have had the effect of compressing the years of economic activity both at entry to and exit from the labour market throughout Europe. At the younger end, it has made it very much harder for young people to get onto the job ladder. Labour market push factors have contributed to the proportion of young people staying in full-time education; many of them, it is argued, are merely 'parking' in educational institutions to await better labour market conditions (Gambetta, 1987). Whatever their reason for being in full-time education, many of these young students also work part-time, as Hutson and Cheung's chapter shows. They demonstrate that many Saturday workers in the Swansea area in South Wales are educational achievers who come from affluent home backgrounds. Employers eagerly seek them for their flexibility and because they are bright, entrepreneurial and upmarket. Saturday working can give wages for one day comparable with the weekly allowance on government training schemes, as well as providing work experience and possible access to full-time jobs. It is not available to young unemployed people because benefit legislation makes part-time working unprofitable. Thus Saturday working may be increasing divisions between young people, and also changing power relationships between young people and their parents.

At the other end of the labour market, economic difficulties are increasingly squeezing people over the age of fifty into early retirement (Laczko *et al.*, 1988). Combining this with the change in the proportion of elderly people, conjures up the image of a new stage of life appearing: a twenty-year period of relatively good health after retiring from the labour force. We shall return to this when we consider household formation below.

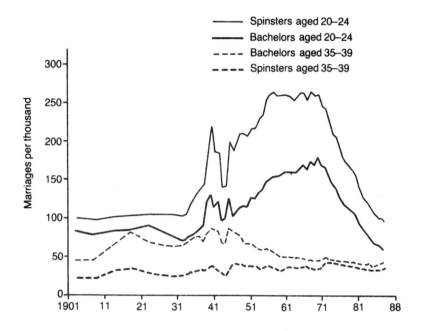

Source   Population Trends, no. 61, Autumn 1990 (HMSO) p. 2; Crown Copyright

Figure 1.2   First marriage rates, 1901–88, England and Wales

Marriage and Child-bearing

One way of assessing changes in the popularity of marriage is to look at the rates of first marriage per thousand population; trends in first marriage rates over the twentieth century in Britain are shown in Figure 1.2. These rates were stable in the early decades of the century, declining somewhat during the 1930s, prompting anxious tracts about the danger of population decline which the authors believed to be such an irreversible part of the modern condition that stringent policy steps needed to be taken if it was to be corrected (for example Leybourne and White, 1940).

The Second World War (unlike the First World War and perhaps in part because of memories of it) produced a flurry of first marriages among the younger age groups (Figure 1.2). Since then, two very different periods can be discerned. Between 1945 and the mid-1960s, marriage underwent a long and sustained boom in popularity. Then, at the end of the 1960s, there was a reversal of the trends, and marriage rates began an equally long and sustained decline. By the end of the 1980s, marriage rates had regained their nineteenth century levels, and there is no evidence of any halting of the decline. The age of first marriage, which had been declining pretty consistently since the 1920s, also began to rise in the early 1970s, and is still rising. Indeed, for a growing minority of people, current trends suggest that they may never marry – 21 per cent of men and 17 per cent of women are estimated not to marry by 50 (Kiernan and Wicks, 1990, p. 6).

Trends in fertility follow a very similar trajectory. Figure 1.3 shows the average number of births to women at two different ages, by 30 and by age 45, over the past 150 years. After a decline of birth rates in the 19th century and first half of the 20th century, the fertility rate began to go up after the Second World War. At the same time, people had their children earlier and spaced their births closer to one another (Cherlin and Furstenberg, 1988). This took many demographers and social analysts by surprise after the population fears of the 1930s; while experts predicted a certain amount of pent-up demand for children after the war, no-one predicted the prolonged hike in fertility rates which followed. However, after the mid-1960s, birth rates dropped to less than replacement level in many European countries. In Britain the nadir was in 1977, since when there has been slight increase, taking fertility rates almost back to replacement level.

As marriage and fertility rates have fallen, cohabitation rates and the rate of births outside marriage have risen. Figure 1.4 shows the trend in the percentage of all births which were illegitimate over the past 150 years. After falling to a low of around 4 per cent at the turn of the century, it stabilised (apart from substantial increases around the two World Wars). But in the past 30 years it has risen steeply to around one in five births. The rising numbers of common-law marriages necessitated a change in the methodology of ascertaining marital status in research enquiries, as we noted in the previous section. This is a trend throughout the industrialised world, and might be interpreted as part of the process of secularisation. Yet the rise in cohabitation is not sufficient to compensate for the decline in marriage rates; as we shall see shortly, there is also a growth in the percentage of single person households.

One important question is the extent to which cohabitation and child-rearing outside marriage act as the modern equivalent of marriage and legitimate fertility. There seem to be two international models for the trends in cohabitation and births outside marriage. The first

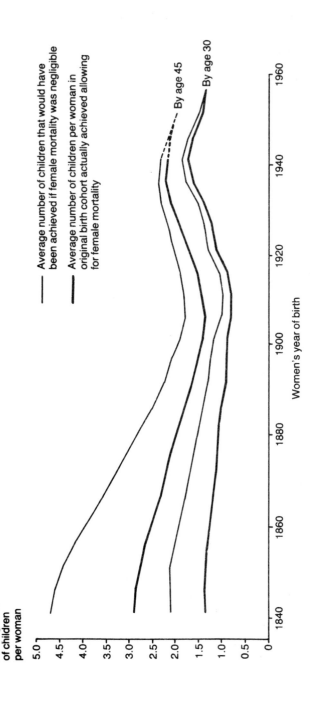

Source *Population Trends*, vol. 48, Summer 1987 (HMSO) p. 9; Crown Copyright

Figure 1.3   Average number of births to women achieved by ages 30 and 45 with and without allowance for female mortality, England and Wales

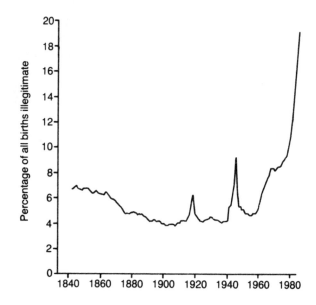

Source   Population Trends, vol 48, Summer 1987 (HMSO) p. 7; Crown Copyright

Figure 1.4   Percentage of all births which were illegitimate, 1838–1985,
England and Wales

is the Swedish model; nearly half of all children are now born outside
marriage in Sweden, but nearly all are born to parents who live together
in a relatively stable living pattern, and the Swedish rate of teenage
pregnancy is uniquely low (Hoem and Hoem, 1988). The patterns in
the United States of America are markedly different, however: the
birth rate outside marriage is lower (one in four births) but is disproportionately composed of teenage mothers, and very few of the children
will be cared for by two parental figures throughout their childhood
(Wilson, 1985). The Swedish trends can more easily be interpreted
as cohabitation being a modern equivalent of conventional marriage,
whereas the US patterns are more widely interpreted as bearing the
hallmarks of poverty and social disorganisation.

Which model best fits the British experience? Concentrating on the
factors which have produced the rapid *growth* in the birth-rate outside
marriage, Ermisch (1990) argues that the trends represent in part at
least, the substitution of cohabitation for early marriage. On the other
hand, other aspects of the *pattern* of cohabitation suggest that the
US model is more fitting; the typical length of a period of cohabitation

is short, for example, resolving quickly into marriage or separation (Haskey and Kiernan, 1989), and less than half the births outside marriage in Britain in 1985 were registered by two parents living at the same address (Kiernan, 1988). Collins (in this volume) makes a useful contribution to this debate by conducting an ecological analysis of the social correlates of areas with high rates of extra-marital childbearing in Britain. She demonstrates a very high association between areas with high rates of birth outside marriage, and those with high unemployment rates and high crime rates, which hardly argues for the Swedish model of changing institutional fashions.

As rates of first marriage have dropped, rates of divorce have risen. In the 1950s, when stricter laws on divorce prevailed, with one party having to show fault in the other party's behaviour, the divorce rate was fairly stable at a little over two per thousand marriages. The 1969 Divorce Reform Act liberalised the law, enabling either party to obtain a 'no-fault' divorce after three years. In the period leading up to and following the Act, the rate climbed to a new plateau of around 13 per thousand marriages, and it has stabilised at this level during the 1980s. But this way of expressing divorce rates does not take into account the changing age-structure of the married population. When age-specific rates are calculated, if the divorce rates prevailing in the mid-1980s were to continue, it has been estimated that around one in three marriages are likely to end in divorce, and that this will affect one in five children (Haskey, 1989a).

Household Composition

There is a contemporary myth about the golden age of an extended family in the past, when three generations and other relatives were more likely to be living under one roof, and when the family played a greater role in economic and emotional support for its members than it does today. This myth has been slowly and systematically dispelled by a wealth of careful historical scholarship emanating from the ESRC Cambridge Group for the History of Population and Social Structure. The world we have lost, Laslett (1965) argues, is not quite the one many imagine. Indeed, the early development of the nuclear family has been linked with the origins of English individualism, as far back as to the thirteenth century, and linked with the development of mobile wage labour (Macfarlane, 1978).

In this volume, Wall, a principal researcher in the Cambridge Group, reminds us that over much of north-west Europe in the past, households

Table 1.1   Distribution of the population by different types of household
(column percentages)

	1961	1971	1981	1987
Married couples with no children	18	19	20	22
Married couples with dependent children	52	52	49	44
Married couples with independent children only	12	10	10	12
Living alone	4	6	8	10
Lone parent with dependent children	2	3	5	5
Other households	12	9	8	8

Source   Kiernan and Wicks 1990, Figure 8; their data is drawn from the
1961 and 1971 censuses and the 1981 and 1987 General Household Survey

were small in size and simple in structure. Apart from one major change
– the exit of co-resident domestic servants as a common household
pattern – there has been little change in the modal household structure
type: married couples with or without dependent children. But of
course, family relationships can extend beyond the boundaries of the
household. As well as needing to know who lives with whom, it is
important to know the proximity of other kin. By carefully tracing
the evidence about the existence of kin either in the household or
nearby, Wall finds, surprisingly, that there has been little change in
the distance of nearest relatives since the mid-nineteenth century.

During the last 25 years, there have been some marked changes
in household composition, as Table 1.1 shows. The largest changes
have involved a decline in the type of living arrangement whereby
the nuclear family overlaps with the household; the proportion of
people living in households composed of a married couple with dependent children declined from 52 per cent during the 1960s to 44 per
cent by 1987. The growth area has been the individualised household
forms: adults living alone and lone parent households, both of whom
accounted for more than twice the number in 1987 than they did in
1961.

Part of the explanation is the growth of elderly lone person households. However, the proportion of non-elderly single person households has also more than doubled, from 4 per cent in 1961 to nine
per cent in 1987 (Kiernan and Wicks, 1990: 19). This household type
is a new one; in the past, young people generally moved from their
parents' home into their marital home, sometimes interspersed with
a period living with an employer, but more often without an indepen-

dent stage in-between. But rising divorce rates and rising purchasing power of young people has led to the formation of more single person households and to the construction of new types of dwellings for this category.

How should we view this new household type, composed of people of working age without either dependents or people on whom they obviously depend? The census view is that they are 'people not in families', on the presumption that families always co-reside. This term almost suggests that they are a deprived group of people. But it is interesting to ask instead whether these younger single householders achieve the same sort of emotional and financial support, friendship and so on, as adults 'living in families'. Bien and his colleagues, on the basis of extensive data gathered by the Youth Institute in München, attempted to find out precisely how people living in varieties of household settings achieved various family tasks. Their conclusion (see chapter 9) is interesting; adults aged between 18 and 59 who lived on their own in the former Federal Republic of Germany had a profile of social and emotional support that was very similar to those living in a family.

The proportion of people living in households composed of a married couple with an independent child (aged 16 or more in the labour market, or aged 19) declined from twelve per cent to ten per cent between 1961 and 1971, but remained static during the 1970s and then began to rise again during the 1980s, both in Britain (Table 1.1) and in North America, (Boyd and Pryor, 1988). This phenomenon seems to be a consequence of the collapse that has occurred in the youth labour market during the 1980s, which greatly reduced young people's ability to form independent households. The desire for independent housing has, however, probably not declined. For some young people dependent on state benefits, single parenthood may have become one way of obtaining independent housing in depressed labour market conditions.

However, it would be wrong to assume that young people who live with their parents are uniformly dependent on them or that the flow of value is uniquely from parent to child. Using data from a longitudinal study of young people's experience in Scotland, Jones' contribution to this volume casts doubt on this model. Jones argues that there is a significant degree of economic reciprocity between parent and child in the household in the short-term: many, especially poorer, households are dependent to an important extent on the contribution that young adults make.

CONCLUSION: POLICY IMPLICATIONS?

This volume represents a set of scientific contributions to the debate about family and household forms in modern Britain. But none of the contributions can stand aside from the cause and effect relationship between such forms and social policy. Social policy institutions operate with a view of what the family is, how people co-reside and give economic support to each other, but they also operate with a normative view of what these relations *should* be, and as such can actually influence predominant patterns of behaviour.

The British system of social security has grown organically. Much of it was developed after the Second World War, in a period when family and household forms were different from those of today. If we cast our eyes broadly over the spectrum of social policy institutions in Britain today, there appears to be some disarray over both what is and what should be the unit for social policy purposes (Roll, 1991). The taxation and pension systems currently treat the married couple as the unit. The tax system is moving towards individualisation, whereby everyone has an individual tax allowance and takes responsibility for their own taxation arrangements. The pension system, by contrast, is coming under pressure to broaden the group of people who can be considered as dependants. The two major institutions which provide people with income at times of need, the National Insurance system and the means-tested Income Support system, operate with different conceptions of the family. The former, insurance-based system still operates with Beveridge's image of a married couple, an inactive wife and dependent children; broadly speaking, inactive men and cohabiting partners have difficulty getting support from this scheme. However, means-tested Income Support takes a wider definition, and cohabiting partners are treated in the same way as spouses. A little reflection suggests that public expenditure considerations easily account for the differences, and explain some of the pressures to broaden the concept of the family for means-tested benefits even further, to include absent fathers and the parents of young adults; both Jones and Collins in their respective chapters are critical of these attempts by policy makers and enforcers to extend family responsibilities into areas where they may lack both legitimacy and effectiveness. The state is also encouraging a transfer of resources to care for the sick and disabled from institutions into 'the community', seeking to expand the already large amount of caring work which is done not only within co-residential families but also outside them.

Social policy, when it is coherent, can have an important impact on social outcomes. One plausible explanation of the major differences in the proportion of women who work full-time in Britain and France, for example, is the very much better child-care support which exists in France than in Britain (Walters and Dex, 1991). Countries with very similar cultural histories can take different paths if their social policy institutions differ markedly; after nearly half a century of separate social and political development, former West Germany has one of the lowest marriage and fertility rates in Europe, and former East Germany has one of the highest. So the formative power of social policy should not be underestimated.

Yet it cannot be fashioned on incoherent or inappropriate concepts of family and household. If policy-makers have inadequate knowledge of the broad range of different ways in which people conduct the personal and domestic side of their lives, and the way in which these arrangements are changing, it is doubtful whether they will be able to fashion effective or rational social policy. Major transformations have taken place in women's participation in the formal economy, in the youth labour market and in increasing pressures towards smaller households. Sociological research has a great deal to contribute by documenting and helping interpret these major social changes.

Notes

1. We are extremely grateful to David Morgan for his careful and lucid comments on an earlier version of this chapter; they particularly influenced the shape and sometimes even the specific content of the first few pages. We would also like to thank Kath Kiernan and Jo Roll of the Family Policy Studies Centre for their help and encouragement with this chapter.
2. These conclusions come from analysis of *Longitudinal Study* data, which are Crown Copyright; we are very grateful to Angela Dale and Brian Dodgeon for producing these figures.
3. *Ibid.*
4. This section draws heavily on a very useful compendium on changes in family and household forms compiled by Kiernan and Wicks (1990).

2 Short-term Reciprocity in Parent-Child Economic Exchanges[1]

Gill Jones

It is generally argued that the parent-child relationship can only be reciprocal in the long term, in that parents care for their children when they are young, while children care for their parents when they are old, the locus of dependence thus moving from the child to the parent over time (see for example Wall, in this volume, and Finch, 1989). Short-term reciprocity is more likely to occur in other relationships, such as those between siblings or friends. Implicit in such understanding is the notion that reciprocity should be equal and balanced. Thus the relationship between parents and their adolescent children cannot be reciprocal, being based on unequal distribution of power and resources.

This view emphasises notions of dependence and independence which may, however, be the stereotype of parent–child relations rather than the norm. In order to progress beyond stereotypes and assumptions, it is necessary to examine the micro-processes which underlie family interactions. In the case of parent–child relations it is particularly important to understand the processes whereby young people grow up while still in the family home. If families are the production centres of a new generation of adults, then children living in the family home must gradually take increased responsibility for themselves and for others, and thus begin to redress the power imbalance between themselves and their parents.

By reassessing reciprocity in the economic relationship between young people and their parents, this chapter identifies a theoretical basis for understanding the transition to adulthood in economic terms. The word 'child' is used throughout to describe a family relationship and 'young person' to describe an individual.

RECIPROCITY

The transition from dependent child to independent adult takes a long time. If indeed its achievement were defined by the development of total reciprocity in the parent–child relationship, the transition to economic adulthood would take most of the individual life course. It is a process whose beginning is far easier to define than its end.

Economic independence begins with the receipt of a personal income from pocket money or from a part-time job, which allows the child to enter the market place, with the power to buy, to barter and to give. The whole process is stratified by social class, however. The young middle-class receive more pocket money, while the young working-class are more likely to take on part-time jobs before the age of sixteen. The class paths of individuals thus diverge at an early stage. In later adolescence they diverge further, with some young people, mainly middle-class, continuing their studies and maintaining their dependence on their parents, and others, mainly working-class, leaving school as soon as possible and entering the labour market. The class distinction holds for other aspects of the transition to adulthood, too: family formation, for example, occurs earlier for the working-class (Jones, 1988).

Any attempt to understand parent–child reciprocity must be undertaken within this framework. Middle-class children remain dependent longer than those of working-class families, whose culture and needs may determine that their young should become economically 'independent' as soon as they can.

By the time young adults have set up their own households and started to form their own families, their economic relationship with their families of origin will have changed. This does not mean that they have become economically independent, however. As Janet Finch comments:

> It appears that the desired relationship is a very subtle blend of dependence and independence which people often regard as quite difficult to accomplish successfully, although they have a fairly clear idea of what they are aiming for (Finch, 1989, p. 169).

Leonard (1980) described the ways in which mothers in South Wales tried to accomplish this aim and achieve a balance between encouraging independence in their adult offspring and maintaining their dependence (and thus their closeness) through 'spoiling' them after they have left home. Gifts increase the sense of obligation of the receiver, the power of the giver and thus the bond of dependence.

The notion of 'generalised reciprocity' was introduced by Sahlins

(1965). According to Sahlins, we should distinguish between 'balanced' and 'generalised' reciprocity, the former involving immediate and direct exchange; the latter involving no expectation of immediate or equivalent return. Most theories of parent–child relations would suggest generalised reciprocity over the long term. Other possibilities exist, however. First, while the parent–child relationship is usually characterised by long-term reciprocity, this does not foreclose the possibility of some reciprocity also occurring in the short term. Next, the extent to which this should be defined as 'balanced' or 'generalised' may depend on the comparative resources of the child and the parents. The exchanges which take place may not be balanced in objective cash terms, but they may still represent equivalent subjective value in terms of the individuals concerned. In all, the blend of dependence and independence in young adulthood may involve a blending of the forms of reciprocity as well.

Most of the research on the economic relationship between young people and their parents has examined the circumstances in working-class families, and particularly families where there is unemployment (Allatt and Yeandle, 1986; Wallace, 1987; Hutson and Jenkins, 1989). The emphasis here has been on the ways in which families negotiate a young person's contribution to the home and the amount of financial help they receive according to a 'notion of fairness' (Allatt and Yeandle, 1986). Changing circumstances require renegotiation.

Power and dependence in families are related not only to age and gender relations but also to an individual's attachment to the labour market and individual income. The power differential between parents and adult children therefore varies according to the labour market positions of both parties. Thus, the child's exclusion from the labour market 'increases the dependence of the child on the parents and renders the problem of parental–child relations even more acute' (Harris, 1983, p. 216). In the terms of Hutson and Jenkins (1989), the families 'take the strain' when their young cannot get jobs, thus presenting a coping front to the outside world. Similarly, the father's own employment status can affect the power relations between himself and employed adult children. Financial contributions from the child to the parent depend both on the power to give and the willingness and/or need to receive and may therefore increase where the child in is employment and earning an income, while the parent is unemployed (Jones, 1991). The negotiation of dependence or independence may thus occur in a context of economic necessity, and reciprocity may increase with poverty. McKee (1987) has shown how some households 'band together' to maximise their resources and pool those that are scarce.

PARENT–CHILD ECONOMIC TRANSACTIONS

The economic relationship between young people (defined here as between sixteen and twenty) and their parents goes beyond purely financial transactions to exchanges in kind, sometimes of a nature which can be converted into cash. Economic help from parents to their children which comes within this category includes the provision of a home, help in providing access to jobs and labour market information. Financial help, in the form of pocket money, clothing allowance, or payment for household tasks, is only one side of the equation. Similarly, though young people may pay their parents for their board, the work many do in the home may also form an integral part of the domestic economy. This chapter can consider only some elements of the economic relationship between parents and children.

The payment of board money to parents is a common phenomenon. Though it has an educational aspect (Hutson and Jenkins, 1989), it may be imbued also with symbolic significance. The practice is expected by parents to 'keep a young person straight' (Wallace, 1987) and may be concerned with issues such as responsibility and the negotiation of identity (Hutson and Jenkins, 1989).

Financial help from parents to children may also have a symbolic aspect. It may, as Leonard (1980) suggested, be a means of keeping adult children close, giving them a sense of obligation to reciprocate in the longer term. However, practice differs according to the families' circumstances (Wallace, 1987; Allatt and Yeandle, 1986; Leonard, 1980). Corr and Jamieson (1989) found that though a common sum for pocket money among 16 year-olds was £5 per week, the amount, and expectations, varied with the financial circumstances of the family. It was less taken for granted in working-class families.

Unsurprisingly, patterns of parental help in cash and in kind have been found to change with age as a child grows up, though the nature of the variation is not entirely clear. Wallace (1987), for example, has indicated the decreasing importance of pocket money and the increasing importance with age of indirect support from parents to young people in the form of food, clothing or cigarettes. Corrigan (1989), on the other hand, suggests that the opposite process may occur: he found that clothing transactions, in particular in mother–daughter relations, may be replaced in adolescence with cash gifts. It is not clear which system gives more responsibility to the young.

Corr and Jamieson (1989) provide some examples of the complex interactions which take place. In one reported case study, a girl who had been receiving pocket money took on a part-time job and her pocket money was stopped. When she lost this job, she did not go back onto pocket money again, but began instead to receive payment for jobs done around the house. It seems that there are circumstances where the process of transition, once underway, cannot be reversed.

The research cited above indicates that economic transactions between young people and their parents may involve payments in cash or in kind; that patterns vary with the economic circumstances of both young people and their families; and that they vary with age, thus forming part of the transition to adulthood. In order to understand the nature of the economic exchanges between young people and their parents, to consider the value of terms such as dependence or reciprocity, we need thus to take account of these patterns and the sources of their variation.

The economic element in parent–child relations is enacted in the context of emotional relationships and often complex family dynamics, and the implicit meanings of economic exchanges are hidden from the survey researcher. The analysis makes use of explicit patterns in seeking to understand the nature of economic exchanges and the interaction between types of exchange.

THE DATASET

The Scottish Young People's Surveys (SYPS) include a series of longitudinal cohort datasets. This chapter makes use of data from the first of these cohorts, a 10 per cent sample of all pupils in their fourth year at secondary school in Scotland during 1983–4. They were first surveyed in spring 1985 (when their average age was 16.75 years) and subsequently in spring 1986 and in autumn 1987 (average ages 17.75 years and 19.25 years respectively). For convenience respondents are subsequently described here as aged 16 in 1985, aged 17 in 1986 and aged 19 in 1987, but it should be remembered that this is a simplification. At the first sweep of the cohort in 1985, response was 81 per cent of the target sample of around 8000 cases. There has since been some attrition but by the third sweep, in 1987, response was still 60 per cent of the 1985 target sample (Ritchie, 1989). The cohort dataset thus provides a large, representative sample of young people in Scotland, allowing comparison according to the basic social divisions of social class, employment status and gender, and additionally allowing the study of change with age.

I have limited the study to cases where young people were living with their parents. The possibility of reciprocity in the relationship between parents and their children living away from home is not therefore considered here, partly for practical reasons. All reported findings are statistically significant unless otherwise stated.

In researching economic transitions using the SYPS, it became necessary to overcome a design problem. We know from the data where respondents were living in 1985, but cannot immediately tell, however, whether those who were paying board or doing housework in 1987 were still living with their parents. This is because the sample was divided into subsets: one subset was asked about board payments and housework while the other was asked where they lived. It is possible, though, to identify indirectly those living in the parental home in 1987. The characteristics of those 32 per cent who have left the parental home are known (Furlong and Cooney, 1990; Jones, 1990): many are in full-time education or living as married. These two groups can be excluded from the analysis of the 1987 data, and Figures 2.4 and 2.5 are based on subsetting in this way. However, some are likely to have left for other reasons, mainly in order to look for or take up work away from home: we can eliminate them too from the 1987 subset by selecting only those whose home town or village has not changed since they were living at home in 1985. In doing this, we are also unfortunately selecting out a few individuals who have moved with their families, but the result is that we can be more confident that, for example, board money paid in 1987 is not in practice the housing cost of an independent household. This approach has been taken where sample sizes permit (Figures 2.2, 2.6, 2.7 and 2.8).

PARENTAL HELP IN CASH

In 1986 and again in 1987 the same respondents were asked: 'Over the past year, have your parents regularly helped you with money?' Figure 2.1 shows the proportion of the cohort who received financial help from their parents in the last year. The question was asked in 1986, when they were seventeen and again in 1987 when they were nineteen. It appears from the figure that daughters are marginally more likely to receive financial help from their parents than sons (69 per cent of daughters and 65 per cent of sons overall). The effect of class of origin varies over time: at seventeen, there were no significant class differences but by nineteen years, clear class differences appear. While the overall proportion receiving financial help from parents has decreased, the decrease is far greater for the children of manual workers. In consequence, only about 40 per cent of working-class children received financial help from their parents when they were nineteen, compared with around 55 per cent of the middle class.

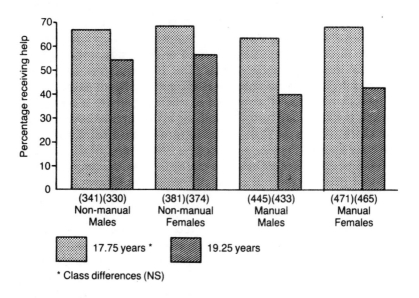

Source   SYPS 1986S, 1987A

Figure 2.1   Financial help from parents at 17 and at 19 years, by sex and father's occupational class

When those in full-time education were excluded in further analysis, class differences (and indeed gender differences) at nineteen years disappeared. About 40 per cent of all nineteen year olds in the labour force received financial help from their parents, regardless of sex or class of origin.

Parental help with money is thus withdrawn as young people become economically independent (Corr and Jamieson, 1989). While young people may still at seventeen years depend on parental help, by the age of nineteen, there is divergence between those who are in employment, and may have been for three years, and those who are still in full-time education and possibly receiving no independent income, although many will in fact have part-time jobs (Hutson, in this volume; Howieson, 1990). Most of those staying in education and receiving parental help are middle-class; working-class children tend throughout adolescence to be much further along the path to 'economic adulthood'.

PAYING BOARD MONEY TO PARENTS

As young people get older and enter the labour market, their contribution to the family economy increases. Once they begin to earn money, even from a part-time job, they are beginning to contribute. Even young children undertakin̖ Saturday jobs can indirectly help out their parents, because by earning, they save their parents in pocket money and perhaps some clothing expenses (MacLennan *et al.*, 1985). Susan Hutson's work, reported in this volume, shows that the same applies to older children.

Labour market entry does not only affect pocket money (Corr and Jamieson, 1989). Once young people leave full-time education, whether or not they are in full-time work, they are expected by their families to pay for their board and keep. SYPS respondents were asked how much they had paid in the previous week towards the cost of board. The amounts varied according to young people's ability to pay: thus those in employment paid more than those who were on youth training schemes, who in turn paid more than the unemployed. (The amounts were usually of £5, £10 or £15 at 16 years and £10, £15 or £20 at 19 years.) The proportion paying in each group varied little, however. Over and above this variation according to ability to pay, patterns varied according to family need: in poorer families (fathers in lower occupational class, fathers unemployed, lone mothers, large families) young people paid more. Gender differences were apparent in the amount paid rather than in the proportion paying (Jones, 1991).

The data in Figure 2.2 show that among sixteen years olds who had left full-time education, 90 per cent of those living with their parents paid board. Those with working-class fathers were more likely to pay board than middle-class children at age sixteen and again at age nineteen (though the class differences were no longer statistically significant among women at nineteen years). Both on leaving school and again at nineteen, the sons of manual workers pay more than sons of non-

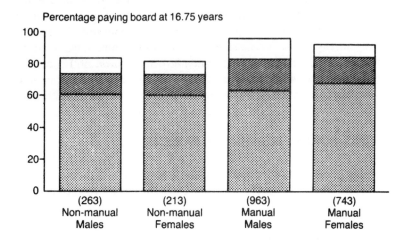

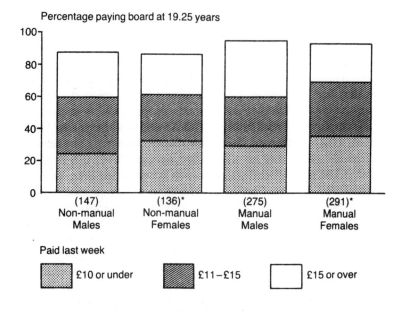

Source   SYPS 1985S, 1987A

Figure 2.2   Paying board at 16 and 19 years, by sex and father's occupational class

manual workers, though class differences diminish with age. While sons paid more than daughters, both paid the same proportions of their income in board money (30 per cent at sixteen and 17 per cent at nineteen years). The semi-arbitrary rates fixed at sixteen seem to become more related to actual earnings with age (Jones, 1991).

The payment of board money appears to be more than purely symbolic, therefore. The amount paid in board money varies both according to the economic circumstances of the family in which the young person lives, and according to the young person's own economic status and age. It is likely that in poorer families, young people are not only paying a higher rate of board money, but are also paying in a higher proportion of the household budget.

PARENTAL HELP IN KIND

The longest-term help given by a parent (at this stage) is in the provision of a home. In early adulthood, young people begin to leave their parents' homes and establish their own households, though the pattern is complex and the process long-drawn out (Jones, 1987, 1990).

At sixteen years, nearly all the SYPS cohort were living with their parents, but by the age of nineteen, many had begun to form households of their own, either with their peers, their partners or alone. Women and the children of non-manual workers were the most likely to have left home, the latter mainly to go to college, and the former also to marry or cohabit (Jones, 1987, 1990). Figure 2.3 thus shows that at nineteen, 82 per cent of men and 71 per cent of women in working-class families, compared with 66 per cent of men and 62 per cent of women in middle-class families, were living with their parents. In practice, it is mainly working-class parents and the parents of sons who are still providing their nineteen year old children with permanent homes, rather than holiday bases.

HELPING IN THE HOME

Sons and daughters may also be able to give help in kind, through carrying out tasks in the home. SYPS respondents were asked how often they had done 'decorating or gardening' and 'cleaning or child-minding' in the last month.

It comes as no surprise to find that the tasks are gendered. Cleaning

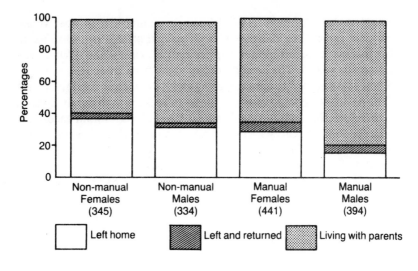

Source SYPS 1987A

Figure 2.3   Whether left home at 19 years, by sex and father's occupational
class

and child-minding were principally done by women (82 per cent of whom did housework three or more times in the last month, compared with only 42 per cent of men). In the case of decorating and gardening the gender difference was, however, relatively small – 50 per cent of women and 61 per cent of men had done decorating or gardening in the last month. Further analysis showed no relationship between doing household tasks and the occupational class of fathers: among young people who have left education and are living with their parents, middle class and working class patterns of housework are the same and equally gendered.

BALANCED RECIPROCITY?

The analysis reported above gives little indication so far that reciprocity is balanced in the parent–child relationship. Certainly, though board money is associated with living at home, it is unlikely that the amount paid by most young people in any way compensates the parents for the actual cost of their keep in the majority of cases (Finch, 1989).

The exception here may be where the family is poor and the young person may be the major breadwinner. Should payments for board be seen as partial reciprocity, supplemented by payment in kind, perhaps in the form of help with housework?

In recent research, Corr and Jamieson (1989) found that some young women felt they should pay less board money than young men, since they helped out in the house. Indeed Wallace (1987) found that while women paid less board money than men, they made up the deficit through payment in kind, principally with housework. These findings suggest that the twin roles of housework and board payments in the economic relationship between children and their parents may differ for men and women.

Does involvement in household tasks bring dispensation from the payment of board money, or should it be regarded as an ancillary form of payment to parents? (Is it either/or, or both?) The answer is not straightforward. First, the relationship between decorating and gardening, and payment of board money (Figure 2.4), is neither statistically significant nor substantively interesting for either sex. In other words, respondents may do decorating and gardening, but this does not affect their board payments.

Cleaning and child-minding, however, are another story. There is a small but statistically significant association between housework and board money for both sexes, but stronger for women (Figure 2.4). The relationship is, however, complex and two processes seem to be occurring. On the one hand, the more housework a woman does, the less likely she is to pay any board at all: thus, 12 per cent of women doing more frequent housework paid no board money, compared with only five per cent of those who did cleaning or child-minding less than twice. This finding tends to suggest an element of dispensation. On the other hand, the figure also shows that among men and women who pay board, the relationship between the amount of housework done and the amount of board paid is positive, in that the more housework done the more board money paid. Only 34 per cent of men and 21 per cent of women who did infrequent cleaning or child-minding paid over £15 per week for their board, compared with 42 per cent of men and 29 per cent of women who did the household tasks more often.

Patterns among women vary by class, however, and Figure 2.5 shows that it is only middle-class women who appear to obtain dispensation from board money when they do housework, since those who did household tasks, whether 'cleaning or child-minding' or 'gardening

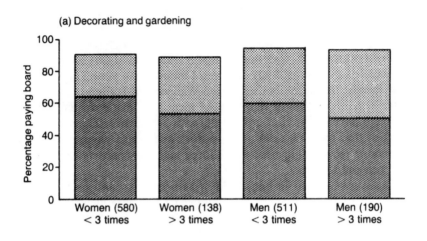

(a) Decorating and gardening

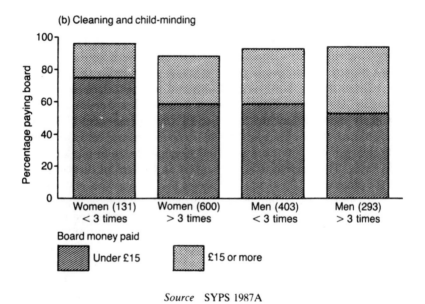

(b) Cleaning and child-minding

Source   SYPS 1987A

Figure 2.4   Paying board at 19 years, by times did household tasks in last month

or decorating' were less likely to pay board money and these negative associations were statistically significant.

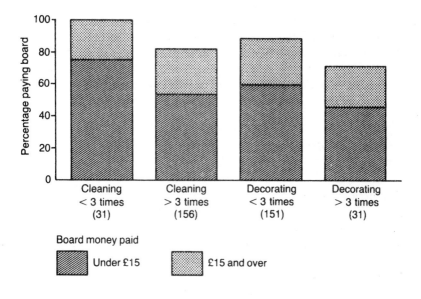

Source SYPS 1987A

Figure 2.5 Paying board at 19 years, by times did household tasks among middle-class women

Middle-class daughters may thus be engaged in a different type of economic relationship with their families from working-class women, or men in either class. Among men, involvement in household tasks is perhaps too infrequent to be worthy of a reciprocal response from the parents. The variation in patterns for women is interesting, though. It raises the question of whether housework is expected of working-class daughters by their parents, and forms a supplement in kind to the cash payments for board, while housework by middle-class daughters is regarded as an alternative to cash payments.

In general, women may be expected to pay both in cash and in kind, while men tend to make their board payments in cash. Gender differences in earnings seem not to be taken into account in these negotiations; even though men and women pay the same proportion of their earnings in board money, young women seem to be obliged to make up the deficit, and thus appear to lose out both in the labour market and in the home in this respect.

This analysis shows the fruitlessness of seeking to put a value either on the contribution a young person makes to the family, or on the benefit they derive from living with their parents. In order to uphold or refute the applicability of the concept of balanced reciprocity in parent–child economic relations, one would have to consider the role and value of contributions in kind as well as in cash, and would have to consider the economic context in which exchanges take place.

THE DEVELOPMENT OF RECIPROCITY AND 'INDEPENDENCE'

The period between Spring 1985 and Autumn 1987 was a period of great change in the lives of the cohort. The move towards economic independence was reflected in their changing economic status – from school to a job, from a youth training scheme to a job, even from a job to child-care. Some young people had already left their parents' homes and moved into accommodation of their own, as students, as parents or as workers. The economic relationships of those living with their parents were also in transition.

The following analysis focuses on cash exchanges. For 1987, the data refer to board money paid at nineteen, and parental help with money in the previous year. For 1985–6, the data refer to board money paid at sixteen, in 1985, and parental help with money over the following year.

Figure 2.6 shows the changing financial relationship between young people who are living at home and their parents at the two dates. Those in full-time education or living as married in 1987 are excluded from this analysis. The figure shows that as young people get older, the proportion receiving financial help from parents decreases and the proportion paying board money increases. One-way help from parent to child becomes less common with age and one-way help from child to parent more common. There appears, though, to be a stage in which two-way exchanges occur, where respondents have been paying board and receiving financial help at the same time.

In practice these stages form part of the transition to adulthood in economic terms. Figure 2.7 shows the individual level process of transition. The different transition routes from left (1985–6) to right

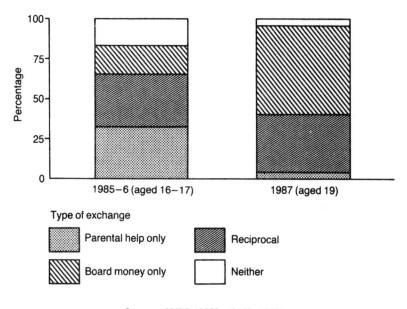

Source SYPS 1985S, 1986S, 1987A

Figure 2.6   Financial reciprocity between young people and their parents
(Among those living at home and not in full-time education in 1987)

(destination in 1987) are shown by the arrows and the groups taking different routes are identified in the centre column. For clarity, 'minority routes', taken by less than five per cent of the subset, have been excluded from the centre column and are not represented by arrows.

Twenty-seven per cent of sons were receiving one-way financial help in 1985; by 1987, most of these had moved either into a two-way relationship with their parents or were solely paying board and receiving no parental help. Those who were in a two-way relationship already in 1985 either continued to be or had moved to solely paying board in 1987. Of those who were solely paying board in 1985, practically none had moved either into a two-way relationship or into a one-way 'dependent' relationship with parents. Where there was no apparent financial exchange between a son and his parents in 1985 (16 per cent), most had begun to pay board and give one-way help to parents in 1987.

By 1987, money was thus generally changing hands between sons and their parents, and increasingly the movement was from parental

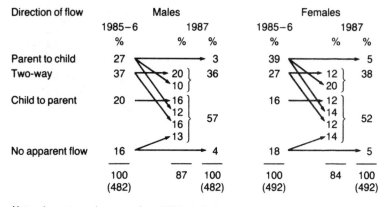

Figure 2.7   Economic transitions, by sex, 16 to 19 years

support alone, through a period of immediate 'reciprocity', towards the payment of board money alone (though this interpretation has to remain speculative, when data are only available for two time-points). Economic 'independence', in these terms, meant increasing responsibility for paying into the family budget rather than taking out of it. Total independence (if defined by no apparent financial inter-actions between young people and their parents) was rare.

The basic pattern for sons holds for daughters too, but there are gender differences in the proportions in each group in 1985 and thus in the route taken between 1985 and 1987. There were practically no gender differences in the destinations at 1987. Women were far more likely than men to be in a dependent relationship with their parents at sixteen–seventeen, and this may be because they were more likely to have remained in full-time education. Most of these had moved into a two-way relationship by 1987. As with men, the majority were paying their parents and receiving no financial help from them at nine-teen years.

The typology of exchanges has thus been placed more clearly in an age context in Figure 2.7. Two-way exchanges appear to represent a transitional stage in the development of economic 'independence'. At this stage, immediate, though not necessarily balanced, reciprocity seems to be occurring. In the next stage, where the young person is paying board but receiving no current financial help from the parents, the concept of short-term reciprocity may be more appropriate, in the sense that the adult child is beginning to pay back for the help provided over time.

Further analysis showed the major (or at least the longer-term) variation to be class, rather than gender, based. In all, 55 per cent of working-class sons and daughters had been in a two-way economic relationship with their parents *at some stage* by the age of nineteen, compared with 41 per cent of middle-class sons and daughters. In other words, sons and daughters go through the same stages between the ages of sixteen and nineteen, though their timing varies. Class differences, on the other hand, persist beyond this period, suggesting that the time-scale of the economic transition to adulthood varies quite considerably between social classes.

It was suggested earlier that reciprocity may increase with poverty. The finding that young people contribute more to the family budget in poorer families (Jones, 1991) suggests that this is to some extent the case. However, it should be stressed that I am referring here to reciprocity at a particular age, rather than at a particular stage in the life course. Since there are class differences in the timing of life course events, the reciprocity observed among the working-class members of the cohort may become apparent over time among the middle class as well.

CONCLUSIONS

The real value of the differentiated concept of reciprocity to this discussion is that it has allowed us to question some previously held assumptions about the parent–child relationship. It makes it possible to examine the nature of the contributions young people make to their parents in cash and in kind, rather than dismiss them as mere tokens. It makes us question other assumptions about the distribution of resources within families. In particular, it brings into focus a grey area between childhood dependence and adult independence and makes us question these very terms.

It becomes clear that adult children, even those living at home with their parents, become less and less dependent on their-parents as they get older. The transition to economic adulthood is not deferred until a young person leaves home: indeed the transitions taking place within the security of the family home may help successful negotiation of the eventual move away from home. The payment of board money, the tasks done in the home, all create a situation in which young people are increasingly contributing to the family economy and becoming full adult family members. The normative roles of dependent child and protective parent thus become obscured: indeed in some families they are reversed, and the 'child' may be the 'bread-winner'.

Social policies appear to be based on notions of dependence and independence without any understanding of how the transition between these states is achieved. For example, though young workers may be independent of their parents, the young unemployed are expected to be able to be dependent on them, right up to the age of twenty-five. This policy seems to take no account either of the needs of young people growing up or of inequality between families, not all of whom can subsidise their young. Nor does it consider the problems of adjustment needed in families if young workers lose their jobs (or indeed the tensions and frictions which could result). We should abandon simplistic language and learn more about the ways in which dependence and independence merge in the transition to adulthood.

Note

1.   The SYPS is jointly funded by the Scottish Education Department, the Industry Department for Scotland, the Training Agency and the Department of Employment. As a Designated Research Centre, The Centre for Educational Sociology also acknowledges the support of the ESRC. My thanks to these sponsors, our respondents, and also to Sara Arber, Cathie Marsh, Janet Finch, and my CES colleagues for their helpful comments. The views expressed are mine alone.

3 Saturday Jobs: Sixth-formers in the Labour Market and the Family[1]

Susan Hutson and Wai-yee Cheung

Anyone who uses a supermarket or a fast food store in any of Britain's major cities on a Saturday will have the opportunity to observe one interesting feature of the youth labour market of the late 1980s: a high proportion of staff are young people, still in full-time education, working part-time. Yet, in the literature and relevant policy statements over the past ten years, these young students-workers have been largely invisible. Their invisibility rests, in part, on the fact that they enter national statistics under their predominant activity, which is 'student'.

The first objective of this chapter is descriptive: to set out the extent of this Saturday job working in an area of South Wales in 1989. We consider any part-time working by 16–19 year olds in full-time further education, whether on Saturday, Sunday or in the week, and attempt to estimate whether or not Saturday job working was increasing. Any substantial growth of these young people substituting for non-student employees in the retail and leisure industries will have important consequences for the labour market, and must be seen alongside the general decline in jobs for school-leavers (particularly marked in unskilled jobs) depicted in Figure 3.1. Moreover, it is likely that habits of earning in the sixth-form, once established, could alter the earning patterns of students in higher education particularly with the increasing financial pressures of fixed grants and the removal of rent subsidies.

As well as having serious consequences for the youth labour market, Saturday job working provides income which can affect family relationships. The second objective of this chapter is therefore to look at money exchange in the family; we shall consider the interplay of the financial aspects of exchange, by which needs and resources are balanced within the household, with the more symbolic aspects of exchange which mark the relationship between parents and children. The discussion therefore complements Jones' examination of board money (this volume). Jones argues that paying board goes beyond the purely symbolic realm, and

45

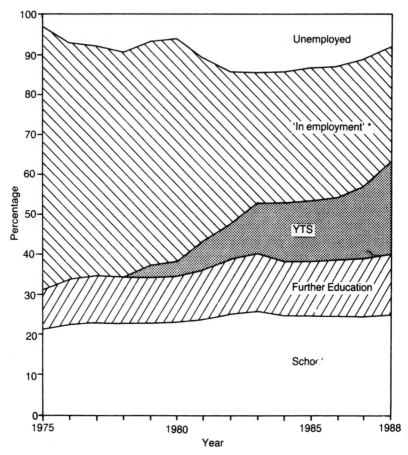

* 'In employment' is a residual category derived by subtracting those known to be
  in the other categories.

Source   Statistical Bulletins 2/87, 14/88, London DES (reproduced from Smithers
                      and Robinson, 1989).

Figure 3.1   Changes in education and employment, 16–18 years, in Britain
                             1975–88

that the amount paid in board money varies according to the economic
circumstances of the family in which the young person lives: in poorer
families, young people pay more. However, our data will suggest an
apparent lack of difference in the amount of pocket and allowance
money given within households of different social class. These

exchanges therefore appear to fall to the symbolic end of the continuum and support the recognition that money exchange within the family or household is not purely financial (Brannen and Wilson, 1987; Pahl, 1989).

Both chapters, however, illustrate the complex way in which young people lose much of their dependence on their parents while they are still living in the family home. Taxation, employment and welfare benefit policies for families and young people which assume that young people living in their parental household are in a relationship of dependency fall wide of the mark.

In setting out the characteristics of Saturday job working and considering money exchange in the family, it is necessary to look at the connection between parental income and the earning of school children. Fyfe (1989, p. 42) suggests that child earnings, by those aged under 16, can be viewed as substitutes for pocket money in poorer homes. Roberts *et al.* (1987), on the other hand, looking specifically at Saturday job working of 16–19 year olds, present a different picture; they suggest that, increasingly, these earners are educational achievers from affluent homes. They note that employers like their ability to pick things up quickly and the up-market atmosphere they help to create. They argue that there has been a change from the traditional association of Saturday jobs with working-class origins and educational failure to towards viewing part-time employment as enabling students to stay on. In support of this argument, the Youth Cohort Study (Courtney, 1989) showed that, while 45 per cent of boys and 52 per cent of girls with four or more 'O' level or equivalent passes were working part-time in the fifth-form, this fell progressively to five per cent of boys and 14 per cent of girls amongst those with no graded results.

THE DATA

Information about Saturday working was sought from a group of young people who had stayed on at school or college beyond the minimum leaving age. In a seven month period in 1989–90, 334 self-completion questionnaires were collected by the authors from young people in two tertiary colleges in West Glamorgan and in one comprehensive sixth-form, which were typical of the area. The sample was purposively drawn to balance the number of first and second year sixth (16 and 17 year olds) on the one hand and A level (academic) and BTech (vocational) students on the other. Slightly more girls were questioned (57 per cent), which reflects their higher staying-on rate. To get some comparative data from a different labour market, 96 young people from a comprehensive sixth-form in Bromley, South London were also questioned; these were all A-level students in their second year in the sixth-form (average age 17).

In order to get at least a qualitative insight into the phenomenon of Saturday job working, interviews with open-ended questions were conducted with young employees of nine city-centre firms in Swansea. The managers of these firms were also interviewed in the same manner. Information about the increase in working was also gained from a brief questionnaire which was sent to the national headquarters of these nine firms; of the seven responding firms, one had circulated its 61 country-wide branches with the questionnaire. Further qualitative data was also collected from in-depth follow-up interviews with some of the parents and in classroom discussions with the young people.

SATURDAY JOB WORKING AND THE LABOUR MARKET

Saturday job working by those in further education was widespread. In South Wales, 77 per cent of girls in the sample and 51 per cent of the boys were working. In London, by contrast, three quarters of both boys and girls were working, thus suggesting that boys would take up Saturday work where suitable jobs were available. Interviews with the nine firms in Wales revealed that young Saturday workers made up 50–60 per cent of the total work force in two fast food firms and 15–30 per cent in five department stores. In the two supermarkets, they made up 64 per cent and 14 per cent of the work force respectively.

In general, rates of pay and hours worked rose by age. Pay rates in Wales varied from £1.50 an hour at 16 to £2.50 an hour at 18. By 18, the pay rate was the same hourly rate as that received by a full-time adult worker. Of the Welsh respondents, 40 per cent of first year students and 58 per cent of second year students were earning over £20 a week in the term time. Time of year was the most important variable in determining the extent of Saturday working as many students worked full-time in the holidays. Eighty-four per cent of students in Wales and 87 per cent in Bromley reported earning over £20 in the holidays with 17 per cent in Wales and 19 per cent in London earning over £80 a week at this time. There were some gender differences in jobs and wage rates. Slightly more girls were found in the lower paid jobs and slightly more boys in the higher paid jobs. Overall,

wage rates were slightly lower in Wales than in London and it appeared
that young people in Wales were work:ng slightly longer hours for
the same money. Thus, both in extent and in the level of wages received
by these young people, Saturday working is important both in labour
market and in household terms and does not deserve the neglect it
has received.

All informants were asked if they had been earning before they were
16. Sixty-five per cent said they had, giving baby-sitting and paper-
rounds as the most common jobs. This is a higher figure than that
from an earlier London sample (MacLennan *et al.* 1985), where 43
per cent were found to be working (excluding baby-sitting) and where
11 and 12 year-olds were as likely to be working as older categories.
However, high rates of young people working in illegal jobs or illegal
hours (56 per cent in the London survey) were not echoed by this
study, principally because the young people in this survey were over
16. At this age, there is virtually no legislation restricting the types
of jobs and hours that can be worked. Moreover most, but not all,
of this sample were working for large city-centre firms with trade union
agreements on pay and conditions. The conditions and pay rates for
smaller firms and for parent employers may well have been different.
Concern over the effect on school-work, leisure and safety, which was
highlighted in the earlier London study, was not stressed by the informants in this study. This may be related to the other, widely held, values
placed on Saturday job working.

The Increase in Saturday Job Working

There are no published national statistics on Saturday job working.
Table 3.1 was therefore specially commissioned from the Labour Force
Survey. It shows that the proportion of young people working part-time
went up by more than a half in a four year period between 1984 and
1988. The rate of part-time working by young people was lower than
that found in West Glamorgan and Bromley, however. The questionnaires returned by the company which had circulated its 61 branches
suggest that the increased recruitment of young Saturday workers
results from explicit policy directives. Sixty-four per cent of the stores
reported an increase in young Saturday staff. The main reasons given
for this increase were, first, a response to their company's national
directive to cut down full-time hours and, second, to profit from the
flexibility in hours that these youngsters could offer. The increase in

young staff was highest in a new area of work – catering within the store. Significantly, high numbers of Saturday job workers were employed in fast food firms which are also areas of recent expansion.

Table 3.1   Persons 16–19 in full–time education who have a part–time job
in Great Britain, 1984 and 1988

Persons aged 16–19 (number in thousands)	All		Male		Female	
	1984	1988	1984	1988	1984	1988
All	3548	3279	1807	1666	1740	1612
In full-time education	1306	1218	648	616	657	603
In full-time education with part-time job	294	438	127	207	167	231
Percentage in full-time education	37%	37%	36%	37%	38%	37%
Percentage of those in full-time education with part-time jobs	23%	36%	20%	34%	25%	38%

Source   Table run by special request from the 1984 and 1988 Labour Force Surveys.

However, the nine managers interviewed and the questionnaires returned from the other six company headquarters denied that there had been a substantial increase in young Saturday job workers. Most firms interviewed employed equal numbers of full-timers, part-time married women and young Saturday staff. The managers interviewed valued full-timers for their knowledge and continuity while they valued married women for their preparedness to work flexible hours on weekdays and their acceptance of the discipline of work. However, young Saturday staff were valued for their availability on Saturdays and holiday periods when customer demand was high and other staff could be on holiday. In most firms interviewed the hours of young Saturday staff were altered from week to week. Furthermore, National Insurance contributions are not payable for staff who earn less than a given threshold (£43 per week at the time the study was undertaken), and rights to various forms of employment protection are denied staff working less that 16 hours per week. There was therefore an economic incentive for firms to prefer part-time workers. Part-timers are also less likely to join unions, and the two fast food firms interviewed who employed the highest proportion of Saturday job workers had no agreements with unions.

School-leavers and Sixth-form Earners

In Britain in 1988, 40 per cent of all young people were in further education while 23 per cent were on a Youth Training Scheme which was compulsory for 16–18 year-olds without jobs (Figure 3.1). Strikingly, the Welsh sample contained a substantial number of young people in full-time education earning more than their peers in full-time training. The Youth Training Scheme Allowance rate was £29.50–£35 a week in 1989. In West Glamorgan, 74 per cent of the sample were earning over £30 in the holidays and 29 per cent of the sample were earning over £30 in the term. Moreover, the parents of young people in full-time education would have been receiving £7.25 a week in child benefit from the state. Very few of the sample (three per cent) paid their parents board money whereas the majority of young people, once they leave full-time education, pay around £10 a week (Hutson and Jenkins, 1989).

Thus, it would seem that the feeling of 'money in your pocket' if you leave school, which was said to underpin working-class culture of the 1960s and 1970s (Willis, 1977), has become an illusion. However, when young people were asked why they decided to stay on in education, the desire for qualifications, better jobs and general expectations of higher education were mentioned while these short-term financial considerations were not.

Are Saturday Job Earners Taking Jobs From Others?

It was clear that very few of these part-time workers intended to remain in this sector of the labour market. The majority (65 per cent) of the whole sample were aiming to go on to higher education. A few said that the Saturday job experience had, in fact, acted as a spur to them to stay on in education and move into more interesting and better paid areas of work. Although the young people were putting these jobs on their CVs and using employers as referees, they were applying for different, full-time jobs or for college places. In general, firms were not looking for management potential amongst these Saturday workers.

The majority of the managers interviewed said that the balance of their work-force had not changed. Some said that the overall expansion of trade, over the last few years, meant that part-timers could be taken on without taking the places of other workers. They pointed out that Saturday working did not appeal to married women with family obligations and that young unemployed people were looking for full-time work and not Saturday jobs. Moreover, work-force proportions can only be changed as workers leave or retire. Turnover rates depend on the structure of the population and the characteristics of the local labour market. For example, several of the managers interviewed in South Wales spoke of a particularly stable market of married women workers due to the lack of other employment in the area. Despite these factors, a local union representative mentioned that some women and young people in the labour force were increasingly looking to Saturday work to supplement low-paid weekly jobs. These people were, thus, in direct competition with these sixth-formers.

In Britain, part-time working is not attractive to people receiving social security benefit, or coming from households on benefit, as almost all of any money earned is subtracted, pound for pound, from the benefit. However, part-time work can lead into full-time jobs and several of the managers interviewed preferred to take on an employee temporarily before offering them a full-time job. It is clear, therefore, that Saturday working could be used as a staging point to a full-time job, not for young Saturday job workers, but for those seeking full-time work within this sector of the labour market if benefit legislation were changed. However, employers may actually prefer to recruit these young educational achievers, as Roberts *et al.* (1987) hint, despite the denial by the Welsh managers interviewed.

Earning and Social Class

The occupational status of the fathers of these young people reflected the different social class profiles of the two areas. In Bromley, 71 per cent were in professional or intermediate jobs whereas in West Glamorgan the figure was only 37 per cent. In West Glamorgan, skilled manual workers made up 22 per cent of the sample as against 10 per cent in Bromley. However, overall, the samples contain more higher status households than a general sample from the two areas would be likely to show, which reflects the educational status of these young people.

The wide distribution of Saturday job working across all class groups indicates that part-time earning has become part of life for those in this age and educational category. However Table 3.2 indicates that, in the Welsh sample, earning appeared to be concentrated in households from the top and the bottom of the social scale. The presence of these educational achievers from affluent households was evident in this table. However, also evident in the Welsh self-completion questionnaires and interviews, were young people from households where the head was a semi- or unskilled manual worker. These young people were often working longer hours and paying for their everyday expenses, which indicated that they were working out of financial necessity. A high proportion of this category (65 per cent) were aiming to go on to higher education and it is likely that their earning was significant in financing themselves through further education. It may appear, to an outside observer, that some young people were working out of financial necessity and making a contribution to the household, whilst others were not. However, the young people themselves did not make this distinction. The majority of the informants said, simply, that they were working for money.

Table 3.2 Father's occupational status of those with a Saturday job: Welsh sample 1989

Father's occupational status	Percentage with Saturday job	(N)
Professional	80	(30)
Intermediate	69	(93)
Other non-manual	56	(57)
Skilled manual	63	(75)
Semi & unskilled manual	69	(39)
No response	68	(40)
All	66	(334)

MONEY EXCHANGE IN THE FAMILY

Money Exchange and Social Class

When a young person leaves school and starts full-time work, there is traditionally a change in the money flow between the generations as Wall (this volume) shows. Jones (this volume) has demonstrated in a Scottish sample that, even before the young person leaves home, there is a gradual growth of independence which for a period deserves to be called balanced reciprocity. If young people's patterns are comparable between Scotland and Wales, these results suggest that Saturday job working occupies a period prior to that where monetary reciprocity is expected. All the young people in the sample, whether they were earning or not, were receiving money from their parents. Eighty-two per cent were given money regularly by their parents and only 12 per cent gave their parents money, either regularly or occasionally. In South Wales, it is on leaving full-time education that pocket money and allowances usually stop and most young people, living at home, begin to pay board. In this context, Saturday job earning is not usually counted as a proper wage. As one mother said: 'I would not dream of reducing his pocket money when he's got a job. Why should I give him less just because he's earning'. It is clear that this is a statement about a relationship rather than about finance.

However, it is important to know the household's economic situation. One would expect richer parents to be giving more money to their children than poorer parents. Informants were asked the question: 'Do your parents give you money? How much do they give you?' The first set of figures in Table 3.3 show that the majority of young people had £2–5 a week at age 15. This had increased to £5–10 a week in the sixth form as the second column makes clear. But interestingly, these amounts did not vary consistently according to the social class of the father or whether or not the young person was earning (Tables 3.4 and 3.5). This would indicate that pocket and allowance money tend to fall towards the symbolic end of a continuum, expressing social relations appropriate between parents and children rather than representing a rational redistribution of earnings within the household.

Table 3.3   Money given by parents: Welsh sample 1989 (column percentages)

Money given by parents	Pocket money at 15	Present weekly allowance
None	8	0
>£2	5	—
£2–£5	56	15
£6–£10	17	36
£11–£15	1	12
£16–£20	—	2
£20 +	—	7
Money when asked	10	1
No response	3	28
Total percentage	100	100
Total number	(334)	(334)

Table 3.4   Amount of present allowance by father's occupational status: Welsh sample 1989 (column percentages)

| | Father's occupational status | | | | | | |
	Pro-fessional	Inter-mediate	Other non-manual	Skilled manual	Semi and unskilled manual	No response	All
>£5	23	15	12	16	21	3	15
£5–10	34	37	39	25	36	43	36
£11–16	3	12	11	16	13	17	12
£16–20	0	2	0	4	0	5	2
£20 +	7	12	4	5	3	7	7
Ask	3	0	2	3	0	0	1
No response	30	22	33	31	28	25	28
Total number	(30)	(93)	(57)	(75)	(39)	(40)	(334)

Table 3.5   Amount of present allowance by earning/non-earning: Welsh sample 1989 (column percentages)

Amount of present allowance	Earning	Non-earning	All
>£5	14	16	15
£5–£10	33	42	36
£11–£15	12	11	12
£16–£20	2	3	2
£20+	6	9	7
Money when asked	2	0	1
No response	31	19	28
Total percentage	100	100	101*
Total number	(221)	(113)	(334)

*The total percentage adds up to more than 100 due to the rounding of the decimal places.

The apparent similarity in the amounts of money parents gave their children indicates that parents at the lower end of the social scale will certainly have been giving their children a larger proportion of their income, and this could have caused hardship. On the other hand, there was evidence, from the interviews, that richer parents were deliberately restrained in what they gave their children. This may have been connected with a middle-class disapproval of over-consumption and a desire to teach their children to manage money. Several of the higher status parents expressed a genuine feeling that they did not have the resources to be over-generous to their children.

This apparent similarity in the money given to children, the wide opportunities for earning, together with the commercialisation of young people's leisure appeared to produce an equality in young people's spending power across social classes. The Welsh findings also showed a lack of consistent difference across classes, or between earners and non-earners, in terms of rates of going out; choices of commercial leisure; hobbies; time spent on homework; or car ownership. Moreover, there were no marked gender differences in these areas, except that some young women reported doing more housework.

Two interviews illustrate the interplay between the symbolic and the economic aspects of exchange between parents and children. Tamsin, at age 16, had taken a summer holiday job in a restaurant. Her parents, both in full-time professional jobs, did not wish her to go on working as they were worried the job would interfere with her homework. They gave her an allowance of £10 a week of which £5 covered school dinners. They knew she needed more money, particularly for clothes. Instead of increasing her allowance, however, Tamsin was given extra money under two specific labels. The first sum was £200 'driving lesson' money given to her for her eighteenth birthday but it was spent on general expenses and not driving lessons. Later, Tamsin had said she wanted to go ski-ing with the school. Her parents asked her if she really wanted to go and she admitted she would rather just have the money. So she was given £200 'ski-ing money' which, again, she used for everyday expenses and clothes. Thus, the money officially laid 'on the table', as an allowance, was very modest and unchanged from week to week. It did not reflect the resources in this high income household. Additionally, more money passed hands, but it was hidden behind special labels. This can go some way to explain the apparent similarity in the amounts given in formal pocket money and allowances across different income levels. In this high income family, at least, money was being passed in other ways – ways not so easily elicited in a self completion questionnaire.

However, it is not only high income families who pass money to children in such ways. Evidence from Wales (Hutson and Jenkins 1989) suggests that most unemployed young people were paying weekly board money to their parents at a similar rate to their working contemporaries. However, mothers were often passing back this money, and sometimes more, in small sums 'under the table' through the rest of the week. Thus, while the symbolic board money remained fixed, parents were attempting to counteract their children's poverty through hidden exchanges.

Sharon, who hoped to go to university, worked 20 hours and earned £30 a week in a supermarket. Her father was a lorry driver, her mother a part-time home-help. In the holidays, Sharon could bring home more money than her father. The previous year she had stopped going out for two months and saved £370 for a holiday, with friends, in Majorca. She paid for all her everyday expenses but her parents gave her £3 a week to put in the bank. At one stage, Sharon said that she was spending all she was getting on herself. She said: 'I could have been doing something for the family. I did feel guilty. I bought things for the house but my mother didn't want me to'. Sharon had given this up, and, at the time of the interview, her mother was now buying her odds and ends although, Sharon said, she did not need them. Here, Sharon's attempts to balance her parents' low earnings with her own money were not accepted. Her parents expected her to spend out on a holiday even when she felt guilty about her leisure spending. In the saving money and the odds and ends they gave her, her parents attempted to maintain the relationship expected between parents and children.

Money Exchange and Young People Earning

Although parents gave similar amounts of regular money to earners and non-earners (Table 3.5), more earners than non-earners were spending their own money in the three areas they were asked about – everyday expenses, clothes, and leisure. Table 3.6 shows a recognised hierarchy of spending among both groups whereby parents consistently paid more for necessary items (everyday expenses) and young people paid more for luxury items (leisure). However, Saturday jobs do not seem to save parents as much as one would expect; when asked, 21 per cent of the earners felt that their jobs did not save their parents any money at all.

Holiday expenditure shows an interesting connection between social class and earning/non-earning. Sixty-nine per cent of the Welsh sample had had a holiday in the previous summer. As one would expect, the higher the social class, the higher the likelihood of a holiday and the higher the likelihood that this would be abroad. Table 3.7 shows that non-earners were as likely to go on holiday as earners. Earners, when they went, however, were likely to make a financial contribution. Of course these figures do not indicate what kinds of holiday these were,

Table 3.6   Expenditure on everyday expenses, clothes and leisure: Welsh
sample 1989 (column percentages)

	Everyday expenses		Clothes		Leisure	
	All	Earners	All	Earners	All	Earners
Parents only	73	67	31	19	17	7
Mixed	11	14	54	62	31	32
Self only	15	19	16	18	50	60
No response	1	0	0	0	1	0
Total percentage	100	100	100	100	100	100
Total number	(334)	(221)	(334)	(221)	(334)	(221)

nor whether there was any significant difference between those paid
for by parents and those contributed to by young people, but the interview data suggested that there was not a great difference. It would
thus appear that some young people were contributing to a holiday
which they might have had anyway. In a similar way, some earners
bought more expensive presents, for family or friends, when cheaper
ones would have been acceptable. However, most spoke with pleasure
of being able to buy a proper present, or contribute to a holiday with
their own money.

Table 3.7   Holiday taking and holiday payment by earners/non-earners:
Welsh sample 1989 (column percentages)

	Non-earner	Earner	All
No holiday taken	35	30	32
Holiday taken – payment:			
Parents only	52	34	40
Mixed	5	21	16
Self only	5	15	12
Total percentage	100	100	100
Total number	(113)	(221)	(334)

Any study of the earning of money by young people in the family
must take note of this importance of *independent* money. This money
is free of parental control. At this age it can be used to claim independence and adult status in the family. This goes some way to explain
why so many young people were working long hours when an outside
observer might see no objective need for it and why some young people
appeared to be working for things their parents might have given them

anyway. Sixty per cent of the sample said they were working 'for money'. For only some was this money, objectively, a financial necessity. For others, in whatever terms they saw it, they were really talking about *independent* money. This was illustrated by one girl who said: 'I need money because I have to pay for everything – holidays, driving lessons, clothes and going out. *It's not that my parents can't afford it.* It makes me feel more independent, knowing that everything I own, I bought.' Another girl answered the question: 'Why do you work?' with: 'To receive money of my own which allows me to be independent of my parents. Therefore, this enables me to spend it on what I want, not on what my parents want. I spend my money on socialising. That's my business'.

Most of these young people did not consider that they might have been given much of this independence anyway. A recent study in South Wales (Hutson and Jenkins, 1989) shows the way in which most parents are willing to concede adult status to children. In this context, allowance money was regarded by both as a step towards greater independence. In fact many young people, on the self-completion questionnaire, regarded this money as their own independent money, comparable with, but usually less than earnings.

The fact that Saturday job wages are seen as independent money can account, in part, for the lack of connection between household income and children's earnings. Moreover, most of this money is spent on the luxury end of the scale – fashion clothes, music, nightclubs, hobbies and drink. Many people, even parents, would agree that young people have a right to these things. They are what 'being young' is about. If most young people tend to spend their money on luxuries, this will have a minimal effect on household income. It also means that some young people can cut or expand expenditure, and so earnings. If many young people are earning for luxuries, rather than subsistence, they can tolerate the flexible hours and wages that employers like so much.

Saturday Job Earning and Values

In addition to money and independence, other values associated with work were mentioned – commitment, effort, achievement, learning about the 'real' world and about the management of money. Although there were complaints of boredom, fatigue and frustration with superiors, one girl described her job in a way not untypical of the survey: 'Where I work, it's enjoyable. All my friends work there and you get paid while working and enjoying myself. Every one of the Saturday girls knows the manager's daughter'.

This modern stress on values is mentioned by Jamieson and Toynbee (1987), who say that parents often ask for housework to be done in order to teach values rather than because it is the most practical way to get such work done. One teacher in the Welsh study said, of Saturday jobs and her academic students: 'It teaches them to deal with difficult situations, with the public and to *take orders with a smile*'.

The positive aspect of this kind of work is shown by the fact that, of those working in Wales, 79 per cent said their parents would encourage them and 83 per cent said they would encourage a friend to find a job. Such a positive attitude to work, which is more often associated with interesting and well rewarded professional jobs, is here being expressed in relation to unskilled jobs. The lack of fit between the qualities of the job and the values expressed is, perhaps, not noticeable to the young people because these jobs form a temporary phase in their labour market careers and because the hours worked are relatively short.

While stressing the values imputed to Saturday job working, it is necessary to look at some of the reasons given for not having such a job. Most gave a mixture of reasons but the two most common single reasons given were 'hobbies' (which included sport) and 'homework'. The majority of first and second year students in Wales reported doing one to two hours of homework a night whilst the second year students in Bromley reported two to three hours. Although the study did not show that earners spent less time on homework than non-earners, two head teachers expressed concern at the increasing hours worked by students. It is likely that, if legislation restricting Saturday job working were to be called for in the future, the values attached to the money earned by both parents and young people would act as a strong check on such controls.

CONCLUSIONS

The extent of Saturday job working is high yet remains officially invisible. As an activity, it does not fall into childhood or adulthood. It is neither full-time education nor full-time work. It does not even fall into the black economy. Saturday job workers do not appear in national statistics. Students of the labour market have largely ignored it and families take it for granted.

Evidence shows, despite management denial, that Saturday job working is on the increase, particularly in new retail markets, and forms part of the general increase in part-time work and casualisation of jobs. It is probable, with the polaristion of a labour market between those who have skills and jobs and those who have neither, that some low-paid workers could supplement weekly wages by doing Saturday jobs. More importantly, if the restrictions on part-time earning were changed for those claiming social security benefit, then Saturday jobs could give a first step into the labour market for those seeking full-time and permanent work in these kind of jobs.

Many of the Saturday job workers in this study could be called educational achievers from affluent homes. This is to be expected in a group staying on in education. However, there were some young people, from the bottom of the social class scale, who were working from financial necessity and using their earnings to take them through further education and on into higher education.

Most young people said they were working for money. Most felt that they could afford to buy more things if they were earning. They did not consider that their parents might have given them these things anyway. If they were not, objectively, working for financial necessity, they were working for *independent* money – money free from the controls of parents. They did not consider that their parents might have given them their independence and relaxed these controls simply as they grew up.

Saturday working was positively valued. Work teaches money management and work skills. It is a slice of the real world from which children in school are usually excluded. The commercialisation of leisure and the current enterprise spirit, pervading both education and work, leads young people, parents and even teachers, to support Saturday job working as a temporary phase in their labour market careers.

If money exchange within the family is seen to lie along a continuum running from the symbolic to the economic then this chapter places pocket and allowance money towards the symbolic end while Jones places board money toward the economic. This apparent contrast suggests that two factors influence where, on the continuum, an exchange lies. The first factor is whether the young person is seen as a child or an adult and here the significant divide seems to be the leaving of full-time education. The board payers have left school. They have become adult contributors into the household in a way that Saturday job students have not. The second factor is the overall resources of the household. If total resources are short, then financial considerations are more likely to prevail. Jones' sample is larger and has a cross-section of a national population. The Saturday job sample was smaller and weighted towards better-off households.

However, the interplay between the symbolic and the economic aspects of exchanges between parents and children is complex. Official sums, or public money laid 'on the table' are likely to have a higher symbolic content than the more private exchanges which often go on 'under the table' and may better reflect the economic realities in the household. It is not only the better off households who make these kinds of payments and parents may resist taking money from children even when their economic circumstance dictate that they should. Throughout all social classes parents support their children and the same family sentiments are expressed.

State policies rely on these sentiments and make two assumptions. Firstly, that parents, whatever their age or their resources, will support their children well into adulthood and, secondly, that all young people can rely on this support. It is clear, therefore, that those young people without families, who lie outside the scope of this chapter, are in a difficult financial position (Liddiard and Hutson, forthcoming). The loans, the gifts, the money 'under the table' and the financial advice will not be available for them.

Much of the Saturday job income was spent on leisure and luxuries. Most parents saw this as an acceptable part of this stage of life, before the adult responsibilities of a family. This is one reason why earnings appear to have a relatively small effect on the standard of living of other household members. However, although this study has suggested that many of these young people were not working out of financial necessity, it must be remembered that until recently it was accepted, by both experts and laypeople, that most married women worked only for 'pin money'. The affluence of some of the households, the youthfulness of the workers, the values which sustain Saturday jobs must not be allowed to hide the low pay and poor working conditions which can belong to these jobs and conceal the fact that part-time earnings by young people can, in reality, make an important financial contribution in some households.

Note

1. The authors would like to thank the ESRC for funding this research (Grant Number R000231510) and Holly Hutson for her contribution in entering the data.

4 Relationships Between the Generations in British Families Past and Present

Richard Wall

In the absence of firm evidence about the nature of the family in the past it is very easy to assume that family and kin ties have become less cohesive than once was the case. Such views helped shape the policies of Conservative governments of the 1980s towards the role of the state in the care of the dependent elderly (Gordon, 1988), but similar expectations were also current in 1957 when Townsend published his study of the elderly in Bethnal Green (Townsend, 1957, p. 3) and further back still, in the 1890s, there were already some ready to allege a growing neglect by children of their elderly parents (Booth, 1894, 1980, p. 26).

Taken at face value, such comments would imply that the British family has been in a state of long-term decline from at least late Victorian times. Yet it is interesting that these three investigations into the circumstances of the elderly – Booth in the 1890s, Gordon's reinterpretation of the New Survey of London Life and Labour of 1929–31, and Townsend on Bethnal Green in the 1950s – all ended by emphasising the significant role of the family in the care of the elderly, even though this was not always, or even usually, transmitted in the form of financial support. My purpose in the present chapter is to re-examine these issues beginning with a reassessment of the frequency with which the elderly (defined here as persons aged 65 and over) lived alone or with other members of their families. This provides a useful starting point since it is those elderly who have no other member of the household to whom they can turn when they fall sick who are most likely to suffer in such circumstances. Moreover it is unlikely that persons living on their own will receive from relatives hidden financial assistance of equivalent value to that derived from relatives who do co-reside (although the extent and direction of resource transfers between household members is a much under-researched area).

Aid in kind as opposed to cash transfers also becomes more difficult when relatives live further away. The distances which separated the homes of parents from those of their adult children, the most likely potential providers of informal care to their ageing parents, will therefore form the second part of our enquiry. Finally, consideration will be given to such hard evidence as there is on the amount of support which children are now, and were in the past, able to provide for their elderly parents. The evidence will often be found to be incomplete, but hopefully it will suffice both to modify expectations as to the additional burdens it is reasonable for the modern state to thrust on to the family as well as to dispel some of the pessimism that dominates current assumptions concerning the family.

THE ELDERLY IN THE HOUSEHOLD

The household and family patterns of the elderly are of particular relevance in connection with the debate which has recently opened up between David Thomson and E. H. Hunt concerning the generosity or otherwise of the nineteenth century Poor Law compared with the benefits handed out by today's welfare state (Thomson, 1984; Hunt, 1989). Thomson has argued that the pensions provided to the elderly poor during the period 1837–63 reached between 69 and 90 per cent of the income of the working-class adult, or adult equivalent (children were counted as 0.45 of an adult), compared with today's pensions which provide only 40 per cent of the income enjoyed by the working class. Hunt has countered this claim in a variety of ways which need not concern us here.

However, both protagonists have missed the point that for many pensioners today, pension income together with other income provided by the pensioners themselves is the only income supporting the pensioners' households. By contrast, as we shall demonstrate below in Tables 4.1 and 4.2, in the past the vast majority of elderly lived with people who would have had other sources of income, principally earnings, from which the elderly members of their households could be expected to draw some benefit.[1] That pooling of incomes among members of the same household occurred at least to a certain extent is suggested by the fact that there are frequent references to the elderly being welcomed into the households of their children because of the income they brought with them in the form of out-relief payments from the Poor Law authorities and (in later times) from pensions (Booth, 1894, 1980, pp. 277, 326; Anderson, 1977, pp. 51–3). The application of the income of the elderly, such as it was, to the general benefit of the household implies some transfer in a reverse direction; otherwise the elderly would not have been willing or able to forgo their income.

Table 4.1 shows the trends in the proportions of elderly living on their own or only with a spouse. By 1985, 36 per cent of persons aged 65 and over in Britain lived on their own. Living alone in old age was rarer, if not totally unknown in pre-industrial England, with under 10 per cent of elderly in rural areas living alone, 11 per cent in the City of Lichfield in 1692, and just six per cent in 1701 in the cluster of settlements that later was to become Stoke-on-Trent. However, it was only during the two decades immediately preceding 1985 that there was to be a rapid progression towards more elderly persons living alone. Indeed, in the middle of the nineteenth century the proportion of elderly on their own may have been even lower than in pre-industrial times.

Nor has the pace of change towards more elderly living alone been constant from place to place. Even in the early 1930s, percentages of elderly people living alone in working-class areas of London were approaching levels typical of the country as a whole in the 1970s. On the other hand, there are communities surveyed after the Second World War where many fewer elderly lived alone – two Welsh communities of the Mid-Rhondda investigated in 1945–6, Swansea in 1960, and Wolverhampton also investigated in 1945–6. Such different residence patterns, judged from the frequency with which households in general took in relatives other than immediate nuclear family members, may have persisted into the 1970s, although they would not appear to have been in existence in the middle of the nineteenth century (Wall 1982). One characteristic, however, was present in all the populations studied, and that was that more elderly women than elderly men were living on their own. This is scarcely surprising given that even in the English past, women out-lived men and were in general, younger on marriage and on re-marriage than their partners.

In addition to the elderly who live alone, note also needs to be taken of those elderly who live with just one other person, namely their spouse. In the late twentieth century, as Table 4.1 again makes clear, this is a frequently encountered situation, representing, for example, the position of 62 per cent of elderly men and 33 per cent of elderly women in 1985 (see Arber and Ginn, this volume). In pre-industrial England it was experienced much less frequently. Once again, the break from patterns typical of pre-industrial times comes late; the proportions of elderly women living only with their spouse after the

Table 4.1   Elderly persons living alone, or alone but for a spouse, Great Britain, sixteenth to twentieth centuries, as a percentage of all elderly persons living in private household

(Sample) Population	Dates	Population aged ≥ 65	Percentage of elderly males and females[1]			
			males		females	
			Living alone	With spouse only	Living alone	With spouse only
Rural English communities[2]	1599–1796	205	2	19	16	17
Lichfield	1692	104	3	24	15	8
Stoke	1701	78	5	10	8	3
Britain	1851	445	5	-	9	-
London	1929–31	2284[4]	19	41	37	22
York	1935–6	2794[4]	6	28	18	19
Britain	1945	3947	6	-	16	-
Mid-Rhondda	1945–6	209	1	17	7	9
Oldham	1945–6	402	8	42	22	21
Wandsworth and St Pancras	1945–6	367	18	45	32	18
Wolverhampton	1945–6	354	9	33	13	15
Bethnal Green	1954–6	203[3]	22	38	28	25
Swansea	1960	434	7	39	19	27
Britain	1962	2500	11	-	30	-
England	1976	2632	16	62	39	32
Britain	1977	4647	14	63	43	31
Britain	1980–1	9123	17	60	45	32
Britain	1985	3708	20	61	48	33

Key 1.   In this table missing data are indicated by hyphens.
2.   Rural English communities: Chilvers Coton 1684, Wetherby 1776, Wembworthy 1779, Corfe Castle 1790, Ardleigh 1796.
3.   Pensioners only.
4.   Working class population only.

Sources   Rural English communities: Lichfield, Stoke, calculated from photocopies of local censuses held at the Cambridge Group. Britain 1851: Anderson (1988, p. 436). London 1929–31: Gordon (1988, p. 26). York 1935–6: Mid-Rhondda, Oldham, Wandsworth and St Pancras, Wolverhampton, all 1945–6, calculated from Nuffield Foundation (1947, pp. 140–1). Britain 1945: calculated from Thomas (1947). Bethnal Green 1954–5: Townsend (1957, p. 24). Swansea 1960: Rosser and Harris (1965, p. 274). Britain 1962: Shanas et al. (1968, p. 186). Britain 1976: Hunt (1978). Britain 1977: (*Social Trends*, vol. 9, 1979, p. 63). Britain 1980–1: (*Social Trends* vol. 13, 1983, Table 2.4). Britain 1985: Derived from Arber and Ginn in this volume.

end of the Second World War are quite comparable to those of pre-industrial England. However, the proportions of elderly living on their own have continued to rise throughout the 1970s and 1980s, while the proportions living just with a spouse appear to have stabilised. When elderly people do live with others, it is interesting to note the nature of the relationship; as Arber and Ginn argue (this volume), different relatives provide different types of support. Table 4.2 shows that approximately half of elderly males in pre-industrial society (in urban as well as in rural communities) would be co-residing with a child, as would more than a third (and 46 per cent in Stoke) of elderly women. On the other hand, few elderly men co-resided with a child who was or who had been married, and even in the case of elderly women, there were never more than a fifth who co-resided with an ever-married child.[2] Rarer still was co-residence with more distant relatives (grandchildren, nephews and nieces and so forth), in the absence of other relatives. Women were more likely than men to live with their married offspring as they more often outlived their spouse and because it was felt to be more easy than it was with elderly men to incorporate them into the households of their children (see Booth 1894, 1980, p. 326; Anderson 1977, p. 52).

Comparison with the family circumstances of elderly people in the later twentieth century is not easy since, despite the frequently voiced concern about the alleged decline in family values, detailed studies of the living arrangements of elderly people are few and far between. A study conducted in 1962 (Shanas *et al.*, 1968 – see Table 4.2) reveals that a third of elderly men and women were then living with a child, a frequency of co-residence which was not far below that of pre-industrial times at least as far as elderly women were concerned. Furthermore, only 11 per cent of elderly men and 12 per cent of elderly women lived with an ever-married child. Yet fewer elderly lived with an ever-married child in Lichfield in 1692, while the proportions found to be co-residing with a married child in Swansea in 1960 exceed those in all three pre-industrial populations.

The dramatic change in the frequency of co-residence with a child, married or unmarried, has occurred since the 1960s. This is implied by the steep rise during the past three decades in the proportions of elderly living with only their spouse (see Table 4.1) and is confirmed by data from the 1971 census (Grundy, personal communication); according to Grundy, in 1971 just 14 per cent of elderly men and 11 per cent of elderly women were co-residing with a never-married child. This places the main period of decline in co-residence with a

Table 4.2 Co-residents of persons aged ≥ 65 residing in private households, Great Britain, sixteenth to twentieth centuries

(Sample) Population	Dates	Percentage of elderly males who live with . . .[1]				
		Spouse	Any child	Ever-married child	Never-married child	Other relative(s) only
Rural English communities	1599–1796	59	49	12	38	4
Lichfield	1692	70	54	8	46	0
Stoke	1701	59	54	3	51	3
Britain	1851	57	45	-	-	5
London	1929–31[2]	68	-	-	-	-
Bethnal Green	1954–5	-	41	8	33	-
Swansea	1960	-	42	21	33	0
Britain	1962	70	33	11	21	-
England and Wales	1971	71	-	-	22	4
England	1977	75	-	-	14	-
Britain	1980–1	74	-	-	-	-
England and Wales	1981	71	-	-	-	-
Britain	1985	75	-	-	11	-

Table 4.2 continues opposite

Table 4.2 continued

(Sample) Population	Dates	Spouse	Any child	Ever-married child	Never-married child	Other relative(s) only
Rural English communities	1599–1796	41	37	17	21	5
Lichfield	1692	21	34	9	25	2
Stoke	1701	26	46	15	31	5
Britain	1851	31	46	-	-	10
London	1929–31[2]	31	-	-	31	-
Bethnal Green	1954–5	-	37	14	23	10
Swansea	1960	-	41	23	18	-
Britain	1962	34	33	12	22	9
England and Wales	1971	35	-	-	11	-
England	1977	36	-	-	-	-
Britain	1980–1	38	-	-	-	-
England and Wales	1981	38	-	-	10	-
Britain	1985	37	-	-	-	-

Percentage of elderly females who live with . . .[1]

Key 1. In this table missing data are indicated by hyphens.
2. A slight underestimate of co-residents as the circumstances of the two per cent of elderly persons resident in two family households are not given in detail and have been excluded.

Sources Bethnal Green 1954–5: calculated from Townsend (1957, pp. 24, 216). England and Wales 1971 and 1981: calculations by Emily Grundy derived from the OPCS Longitudinal Study. Other populations: see Table 4.1.

never-married child in the 1960s with very little further change occurring during the course of the 1970s.[3]

In another respect, Table 4.2 indicates rather less of a change between pre-industrial times and the present, and that is in the frequency of co-residence with a spouse (whether or not others were present in the household). At first sight this might seem surprising as the higher mortality of pre-industrial times might have been expected to leave many more people to experience old age as widowers or widows. But remarriage was more common in the past while probably more importantly life expectancy has improved more for women than for men, lengthening the period in old age which women spend as widows but shortening the period of time when men are widowers. As a result, women in pre-industrial England were marginally more likely than elderly British women in the late twentieth century to be living with their spouse. For elderly men, the position is a little more different now from what it was in the past. Today, 75 per cent of men have a spouse present in their household, compared to 59 per cent in rural pre-industrial England and Stoke-on-Trent in 1701.

In the past, elderly women were more likely to live with a child than with their spouse. However, with elderly men the situation was reversed. In other words, if we make the assumption that the significant ties are those that involve co-residence, then for women in old age it was ties that crossed generations that were important while for elderly men the ties within generations were the critical ones. Nowadays, for elderly women as well as for elderly men, co-residence with a spouse is more common than co-residence with a child. However, the major break from the family patterns of the past is the much reduced incidence after the 1960s of co-residence between elderly parents and adult children. If our notions are correct about the pooling of income by members of the same household, it is only in the last couple of decades that it has become unusual for elderly persons to be supported both by a state pension and the earnings of a younger adult.

PROXIMITY OF PARENTS AND THEIR ADULT CHILDREN

Overlapping, however, with the ties that linked one household member to another, were other ties that extended beyond the boundaries of the household, to children living elsewhere, to other relatives, and to friends and neighbours. Our concern here is with the residential proximity of parents and their adult children. Such information is available from special censuses of three small rural communities dating from the late eighteenth and early nineteenth centuries. The censuses are 'special' in that they record the current residence of all children whose parents still remained within the communities concerned, making it possible to calculate both how many married children were living within a given distance of the parental home (see Table 4.3) as well as how close to the parental home was the residence of the nearest child (Tables 4.4 and 4.5).

Locating strictly comparable data was not easy. No standard scheme has emerged for measuring distances between parents and children; some researchers have grouped distances into broad categories while others have chosen much narrower distance bands or simply referred to the proportion living within a particular locality, the area of which is left undefined. A further problem is that a given distance will have been a more significant barrier to regular contact before the car became widely available. Distance is also likely to represent more of an obstacle to the parent than to the child, and for certain purposes which may have been of vital importance in one time period but not in another. To take one particular example, Sheldon's definition in 1948 of a relative living within five minutes as living 'near', as that was the maximum distance that could be allowed for the transport of a hot meal without the need for re-heating, has ceased to be relevant with the development of new technology cutting the time required in food preparation and re-heating. Nevertheless, making some crude adjustments we shall see that a significant proportion of parents and children have always lived within relatively close proximity (under five miles). Just as expectations concerning the super-mobility of members of families today can be successfully challenged, so too we can demonstrate that expectations that pre-industrial villagers were always in close contact with their kin are equally wide of the mark.

Consideration is given first in Table 4.3 to the distances separating married sons and daughters and their parents (regardless of the age of those parents). It should be stressed that the percentages of children resident in the same household as their parents, although they look similar to those given above in Table 4.2, are not comparable. On this occasion we consider not how many elderly parents lived with a married child, but how many married children, with a parent still alive, actually lived with that parent (and not all parents were over the age of 65). As Table 4.3 makes clear, very few such children did in fact co-reside with a parent even in rural England in the eighteenth

and nineteenth centuries. As these children's expectations are likely
to have at least been conditioned in part by the reality that surrounded
them, we may say with some degree of confidence that children from
these pre-industrial communities would not have anticipated spending
their married lives in the parental home. Yet the parental home and
the children's marital home were usually not that far away. Almost
half the married sons and about a third of the married daughters in
Stoke Poges in 1831 and in Caunton in 1846 lived in the same parish
as their parents. In Cardington the proportions resident in the same
parish as their parents were lower but even in Cardington, most migration had been local in nature: more than six out of ten married
sons and almost eight out of ten married daughters were living within
ten miles of their parents' home.

Higher proportions of married sons and daughters lived within five
or ten miles of their parents in some communities in the second half
of the twentieth century. The advantage of the long historical perspective is that it enables us to see both northern farmers in 1960 and
Swansea in 1960 as forming particularly tightly knit communities. The
real surprise, however, is that in a cross-section of the English population in 1951, the proportion of married sons and daughters living within
two kilometres of their parents exceeded in some cases the proportions
resident within a wider radius (the same parish as their parents) more
than a hundred years earlier.

Since the 1950s, the pattern of migration has changed significantly
and it is unfortunate that for this more recent period it has not been
possible to find a representative population. All we have available are
the results of a study of five towns conducted in 1983. The study is
far from ideal for our purposes as it comprised two-child families only,
and excluded all instances where parent and child co-resided. Even
with these limitations, however, it is worth pointing out that almost
a fifth of the sons and a quarter of the daughters included in this
1983 sample were resident within two kilometres of their parents and
that a third of the sons and 40 per cent of the daughters were located
within five kilometres. In all probability, these are lower proportions
than would have lived within such a restricted radius of their parents
in the eighteenth and nineteenth centuries, but the differences are not
that great, indicating how inappropriate it would be to draw sharp
contrasts between an 'immobile' past and a 'mobile' present.

We now need to consider the same migration pattern from the parents' perspective by calculating the distance between the parent and
the married child who lived closest. Table 4.4 shows that half of the

Table 4.3   Residential proximity of parents and their married children, England, eighteenth to twentieth centuries (cumulative column percentages)

Distances from parent(s)[1] (cumulative percentages)	Cardington Bedfordshire 1782	Stoke Poges Buckinghamshire 1831	Caunton Nottinghamshire 1846	England 1951	Swansea Glamorgan 1960	Northern farmers c. 1960	Five towns 1983
Married Sons:							
Same household	5	4	2	-	-	6	-[7]
Same parish	26	46	48	30[2]	26[4]	63	18[2]
Under 5 miles	49	-	66	47[3]	71[5]	-	34[3]
Under 10 miles	64	-	86	-	80[6]	74	-
Married Daughters:							
Same household	10	0	0	-	-	4	-[7]
Same parish	22	34	30	32[2]	42[4]	37	25[2]
Under 5 miles	57	-	60	49[3]	80[5]	-	40[3]
Under 10 miles	78	-	84	-	85[6]	83	-
Numbers:							
Sons	(38)	(26)	(45)	(283)	(383)	(35)	(408)
Daughters	(40)	(38)	(47)	(289)	(408)	(81)	(436)

Key 1. In this table missing data are indicated by hyphens.
2. Within two kilometres (1.24 miles)
3. Within five kilometres (3 miles)
4. Same locality of Swansea
5. Other part of Swansea
6. Within twelve miles
7. No families with co-resident children were included in the sample.

Sources Cardington, Stoke Poges, Caunton, calculated from local censuses held at the Cambridge Group. Coverage of the first two limited to labouring and cottage families and others of equivalent status. England 1951: Parents of married couples interviewed in 1983, not all necessarily married in 1951, see Warnes (1986, p. 1591). Swansea 1960: Rosser and Harris (1965, p. 212). Northern Farmers c. 1960: Nalson (1968, p. 79). Five towns 1983: Warnes (1986, p. 1591). The towns are Maidstone, Stockport, Merton, Melton Mowbray and Oakham with three adjacent villages. At least one parent had to be of statutory pensionable age. All had two (not necessarily married) children with whom they were in contact but with whom they did not co-reside.

Table 4.4   Proximity to parent(s) of nearest married child, England,
eighteenth to twentieth centuries (row percentages)

		Percentage of children within given distance of parental home				
	Date	Same household	Same parish	Elsewhere	Total	N
Nearest married son:						
Cardington	1782	8	33	58	100	(24)
Stoke Poges	1831	6	44	50	100	(16)
Caunton	1846	4	58	38	100	(26)
Nearest married daughter:						
Cardington	1782	14	18	68	100	(28)
Stoke Poges	1831	0	55	45	100	(20)
Caunton	1846	0	48	52	100	(33)
Nearest child:						
Cardington	1782	16	24	61	100	(38)
Stoke Poges	1831	4	63	33	100	(27)
Caunton	1846	3	64	33	100	(39)
Bethnal Green	1954-5	15	59[1]	27	100	(164)

Key 1. Within a mile of the parental household.
Sources Bethnal Green 1954-5: calculated from Townsend (1957, pp. 24,
32). Children resident in the same dwelling, but not in the same household,
(9 per cent of the total) have been classed as resident in the same parish for
the purpose of the table. Other populations: see Table 4.3.

parents of a married son and daughter in Stoke Poges and Caunton
had at least one son or daughter living in the same parish, although
not usually within the parental household. Whereas many of the children established their homes outside the parish of their parents (see
Table 4.3) the majority of parents could nonetheless still anticipate
that a married daughter or a married son would remain in the same
parish. Not all families conformed to this pattern however. One in
three were in the situation where the nearest married child did live
elsewhere, presumably beyond easy daily contact, and in Cardington
it was closer to two in three. It is also worth stressing that the proportions of parents with married children living in the parish was somewhat
less even in Stoke Poges and Caunton than the proportions of parents
with a married child living within a mile of the parental household
in Bethnal Green in 1954-5 (Townsend, 1957).
Comparison with the situation in the later twentieth century, how-

ever, ought not to rest solely on the results from one undoubtedly closely knit community. We have, therefore, felt it necessary to complement the earlier analysis with another, restricted to those parents over the age of 65 but including the never-married in addition to the married children.

Table 4.5   Proximity to elderly parent(s) of nearest child, England, eighteenth to twentieth centuries (row percentages)[1]

	Date	Same household	Same parish	Elsewhere	Total	N
Cardington	1782	25	33	42	100	(12)
Stoke Poges	1831	0	75	25	100	(8)
Bethnal Green	1954–5	52	33	15	100	(167)
Swansea	1960	50	18	32	100	(327)
Britain	1962	42	24	34	100	(1911)
Four towns	1977	14	35[2]	51	100	(1646)
Five towns	1983	–[3]	36[4]	–	100	(432)

Key   1. In this table missing data are indicated by hyphens.
2. Same street or neighbourhood but presumably extending up to five miles as a distance from parent(s) of five or six miles is the next category to be specified.
3. No families with co-resident children were included in the sample.
4. Within one kilometre (0.62 miles). Fifty-eight per cent of couples lived within five kilometres (three miles) of a child.

Sources   Four towns 1977: calculated from Abrams (1978). The four towns are Hove, Merton, Moss Side and Northampton. Children resident in the same dwelling, but not in the same household have been classed as resident in the same parish for the purpose of this table. Five towns 1983: Howes (1984, p.10). The same survey is used by A. M. Warnes (see above, Table 4.3). Other populations: see Tables 4.3 and 4.4.

The results are presented in Table 4.5 and indicate that the elderly inhabitants of these eighteenth and early nineteenth century communities were no more likely to have their children close to hand than were their counterparts in the mid-twentieth century. In two of these mid-twentieth century populations (Swansea and Bethnal Green), more than half the elderly parents still had a child in their own household, while more than two-thirds had a child either in their own household or in the vicinity. Results for Britain as a whole in 1962 were not dissimilar. Certainly, migration patterns have changed since the 1950s, yet even these would not appear to have produced great distances between elderly parent and nearest child. For example, 58 per cent of the elderly in the five towns survey of 1983 were found to be living within three miles of their nearest child – exactly the same percentage as lived within the same parish as their elderly parents in Cardington in 1782.

Establishing that certain families lived in proximity to their kin does not, of course, indicate that they were in contact with each other but only that such contact was possible. What use was made of the proximity would be influenced by the occupations, the ages, and the genders of the respective parties. In their investigations of communities in the East End of London in the 1950s, Young and Willmott laid great stress on the social and emotional ties between mothers and their married daughters (Young and Willmott, 1957). In pre-industrial rural communities, on the other hand, ties between parents and married sons may have been relatively stronger; we have seen already (Tables 4.3 and 4.4) that, if anything married sons lived closer to their parents than married daughters.

ASSISTANCE IN MONEY AND KIND

Having considered the residential proximity of elderly parents and their adult children, we now need to measure whether there was any major change over time in the proportions of elderly parents who received financial or other forms of assistance from their children. Even in the past, however, many elderly people had other sources of aid on which they could call, including their earnings and savings and in the case of severe hardship, in the English case, the support of the community through the Poor Law.[4] Accordingly, we will try to determine the changing balance in support for the elderly between their families on the one hand and either the community or their own resources on the other.

The local censuses which have served us well for historical evidence up to this point are far less informative on these matters, containing only the occasional reference to assistance being provided to the elderly by their children or by neighbours.[5] It is inevitable that much of the contact that occurred with kin and neighbours is simply not going to be recorded in the surviving documentary evidence. Two sources, however, repay careful attention. The first is the family histories which accompany the family budgets of peasants, artisans and labourers across Europe collected by the French social scientist Frederic Le Play and his followers in the middle of the nineteenth century. The second is Charles Booth's account of the material circumstances of elderly people from all social classes living in rural communities in England and Wales in 1892 (Le Play, 1855, 1877–9; Ouvriers des deux mondes, 1857–99; Booth, 1894, 1980).

The procedure followed by Le Play was to select one family for detailed study as representing a region or social group and doubts have been expressed about whether one family can ever be typical. Moreover, although he made great efforts to ensure that these families were drawn from regions right across Europe and from a broad spectrum of different occupations (Wall, 1983a, pp. 30–1), he omitted from his study all middle- and upper-class families. Other biases may have been introduced by the strength of Le Play's ideology which favoured the patriarchal or stem-family, where power resided with older males acting as household heads (Laslett, 1972, pp. 16–21; Silver, 1982, pp. 76–80). Le Play's concern with morality and social harmony may also have lead him to portray certain relationships, particularly those between parents and children and employers and employees in too positive a light (Silver, 1982, 73–4), and on the same grounds his account of attitudes towards the elderly could be seen as suspect. In what follows, therefore, we try and guard against biases of this sort by focusing on Le Play's exceptionally careful documentation of the material resources of the elderly, about which there should be less dispute. A close reading of Le Play's account of the circumstances of the individual families enabled the elderly to be classified as alternatively independent or dependent according to whether they received a significant measure of support from their children. The line between what was, and was not, to be considered significant was not easily drawn, but the principle followed was to class as significant all resource transfers without which the standard of living of the parents would have been markedly worse.

It has to be emphasised that, in thus classifying an elderly person as dependent (or independent), this is simply in relation to their offspring and not in any absolute sense. In particular, it ought not to be assumed that because we have classed some elderly as self-supporting as far as their families were concerned, that none of them were in receipt of state support or charitable handouts. Equally, it would be incorrect to infer from the provision of pensions and annuities or the offer of a place in the child's household that relations between parent and child were inevitably harmonious. Le Play in fact documents many instances to the contrary; indeed it is probably more realistic to expect heightened rather than reduced tension where living standards were low and parents and children were competing for scarce resources (see Wall, 1983a, p. 34).

Analysis of the material collected by Le Play and his followers is presented in Table 4.6. This indicates that, in the nineteenth century, rather more than half of elderly labourers, craftsmen and peasants in Europe were financially independent, compared with just over a third who were financially dependent on their offspring. Independence was, however, achieved in a variety of different ways. The largest single category was the 45 per cent of elderly who were supporting themselves from their own resources, relying either on earnings or on savings which they had accumulated over the years. A further nine per cent headed a household which included at least one of their children, but where it is clear that the control of the household remained in the hands of the older generation. These too have been classed as independent elderly.

Table 4.6   The older generation: independence and dependence in Europe in the middle and late nineteenth century (column percentages)

	N	per cent
Independent:		
Household head: offspring dependent	(8)	9
Supported from own sources	(42)	45
Dependent:		
Pension or annuity from offspring's resources	(11)	12
Direct support from study family	(13)	14
Direct support from another sibling	(6)	7
Co-resident with study family	(13)	14
Total	(92)	100

Sources   Ouvriers des deux mondes (1857–99), and Le Play (1855, 1877–9). Case studies of families in Greater Russia are excluded.

The dependent elderly were divided in equal proportions between those who had been incorporated into the household of a child, and those who had also been maintained by the family of the child but in their own households, together with a much smaller group receiving support from the sibling of a member of the family under investigation.[6] Occupying an intermediate position between independence and dependence were those elderly whose children provided them with an annuity or pension. These elderly, too, were technically dependent on their offspring for their livelihood, but perhaps they are best seen as semi-dependent, since such arrangements could not be changed simply because the child wished it, whatever the circumstances. Typically such arrangements came into being following a contract between parent and child by which the parent handed over control of the farm or other enterprise in return for a guaranteed income in old age.

What is particularly interesting in all this is that many, if not a majority, of the elderly whose lives were documented by Le Play and others using his methods, were not just residentially, but financially independent of their children. This result is all the more significant because the family histories collected by Le Play can also be used to show how regularly parents were able and prepared to help their children on marriage or later in life should the need arise. Sixty per cent of the children received such help against the 35 per cent of their children who helped their parents in their old age (see Wall, 1983a, pp. 23–8 for further details on resource transfers affecting young married couples).

In short, in the nineteenth century, aid was more often being channelled down the generational chain than it was being channelled up. Wealth, after all, in general resided with the older generation, and needs with the younger. Some demographers have argued that the high level of fertility before the 1920s was precisely because parents anticipated benefiting from the labour power of their children (cf. Smith, 1981 referring to Caldwell, and Smith, 1984). These data suggest this interpretation is incorrect: if wealth did accumulate in this way, it would appear that it was speedily returned.

The second of the sources to provide information on resource transfers within families, as was mentioned above, is Charles Booth's survey of the elderly in rural areas of England and Wales in 1892. This survey has one great advantage over the material collected by Le Play in that Booth attempted to show what proportion of the population over the age of 65 was receiving, either in money or kind, income support from a variety of sources including the Poor Law, charity, their own earnings and means, and any financial aid from relatives. This enables us to compare the frequency of support by relatives with that derived from other sources. Unfortunately, there is little hard information on the amounts received, although Booth considered that both the amounts transferred by relatives (principally children) and the numbers of elderly who benefited thereby surpassed the levels of aid received from the Poor Law and from charity (Booth, 1894, 1980, pp. 325–6, 341). Booth also comments that earnings and means were

often very small even when they were the principal forms of maintenance.

Table 4.7 shows the frequency with which relatives provided assistance to the elderly person, irrespective of whether any was also forthcoming from other quarters. Altogether, one in four of the elderly
in the 1892 survey received some support from their relatives. This
is more, as Booth himself had indicated, than were assisted by the
Poor Law or by charity but considerably less than the numbers supporting themselves either from earnings or savings. Booth's survey of 1892,
therefore, like the family histories collected earlier by Le Play, indicates
that the great majority of those who had succeeded in reaching old
age were not financially dependent on their children. Moreover, even
were we to adopt a much broader definition of dependency and class
as dependent elderly any who, according to the survey, received some
support from their relatives, charity or the Poor Law, we still find
a situation where a narrow majority of the elderly (55 per cent) would
be classed as independent. Furthermore, it was even rarer for an elderly
person to be totally dependent on relatives; only five per cent of all
the elderly persons in Booth's survey were in this position (Table 4.7).
Indeed, total dependency on any one source of income other than
earnings or savings was somewhat unusual. Thus, five per cent were
exclusively dependent on the Poor Law for their support, and just
one per cent on charity, while under a quarter relied entirely on earnings
or enjoyed means of their own.

Another way of using Booth's data to investigate the contribution
made by relatives to the income of the elderly is to examine in detail
how the various sources of income could be combined. Table 4.8 shows
that combinations of income source were of particular importance for
those who depended to a greater or lesser extent on the Poor Law,
charity, or relatives. By contrast, the majority of those who had earnings or means of their own had just one source of income, with just
one in ten elderly in these groups receiving some support from relatives.
Of particular interest are the patterns of support of those who were
at least partially dependent on the Poor Law. Nearly a quarter of
those supported by the Poor Law had no other source of income.
This is comfortably surpassed by the proportions dependent on the
Poor Law and charity (38 per cent) or on the Poor Law and relatives
(also 38 per cent) although it is larger than the proportion with some
earnings. Even this figure of 38 per cent, however, should not be considered a high level of support by relatives. The late nineteenth century
was a special period in the history of the Poor Law when children

Table 4.7   Sources of income of persons aged ≥ 65 in rural England and Wales in 1892 (cell percentages)

Source of support	Sole method of support	Partial or sole support[3]
Poor Law[1]	5	22
Charity	1	13
Relatives	5	25
Earnings[2]	24	46
Own means	23	34
N =	(9125)	(9125)

Key   1. That is, receipt of out-relief (relief outside the workhouse) from the Poor Law. According to Booth, temporary or medical aid was probably discounted. Paupers belonging to the communities investigated but residing in the union workhouses were excluded.
2. Includes cases of elderly wives whose husbands were earning
3. Combinations of sources of support are possible, hence the percentages do not sum to 100.

Source   Booth (1894, pp. 339–40).

were being pressed hard by the Poor Law authorities to assume responsibility for their elderly parents (Thomson, 1984; Anderson, 1977).

Of course, much of the help provided by children almost certainly did not take the form of a contribution to the income of their parents. Booth includes a little evidence on this elsewhere in his report (Booth, 1894; 1980, pp. 376–7, 379–80, 397–8, 400–1, 406–7, 413–6). A careful scrutiny of this material, restricted to individuals with surviving children, and defining assistance in such a way that it includes all instances of co-residence with children, and of help of all kinds, with cash, rent payments and help with housework provided by the children living elsewhere, indicates that between 70 and 83 per cent of these elderly people were 'helped' by their children: far more in other words than benefited from their financial support (see Table 4.7).[7]

The hardest task of the chapter is to try and compare these findings about levels of assistance from relatives in 1892 with more recent data. Both needs and contact patterns of the elderly have changed so much over the course of the twentieth century that it is difficult to compare levels of assistance, however fully documented they may be in particular enquiries. Nevertheless, a number of studies do indicate whether any income was received from children. In Liverpool in 1930, only three per cent of pensioners had some support from their children (Jones, 1934, pp. 261); similarly, four per cent received support in four towns

82

Table 4.8 Combinations of income sources of persons aged ≥ 65 in rural England and Wales in 1892 (cell percentages)

Source of support	Total benefiting	Sole source	Additional source of income[1]				
			Poor law	Charity	Relatives	Earnings	Own means
Poor Law[2]	2008	23	-	38	38	16	14
Charity	1664	7	46	-	41	32	-
Relatives	2304	21	33	29	-	20	14
Earnings	4244	52	8	13	11	-	16
Own means	3136	68	-	-	10	22	-

Key 1. Combinations of sources of support are possible, hence the percentages do not always sum to 100. Missing data are indicated by hyphens.
2. See Table 4.7, Note 1.

Source Calculated from Booth, (1894, 1980, pp. 339–40). Certain combinations, such as persons receiving charitable or parish support while having some means of their own seem not to have been encountered.

investigated in 1977 (Abrams, 1978, p. 54). However, in Bethnal Green in 1954–5, a very much higher proportion was recorded – fully 61 per cent (Townsend, 1957, p. 62).

The equivalent figure from 1892 would be the 25 per cent whom we estimate received a major boost to their incomes as a result of their children's contributions. Significantly, several of the surveys conducted prior to the 1960s (Liverpool in 1930 is the clear exception) imply a frequency of support not far short of this level.[8] Certainly, it is not possible to detect any major change in the frequency with which the elderly were supported by relatives following the introduction of state pensions early in the twentieth century. On the contrary, well after the introduction of pensions, a substantial minority of elderly persons were continuing to receive some financial support from their relatives. Unfortunately, the situation in the last three decades is less clear in that there is only Abrams' four towns study of 1977 suggesting that support from relatives has become rare. If this finding can be confirmed by studies of other types of community it would indicate a significant falling off in the level of support from relatives during the very decades Thomson identified as seeing a marked improvement in pensioners' incomes relative to other groups in the population (Thomson, 1989).

On the more generous definition of assistance, involving aid in kind as well as in cash and help with various household tasks, a slightly different picture emerges. The 70 or 83 per cent of elderly being helped by their children in 1892 was higher, although not always substantially higher, than that recorded by later surveys. For example, 75 per cent of elderly were 'assisted' in cash or kind in Bethnal Green in 1954–5, 59 per cent according to the 1962 enquiry, while 42 per cent reported they were helped by relatives 'when they visit' when Audrey Hunt completed her research in 1976 (Townsend, 1957, p. 62; Shanas, 1968, p. 205; Hunt, 1978, p. 97). The categories available for comparative purposes are undoubtedly crude and the margin for error great. Taken at face value, however, the various surveys imply that even by the 1950s it was becoming less common for the elderly to rely on their relatives for assistance of a non-financial character than had been the case at the end of the nineteenth century. All the same, such assistance continued to be given, sometimes to a majority of the elderly. In addition, the need of the elderly for such help from relatives may have lessened as more and more people entered old age in better health, while any decline in such assistance may, in any case, have been counterbalanced to some extent by improvements in the quality of relationships once they no longer involved the transfer of scarce resources (Anderson, 1977, p. 59).

CONCLUSION

In this chapter, long-term changes in relationships between the generations have been investigated using the evidence of patterns of co-residence, residential proximity of parents and their adult children, and resource transfers between child and parent. On each occasion, there has been some contrast between 'past' and 'present' but usually not a sharp one. There have been some basic continuities in household composition over the course of several centuries, notably, for example, in that more women than men are likely to be living on their own in their old age. Where there has been change in residence patterns, it is only in the last thirty years that these have become marked with a rapid expansion of the proportions of elderly living alone, or alone but for a spouse. Co-residence with a child has become much more unusual. It is also possible that the 1960s saw changes in the proportions of elderly receiving financial support from relatives.

Nevertheless, on the basis of the evidence that has been presented, it is apparent that claims that the family is in terminal decline (and has been since the nineteenth century if not earlier) are unjustified. It is also worth emphasising that in the past the family had only a minority role to play in securing the financial well-being of their elderly relatives. Much more common, was for the responsibility of the elderly to be shared between the state, the family and other charitably minded individuals.

Notes

1.   Consideration is confined in Tables 4.1 and 4.2 to the household and family patterns of all elderly persons and a more exact comparison would require information on the household and family patterns of the elderly poor in the nineteenth century and earlier (as support from the community from the Poor Law was offered only to those deemed to be in need). However, a recent authoritative study of the poor in an Essex agricultural community at the end of the eighteenth century and in a neighbouring de-industrialising one early in the nineteenth century reached the conclusion that the poor could not be distinguished from the majority of the population 'in terms of specific features of size, composition and structure of the household' (see Sokoll, 1988, p. 324).

2.   Some under-count of children separated from their spouse or widowed

is likely as the marital status of persons recorded as child of the head is frequently omitted from the enumeration of local populations during the pre-industrial period.

3. So great is the change suggested for the 1960s, from 22 per cent of elderly living with a never-married child to 14 per cent for men or 11 per cent for women in 1971, that there is justification for some suspicion that the 1962 survey of the elderly may have over-estimated the frequency with which the elderly lived with a child. (For an admission that there might have been an under-count of the very elderly in the sample and of the elderly who lived alone, see Shanas *et al.*, 1968, Appendix A, pp. 458–9).

4. In other European countries, different institutions regulated the support of the poor and provision for them was not always so generous, see Woolf (1986), pp. 186–94; van Leeuwen (1986), p. 7.

5. See for example the local census of Corfe Castle in 1790, reference to Abraham Croker 'blind. He is maintained by his children, and etc.'; and the local census of Warmsworth, Yorkshire in 1829, reference to Charlotte Jackson in house number 4 waiting gratuitously on the Bennetts aged 85 and 83 in house number 1. Copies of these censuses are in the Library of the ESRC Cambridge Group.

6. There may, however, be a slight under-reporting of the incidence of co-residence between parent and child given the implication of Table 4.6 that even on the maximising assumption that the siblings of family members always incorporated the parent into their own households, only 30 per cent of the members of the older generation co-resided with a child. This seems on the low side compared with the 49 per cent of elderly males and 37 per cent of elderly females indicated in the local censuses of pre-industrial rural England as co-residing with a child, see above Table 4.2. Furthermore, over much of Southern and Eastern Europe in the past higher proportions of elderly with co-residing children could be anticipated than was the case in England (Wall, 1983).

7. That there are two percentages reflects the fact that the descriptions given by Booth do not always make it clear whether there were any surviving children. Assuming that where children were not mentioned that the elderly were actually childless, produced the higher of the estimates of assistance from children because it removed a number of elderly from the category of those assumed to have children but whose children did not provide assistance.

8. Apart from those studies that have already been mentioned, there are the seven per cent (or 39 per cent if co-residents are included) of working-class elderly in London supported by their children in 1929–31 (see Gordon, 1988, p. 34), the 16 per cent said to have such support according to a national sample of elderly over the age of 60 in 1945 (Thomas, 1947, p. 56), the 23 per cent of persons over the age of 60 in a survey taken for the purpose of assessing the housing needs of elderly people in Hamilton in 1950 (Gray and Beltram, 1950, p. 13), and the 24 per cent of the national survey of 1962 (Shanas *et al.*, 1968, p. 205).

5 'In Sickness and in Health': Care-giving, Gender and the Independence of Elderly People[1]

Sara Arber and Jay Ginn

In sociology, research on the family and the distribution of labour and resources within the household has tended to ignore elderly people, focusing on younger people's changing patterns of employment and domestic work. Feminist sociologists, who might have recognised a parallel between the long neglect of gender and the current invisibility of elderly people in sociology, have stopped short of later life (Arber and Ginn, 1991). Elderly people have figured primarily as another unfairly shared burden on younger women as carers.

This contrasts with the voluminous social policy literature on elderly people, in which they have been 'welfarised', seen primarily in terms of their needs as recipients of state pensions, health and welfare services. A well-intentioned 'compassionate ageism' has enhanced elderly people's visibility but contributed to a pathology model in which elderly people are seen mainly in terms of disability, poverty, isolation and role loss. This has reinforced a prejudicial stereotype of elderly people as a dependent group, separate from and different from the rest of society.

In most economically developed societies, there is concern about the implications of the growing proportion of elderly people in the population, especially those over age 75 and 85. In Britain the numbers over 85 were 57 000 in 1901, 552 000 in 1981, and are expected to exceed one million in 2001. These trends cannot be disputed, but their interpretation depends on societal values and political priorities, as well as on the association between age and functional capacities. Forecasts of escalating costs of meeting the health and welfare needs of elderly people, including residential care, have reinforced the government's preference for community care (DH, 1989), which in practice transfers more of the costs of care from the state to individuals.

Associating calendar age with dependency and burden ignores the social construction of dependency, improvements in health in successive cohorts, and the positive capacities of elderly people (Thane, 1988). Ageist views, especially those which portray elderly people as dependent and passive, conceal the activities of elderly people as informal carers themselves, and the diversity of household situations in which they live.

The dominant concern of the care-giving literature has been the burden faced by those caring for frail elderly relatives (Biegel and Blum, 1990; Braithwaite, 1990), rather than the preferences and needs of elderly people themselves. The focus of Equal Opportunities Commission research (EOC, 1980, 1982) and feminist writers (Dalley, 1988) has been how caring responsibilities disadvantage women. Elderly people are conceptualised as a passive object to be cared for. This is exemplified in the government survey of *Informal Carers* which aimed to estimate the demand for services, assuming that carers are the key actors in articulating these demands (Green, 1988, 1990).

Another research strand reinforcing the view of elderly people as objects is the literature on family obligations to care for kin. Finch's work (1987, 1989) focuses on the negotiation of normative obligations about who should care for elderly relatives unable to manage on their own. Elderly people themselves are not expected to have an active input or to express a preference in this process, and the solutions adopted are those which suit the potential carers (Finch and Mason, 1990a, 1990b). The implicit assumption is that elderly people are no longer active agents with power to control their own lives; in this sense they have lost their humanity.

Most studies give a one-sided account of the caring relationship, neglecting the view of the person cared for, and British terminology reflects this in the value-laden term 'dependant'. We shall follow American practice (Biegel and Blum, 1990) in using care-recipient and caregiver to signify a more equal relationship.

DEPENDENCE AND INDEPENDENCE

Advancing age is associated with decline in physical capabilities, and increasing likelihood of dependence on others for help with personal and domestic activities. Loss of autonomy is seen most vividly in institutional care, with Goffman (1963) providing a classic condemnatory statement in *Asylums*. Although the worst aspects of institutionalisation may no longer occur, in most currently available organisational settings the actions of residents are constrained by inflexible routines. Accounts of the ill-effects of institutional care (Townsend, 1962; Brown, 1973) have provided part of the underlying rationale for promoting community care (Griffiths Report, 1988; DH, 1989), this being seen as more likely to preserve independence. Closure of publicly-provided residential care homes and long-stay hospitals has often been justified on these grounds. But this neglects both the potential for autonomy in new forms of residential care (Foster, 1990), and the likely effect on elderly people of enforced dependence on relatives in certain caring contexts. Foster has begun to question the ideological equation that institutions are necessarily 'bad', arguing that it is time analysts and particularly feminists took a more critical and positive look at the potential of institutions. Community care may not always be ideal from the perspective of the person receiving care. This chapter argues that community care needs to be conceptualised in terms of a range of caring contexts – institutional care may be preferable in some circumstances.

In spite of the view of the Conservative government (Jenkin, 1977; DHSS, 1981) that the family is the most natural and preferred source of care for those needing help, there is evidence that elderly people would often prefer to rely on state services than their children (Sixsmith, 1986; West, 1984). Similarly in the USA (Crystal, 1982), the majority of elderly people would prefer to go into a nursing home than live with adult children. The minority of recent UK research which has taken the perspective of the elderly person (for example Wenger, 1984; Qureshi and Walker, 1989) demonstrates that they are anxious not to become dependent on their children. Qureshi and Walker state:

> Elderly people do not give up their independence easily; with few exceptions they are reluctant subjects in caring and dependency (1989, pp. 18–19).

However, there has been little recognition that an elderly person's independence and scope for autonomy varies in different caring contexts within the community.

In later life, chronic health problems often impact on a person's physical and social functioning, such as ability to walk and dress oneself. Disability refers to how much difficulty a person has in doing routine activities on his or her own. Dant (1990, p. 21) reminds us that physical disability leads to dependence on others when it cannot be compensated for by other resources (for example with wheelchairs, aids and adaptations). Disability is conceptually distinct from dependence, the extent to which someone receives help from another person for personal or household tasks (Verbrugge, 1989a). Braithwaite argues thus:

> The prospect of becoming dependent on others for basic needs is regarded with trepidation by most of us. Dependency in adulthood threatens cherished values of self-respect and human dignity (1990, p. 1)

However, the degree of physical dependence is not necessarily related to loss of autonomy. In some caring contexts the care-giver takes over not only the elderly person's physical care, but also the scheduling of their lives, their finances and their decision-making, a situation exemplified in the title of the Radio 4 programme 'Does he take sugar?' When this happens, frail elderly people are deprived of most of their opportunity for autonomous action. They may also have very restricted use of personal space (Marsden and Abrams, 1987). Thus the degree of social dependence may vary between caring relationships.

Since access to caring resources is a key factor in mediating the relationship between disability and dependence, this chapter will focus on access to different types of caring resource. Alternative caring contexts are analysed, in terms of the elderly person's relationship to their carer, and whether care is provided within the care-recipient's own home or not. We argue that the caring context is likely to have profound implications for the sense of autonomy of the care-recipient, and suggest that elderly women are disadvantaged in being less likely to have access to caring resources which preserve their sense of independence and control over their own lives.

We discuss below how three essential aspects of self-identity may be threatened by disability, and the ways in which different living arrangements influence an elderly person's opportunity to maintain self-identity.

PRESERVATION OF SELF-IDENTITY

Caring contexts vary as to whether they facilitate a frail elderly person acting as an autonomous agent, and influence three other aspects of personal identity. Although elderly people strive to preserve all three, there are gender differences in the nature of the first.

(1) Maintenance of Roles Salient to Personal Identity

Elderly people seek to express aspects of their self identity which are particularly salient to them as individuals, perhaps through continuation of their occupational role identity or a hobby or pastime. Some of the roles which are central to self-identity are related to gender socialisation, so that for the majority of women performing domestic tasks such as cooking, washing and cleaning is fundamental to their self-identity (Graham, 1983). For men, different tasks may be important. Men are more likely to accept (and to welcome) help with domestic tasks at an earlier stage of physical disability, whereas women may resist this assault on a primary aspect of their self-identity.

(2) Presentation as a Competent Adult to External Audiences

Although ability to perform personal and domestic tasks tends to decline with increasing physical frailty, elderly people are likely to try to preserve their image as a competent adult so that others outside the household remain unaware of any deficiency. Finch (1989) notes the importance of such external audiences. Among elderly married couples where one spouse is disabled, husbands and wives are likely to collaborate to maintain an image of normality to outside audiences (Parker, 1989; Ungerson, 1987).

Research on the families of unemployed men has parallels with caring among elderly married couples. McKee's research (1987) illustrated how the household rallied round to preserve the sense of personal identity of the husband and give the impression that the whole family was coping. She argued that there was a cultural assumption that married couples should be self-sufficient, and that marital privacy was primary. Help from others outside the household, which could not be reciprocated, was often resisted.

The same process is likely to occur where one partner is physically frail, their spouse providing the support necessary to preserve the appearance of integrity of the family as a unit. From the point of view of the care-recipient, such a caring context maximises their appearance of competence in the eyes of the outside world.

(3) Reciprocity and Felt Sense of Burden on Others

Finch's work on family obligations (1987, 1989) shows that kin generally seek to reciprocate obligations so that a balance is maintained.

Only in a few situations, such as the provision of services and gifts from parents to children, and from grandparents to grandchildren, is it acceptable for obligations to remain out of balance. Wall (this volume) argues that there is now and always has been a net flow of goods and services from parents to their adult children. It may therefore be particularly difficult for elderly people to accept dependence on their adult children which represents a reversal of the normative flow of obligations.

Neither Finch nor Qureshi and Walker (1989) discuss reciprocity between spouses. However, Dalley states:

> spouses are happy to care reciprocally for each other; this seems to be one of the implicit bargains of the marriage contract – but willingness to care for other dependants (and to be cared for) is highly relationship- and context-specific (1988, p. 11).

In this chapter we follow Dalley and assume that, in marriage, reciprocity is long-term and general. Spouse care is implicit within the legal marital contract and explicit in the religious one: 'in sickness and in health'. It is essentially non-negotiable. Frail elderly people with access to care from their spouse can be considered to be living in a preferential caring context. A short-term imbalance of care-giving services is seen as acceptable. This is not meant to imply that elderly spouses never resent such a caring role and the consequent restrictions on their life (Connidis, 1989).

Thus caring relationships where there is an attempt at balance are qualitatively distinct from those between spouses. Restoration of balance may be negotiated in a complex way, and involve reciprocation through provision of different types of services (Finch, 1989). Where a frail elderly person is cared for by an adult child, balance cannot be restored, since the care-recipient is unable to reciprocate (except perhaps in financial terms through money gifts/loans or the promise of inheritance). Elderly people are therefore likely to feel themselves to be a burden on the care-giver in this situation (Qureshi and Walker, 1989). Finch notes 'Older people are acutely conscious of the possibility of making too many demands, and commonly try to avoid a situation where they have to rely on their children too much' (1989, p. 39).

Frail elderly people in need of support wish to minimise the extent to which they are breaking norms of family reciprocity and their sense of being a burden on others, but caring contexts vary in the extent to which both parties see the carer's role as burdensome. We show below that frail elderly women are more likely than equally frail elderly men to be in a caring context where they are likely to perceive themselves, and are perceived by others, as a burden.

CARING CONTEXTS AND THE PRESERVATION OF
AUTONOMY AND SELF-IDENTITY

Frail elderly people wish to maximise personal autonomy, preserve a positive self-identity, maintain the appearance of competence to external audiences, and minimise their burden on others (in terms of unreciprocated obligations). These aims broadly coalesce within different caring contexts. Figure 5.1 is a proposed hierarchy of caring contexts in terms of their preference from the elderly person's perspective. The ordering has been derived by interpreting the relevant literature on caring and from our previous research. Spouse care is preferable, followed by care from same generation relatives within the household (for example siblings), and care by adult children or non-kin living in the elderly person's own household. Care provided within the elderly person's own household is likely to be preferred over care provided by relatives who live elsewhere, as it affects the extent to which they are likely to perceive themselves (and be perceived by the carer) as a burden.

Finch notes that 'Sharing accommodation with relatives on a permanent basis is not regarded as a desirable option in contemporary British culture' (1989, p. 22). A key distinction is whether the care-recipient lives in their own household, where they can expect greater independence, or in the household of the care-giver. In the frail elderly person's own home, long-term co-residence with the care-giver is more likely. Here, the elderly care-recipient may, despite physical dependence, have considerable power over their care-giver, for example continuing a dominant parent–child relationship (Lewis and Meredith, 1988). There is likely to be a continuity of reciprocity at some level, even where most of the personal care tasks are performed by the care-giver.

Where an elderly person lives in the home of their care-giver, co-residence is more likely to have been established because of the care-recipient's need for support. The tensions in such co-residence in the past are described by Le Play (1855) and by Anderson (1977) who give graphic illustrations of elderly people as prisoners in their children's homes. A long-term relationship of reciprocity is less likely, and the care-recipient will have been defined from the outset as a depen-

A. *In elderly person's own home: – Self care*

B. *In elderly person's own home: – Care provided by co-resident:*
  - (i) Spouse
  - (ii) Other same generation relative
  - (iii) Child or non-kin

C. *In elderly person's own home: – Care provided by extra-resident:*
  - (iv) Child
  - (v) Other relative
  - (vi) Neighbour, friend, volunteer

D. *In Care-giver's own home – Care provided by co-resident:*
  - (vii) Unmarried child
  - (viii) Married child

Domiciliary support services, such as home helps and community nurses, may provide an enabling role for the frail elderly person in any of these caring contexts.

Figure 5.1   Proposed hierarchy of elderly person's preference for caring contexts

dant, with consequent loss of autonomy and limited opportunity for reciprocation (Arber and Gilbert, 1989a). It is a less desirable caring context from the point of view of the elderly person, and is more liable to break down than care in the elderly person's own home (Braithwaite, 1990).

The preceding discussion has suggested that in varying ways the caring context is crucial to an elderly person's autonomy. The rest of the chapter examines the receipt of care by frail elderly people in the community, and how gender influences the likelihood of receiving care from different care-givers.

DATA AND METHODS

The General Household Survey (GHS) provides a large and nationally representative sample of people living in private households. It achieved an overall response rate of 82 per cent (OPCS, 1987) in the 1985 survey, in which nearly 4000 people over age 65 were interviewed. Moreover, in that year, extra information was sought on the level of disability of elderly people and self-reports of who provides assistance with various personal care and domestic tasks.

A scale of disability was developed based on an elderly person's ability to perform six activities: climbing stairs, cutting toenails, walking down the road, washing all over and bathing, getting round the house and getting into and out of bed. Each activity was coded in two ways: firstly, 0 if the activity could be done easily and 1 if only with difficulty or if it could not be done unaided, and secondly, 0 if it could be done unaided and 1 if it could only be performed with help. These items formed a Guttman scale with a maximum score of 12, similar to an earlier scale developed on the 1980 GHS (Arber *et al.*, 1988).

Contrary to media images of the growing burden of elderly people, disability and the provision of informal care is restricted to a small minority of elderly people. Half the population over age 65 have no disability and a quarter only mild disability (score 1–2; they have difficulty cutting their toenails). The 11 per cent of elderly people with severe disability (score of 6–12) use most of the formal health and welfare services (Arber *et al.*, 1988) and the majority of informal caring resources. They will generally be unable to walk down the road unaided, or bath or go up and downstairs unaided. Four per cent of elderly people have very severe disability (score 9–12), and would generally have difficulty getting around the house.

GENDER DIFFERENCES IN DISABILITY

As is well known, disability is strongly gender differentiated; 70 per cent of elderly women and 83 per cent of men have no disability or only a minimal level (score 0–2), and twice as many elderly women (14 per cent) as men (seven per cent) are severely disabled (Table 5.1). Three per cent of elderly men but five per cent of elderly women are very severely disabled.

The overall gender difference in physical health in later life is partly due to women's greater longevity. There are more women than men in older age groups; 21 per cent of elderly women are aged 80 and over compared to 13 per cent of elderly men (row percentages on Table 5.1). Women at each age are more likely to become disabled than men (Verbrugge, 1984a, 1984b, 1989), but, what is less widely appreciated, the gender differential increases with age. Among those over 85, a fifth of women compared to a tenth of men are very severely disabled (score 9–12) and would require a carer's constant support. In short, although men are disadvantaged in having a shorter life expectancy, women are disadvantaged by their poorer physical health

Table 5.1 Disability level of elderly men and women by age (column percentages).

| | Age group: | | | | | | | | | | | |
| | 65–69 | | 70–74 | | 75–79 | | 80–84 | | 85+ | | All | |
	M	F	M	F	M	F	M	F	M	F	M	F
None	72	63	63	49	54	35	37	24	14	11	60	43
Slight (1–2)	17	23	24	29	26	32	30	26	34	19	23	27
Moderate (3–5)	6	9	8	14	10	17	22	25	29	27	10	16
Severe (6–8)	3	4	3	5	5	10	7	15	14	22	4	9
Very severe (9–12)	2	2	1	2	6	5	4	9	10	21	3	5
Total	100%	100%	100%	100%	100%	100%	100%	100%	100%	100%	100 %	100%
N =	(522)	(588)	(437)	(615)	(324)	(493)	(135)	(269)	(59)	(188)	(1477)	(2153)
Row % Men	35%		30%		22%		9%		4%		100%	
Row % Women		27%		29%		23%		12%		9%		100%

Source General Household Survey, 1985 (original analysis)

(increasingly with advancing age) which leads to their needing more care than comparable elderly men.

CARING RESOURCES AND CARING CONTEXTS

The key caring resource for many elderly people is provided by their spouse. Such care is expected as of right. There is substantial gender inequality in access to spouse care, because of differences between men and women in age at marriage, mortality, and chances of remarriage. Nearly three-quarters of elderly men, but under two-fifths of elderly women, were married in 1985. Among those over 85 (the group with the highest proportion of severely disabled) over five times more men (41 per cent) were married than women (8 per cent).

Concern about the increase in numbers of very elderly needs to be tempered by an awareness of the parallel increase in the proportion of elderly people who are married and thus have a spouse available to provide care should they need it. During this century, there has been a thirty per cent increase in the proportion of elderly men at each age who are still married and therefore have a spouse as a potential care-giver should they need help with domestic and personal self-care tasks (OPCS 1974, Table 5). Among 1985 GHS respondents, 66 per cent of men aged 75–84 were married compared with 44 per cent in the census of 1911, and the comparable figures for women of the same age were 24 per cent and 17 per cent. The increase this century in the proportion of elderly women who are married has been smaller than the increase for men.

An opposite trend in the latter half of this century has reduced the availability of co-resident carers: the increase in the proportion of elderly people living alone. As Wall (this volume) shows, this rose from 12 per cent in 1945 to 36 per cent in 1985. Both Wall and Finch (1989) suggest that this trend reflects greater financial independence among elderly people, and a preference for living alone rather than being dependent on younger kin. Although policy commentators have interpreted the growth in number of elderly people living alone as signalling the demise of the family as a caring institution, this trend in fact probably reflects instead the preferences of elderly people themselves to remain independent and to minimise their sense of burden on others, particularly their adult children.

The proportion of elderly people who are severely disabled varies between living arrangements (Table 5.2). It is lower for elderly people

living alone (12 per cent) or as part of a married couple (nine per
cent), and higher among elderly siblings who live together (17 per cent),
and widowed who live with an unmarried child (18 per cent). The
highest proportion with severe disability are elderly people who live
with their married children (25 per cent).

*Table 5.*2   Percentage of elderly people who are severely disabled in different
living situations

	%	
Lives alone	12	(1315)
Elderly married couple	9	(1820)
Elderly siblings living together	17	(181)
Widowed elderly with unmarried child	18	(134)
Elderly with married child	25	(182)
All elderly	11	(3632)

Source   *General Household Survey*, 1985 (original analysis)

   We suggested earlier that elderly people will prefer to be cared for
in their own home than in the home of their care-giver. The GHS
data allow us to distinguish whether the elderly person is the householder (lives in their own home) or whether they are the parent of
the householder (live in their child's home). Under one-fifth of elderly
people living with an unmarried child live in the child's home. This
increases to one-half for elderly people living with a married child.
There is little evidence that an elderly parent moves into an unmarried
child's house because of increasing disability. This contrasts with
elderly people co-resident with a younger married couple. Almost two-
fifths of elderly parents who live in their married child's house are
themselves severely disabled and are likely to require care, suggesting
that such households are often formed because of an elderly person's
increasing frailty.
   A disabled elderly person moving into the household of a younger
married couple is likely to produce conflict for the carer (Arber and
Gilbert, 1989a, 1989b) who also has competing obligations to her husband and children. The care-recipient is likely to be perceived by their
carer as a burden (Marsden and Abrams, 1987; Nissel and Bonnerjea,
1982). Since the majority of physically frail elderly people are aware
of how others see them, they are likely to internalise this perception
of themselves as a burden, and as a source of strain to the carer.

The significance of these different household arrangements for a frail elderly person needing assistance lies in the different implications they are likely to have for that person's self-identity and their degree of autonomy. Gender influences the likelihood of receiving care in different caring contexts. Two factors determine the nature of care for elderly disabled people, (i) the relationship between the elderly person and their co-resident kin, and (ii) whether the elderly person lives in their own house, or in that of their carer. Gender differences on these two dimensions are summarised in Table 5.3. Almost half of elderly women live alone compared to only a fifth of men, and very severe disability (scores 9–12) reduces the chances of either sex living alone. Among very severely disabled elderly men, 69 per cent live with their spouse, compared with only 27 per cent of women. Very severely disabled elderly women are much more likely to live in another's household. Table 5.3 suggests that elderly disabled women move to live with others, mainly their adult children or elderly siblings, but there is no comparable trend for elderly disabled men. Very severely disabled women are over four times more likely than similar men to live in the home of their adult children, where they are most likely to be seen, and see themselves, as a burden.

GENDER AND HELP WITH PERSONAL AND DOMESTIC TASKS

A key aspect of the maintenance of autonomy and a positive self-image for elderly people is the extent to which others provide for their personal self-care and domestic needs, and the nature of the kin relationship to the carer. Figure 5.1 proposed a hierarchy from the elderly person's perspective of the desirability of receiving care in different caring contexts. We are concerned now with three questions: first, how the caring context of elderly people is associated with the level of help provided; second, whether there are gender differences in the amount of help received with personal care and domestic tasks; and third, how the caring context and the elderly person's gender influence the relative amount of support provided by care-givers within the same household, by informal carers living elsewhere and by formal services.

Where elderly people in the GHS said they could not perform various personal and domestic tasks, or said they could only do them with difficulty, they were asked who usually helped them or performed these

Table 5.3   Caring contexts for elderly men and women by level of disability (Column percentages)

	Not disabled (0–5)		Severe disability (6–8)		Very Severe disability (9–12)	
	Men	*Women*	*Men*	*Women*	*Men*	*Women*
Lives alone	20	48	26	52	14	29
Lives in own household:						
with spouse	71	37	58	31	69	27
with others (mainly						
adult children)	6	8	9	9	7	18
Not in own household:						
with adult children	2	3	6	6	5	21
with others	2	3	–	2	5	4
	100%	100%	100%	100%	100%	100%
N =	(1370)	(1853)	(65)	(189)	(42)	(113)

Source   General Household Survey, 1985 (original analysis)

tasks for them. For each task, a maximum of three different people could be named as helping. The total number of people mentioned was summed separately for the personal tasks and for the domestic care tasks.

Personal Tasks

We analyse first assistance with personal tasks, such as climbing stairs, washing and bathing, getting in and out of bed (usually referred to in the American literature as 'Activities of Daily Living'), and in the next section examine help with domestic tasks such as shopping, washing clothes, cleaning floors and cooking, ('Instrumental Activities of Daily Living'). For both personal activities and domestic tasks, the amount of support, as indicated by number of sources of help, increased with level of disability (Table 5.4).

Ninety-three per cent of men and 86 per cent of women performed personal care activities unaided (Table 5.4a). Overall women received help from more sources than men simply because they were more likely to be disabled. There were no consistent gender differences within each

women with climbing stairs, feeding, getting to the toilet, shaving/brushing hair, bathing, washing face/hands, walking inside the house (column percentages)

Number of Sources	Disability Level: 0		1-2		3-5		6-8		9-12		All	
	M	F	M	F	M	F	M	F	M	F	M	F
None	100	100	99	98	86	78	28	37	7	8	93	86
1	–	–	1	2	12	18	46	39	26	21	4	8
2	–	–	–	–	1	3	22	16	21	37	2	4
3 or more	–	–	–	–	–	1	5	8	45	34	2	2
N =	100% (883)	100% (933)	100% (340)	100% (579)	100% (147)	100% (341)	100% (65)	100% (189)	100% (42)	100% (113)	100% (1477)	100% (2155)

(b) Help with domestic care tasks by level of disability* Number of sources of help received by elderly men and women with shopping, sweeping floors, washing laundry and cooking (column percentages)

Number of Sources	Disability Level: 0		1-2		3-5		6-8		9-12		All	
	M	F	M	F	M	F	M	F	M	F	M	F
None	63	93	51	83	35	47	20	14	5	8	54	72
1-2	26	7	31	15	33	44	28	55	9	15	27	19
3-4	11	–	16	2	25	7	31	17	31	22	15	4
5 or more	1	–	3	1	7	3	22	13	55	55	5	5
N =	100% (883)	100% (933)	100% (340)	100% (579)	100% (147)	100% (341)	100% (65)	100% (189)	100% (42)	100% (113)	100% (1477)	100% (2155)

*For each task up to three different helpers could be given by the respondent.

Source General Household Survey, 1985 (original analysis)

level of disability. However, there were substantial differences in the amount of support provided in each of the three main types of living arrangements – living with a spouse, living alone, and living in a two- or three-generational household. Unfortunately, the numbers are too small if the entire table is subdivided by the number of generations in the household or whether the elderly person was the householder or not. Since the level of support is associated with the degree of disability of the elderly person, we consider only those with severe disability.

Severely disabled elderly people living alone received support with personal care from fewer sources than those living in a married couple or a multi-generational household (final two rows of Table 5.5). Within each type of living arrangement there were only small gender differences in the average number of sources of help with personal tasks to severely disabled people. Among elderly married couples, men received somewhat more support than women, 26 per cent received help from three or more sources compared with 16 per cent of women. On the other hand, among those living alone or in multi-generational households elderly women received help from more sources than equivalent elderly men.

Who provides care has implications for whether care is received as of right, or is the product of negotiations as to the nature of obligations of different relatives. Although those living alone received less support with personal tasks, they were more likely to receive it from formal services than other elderly people, and were the only group who received help from friends and neighbours. Thus they were more dependent on the state and neighbourly care and less dependent on relatives. Despite this more varied dependency, relatives still provided about half the sources of support with personal tasks for elderly people who lived alone.

Elderly wives provided virtually all the support with personal tasks for their severely disabled husbands, with a similar pattern for husbands caring for their wives. The frail elderly who were married therefore received their personal care primarily from their partner, which must have had advantages for their self-identity and sense of autonomy as outlined earlier. Only small amounts of care were provided by formal services (district nurses and home helps), and by other relatives within and outside the household. The frail elderly living in multi-generational households had a similar profile to the married frail elderly in terms of receiving most of their personal care from members of their household, but the burden of felt obligations to a married daughter or daughter-in-law was probably very different compared to situations in which a husband or wife was the care-giver.

Table 5.5   Who helps with personal care tasks.* Average number of times different carers were mentioned who provided help with personal care tasks to elderly men and women with severe disability in different living arrangements. Personal care tasks were: climbing stairs, feeding, getting to the toilet, shaving/brushing hair, bathing, washing face/hands, walking indoors

	Lives alone			Married couple			Multi-generational household		
	Men	Women	All	Men	Women	All	Men	Women	All
Co-resident care:									
By spouse	–	–	–	1.62	1.30	1.44	(0.36)	0.07	0.12
By adult child or other in household	–	–	–	0.06	0.06	0.06	(0.82)	1.55	1.43
Care from outside the household:									
Other relative	0.30	0.54	0.51	0.06	0.07	0.06	(0.27)	0.10	0.13
Friend/ neighbour	–	0.16	0.14	0.01	0.01	0.01	–	–	–
Formal services	0.39	0.29	0.31	0.10	0.10	0.10	–	0.16	0.13
Paid care	0.09	0.01	0.02	–	–	–	–	–	–
Average number of sources of help	0.78	1.01	0.97	1.85	1.53	1.67	(1.55)	1.88	1.83
% receiving 3 or more sources of help	4	9	8	26	16	20	9	31	27
N =	(23)	(131)	(154)	(68)	(88)	(156)	(11)	(58)	(69)

* For each task up to three different helpers could be given by the respondent

Source   *General Household Survey*, 1985 (original analysis)

Domestic Tasks

In contrast to the lack of overall gender difference in help with personal care tasks, there was a striking gender difference in help with domestic tasks (Table 5.4b). Nearly two-fifths of men without disability reported receiving help, compared with only 7 per cent of equivalent women, and half of men with slight disability (score 1–2) received help.

For each level of disability, men received more domestic help than women. This reflects gender differences in the salience of domestic work for self-identity as well as in the views of others about the abilities of men and women to perform such tasks. Women may have been reluctant to give up performing such tasks, even if they had great difficulty. For example Wright (1983) found that severely disabled elderly women often struggled to continue to prepare meals for their unmarried sons. However, among the most severely disabled there was no gender difference.

The level of domestic support to severely disabled elderly people living in different situations is shown in Table 5.6 (and can be contrasted with personal support in Table 5.5). The highest level was provided to those living in multi-generational households and the lowest to elderly people who live alone, with married elderly people in an intermediate position.[2] Only in multi-generational households did women receive help from more sources than men; 57 per cent of severely disabled elderly women in multi-generational households received five or more sources of domestic support compared to only a fifth of comparable women living alone or with their husbands. This suggests that elderly women living with their adult children are more likely to be dependent domestically than comparable women living in other settings.

In multi-generational households, virtually all domestic care was provided by household members, whereas elsewhere there was a greater diversity of providers. For married couples there was a gender difference: wives provided approximately 95 per cent of all the domestic support for their disabled husbands, whereas husbands provided only about three-quarters of the domestic support for disabled wives, the remainder being supplied by formal services and other relatives. Thus elderly husbands were not such comprehensive care-givers in the domestic arena as elderly wives who cared for their husbands. This contrasts with personal care where, as we showed above, there was equivalent support by husbands and by wives.

Disabled elderly people living alone received more assistance from formal services than in other caring contexts. But this group was still reliant for nearly half their domestic help on relatives living elsewhere and may have felt a burden on these care-givers. Friends and neighbours also performed a significant role, unlike in other caring contexts. Although such care may have been less reliable than care from relatives or the state, it may have resulted from reciprocal relationships, and therefore have generated less sense of burden in the elderly person.

Disabled elderly people who lived with adult children were entirely dependent on them for domestic support, and the amount of support they provided was very great. This may have increased their dependence in ways which threatened self-identity, especially for disabled elderly

'In Sickness and in Health'

Table 5.6 Who helps with domestic care tasks.* Average number of times different carers were mentioned who provided help with domestic tasks to elderly men and women withsevere disability in different living arrangements. Domestic care tasks were: shopping, sweeping floors, washing laundry and cooking

	Lives alone			Married couple			Multi-generational household		
	Men	Women	All	Men	Women	All	Men	Women	All
Co-resident care:									
By spouse	–	–	–	3.32	1.94	2.54	(0.91)	0.07	0.20
By adult child or other in house	–	–	–	0.01	0.06	0.04	(2.73)	3.93	3.74
Care from outside the household:									
Other relative	1.09	1.20	1.19	0.04	0.24	0.15	(0.18)	0.07	0.09
Friend/ neighbour	0.30	0.31	0.31	0.01	0.05	0.03	–	0.05	0.04
Formal services	1.09	0.95	0.97	0.10	0.20	0.16	–	0.03	0.03
Paid care	0.22	0.07	0.09	0.01	0.07	0.04	–	–	–
Average number of sources of help	2.70	2.53	2.55	3.51	2.56	2.97	3.82	4.16	4.10
% receiving 5 or more sources of help	22	17	18	37	22	28	36	57	54
N =	(23)	(131)	(154)	(68)	(88)	(156)	(11)	(58)	(69)

*For each task, up to three different helpers could be given by the respondent.

Source General Household Survey, 1985 (original analysis)

women. Since the majority of frail elderly men were married, they could rely almost exclusively on care provided by their wife, receiving very little care from outside the household, or from the state.

CONCLUSION

This chapter has shown the importance of studying the contexts in which frail elderly people receive care, and has pointed to some of the implications of different living arrangements for elderly people's maintenance of self-identity and autonomy.

Men are advantaged in terms of both health and caring resources.

In each age group, elderly men are less likely to be disabled than women, and for each level of disability, men have more access to privileged caring resources, provided as of right, than equivalent women. We suggest that this gives them greater opportunity to preserve their self-identity and minimise their apparent disability to external audiences. Disabled elderly women, in contrast, are more likely than men to be perceived, and to perceive themselves, as a burden simply because they are more likely to live alone or in the home of an adult child. This inequity in access to care is compounded by elderly women's lower average income (Ginn and Arber, 1991). The limited access of older women to both financial and caring resources is a poor deal for 'the carer sex' after a lifetime of unpaid work looking after children, husband and others, often in addition to waged work.

The numbers of disabled elderly people being cared for in the community in living arrangements which are not ideal for their personal autonomy and self-identity could be minimised by policies to expand their options, so that moving to live with adult children could be chosen from among alternatives. These might include the provision of collectively subsidised and democratically managed residential schemes where elderly people could exercise autonomy and maximise their capacity for self-care, and where relatives could share care with staff (Foster, 1990). Pension schemes which removed gender bias by fully compensating those whose work is unpaid would allow elderly women more room to manoeuvre, and reduce dependence on relatives. While recognising the needs and wishes of elderly people, we should, as Thane (1988) has urged, develop policies which treat elderly people as a resource rather than a burden.

Notes

1. This paper is based on a project on Community Care and the Elderly funded by the ESRC (Grant No. R000231458). We are indebted to the ESRC Data Archive, University of Essex, and to the University of London Computing Centre for access to the 1985 General Household Survey, and to the Office of Population Censuses and Surveys for permission to use the GHS data.
2. More detailed analysis was undertaken by level of disability. This showed that the higher level of informal care provided to elderly people living in multi-generational households could not be explained by differences in disability level between elderly people in each of the three living situations.

6 Rational Choice and Household Division

Alan Carling

There is only one task in social theory more daunting than the attempt to persuade sociologists that there is something in the theory of rational choice; and that is the attempt to persuade economists that there is something in any theory other than rational choice.

Relatively undaunted, I shall argue that rational choice is necessary to but insufficient for an adequate theory of household division, hoping at the very least to please sociologists with the insufficiency argument and economists with the necessity argument.[1]

RATIONAL CHOICE

A rational-choice approach is one that brings an optimising calculus of means and ends to bear upon human behaviour. The optimand might be money or labour-time or social status, or a more general utility function containing entries for these and/or other variables. The optimising agent might be a human individual – as throughout this chapter – or a collective actor. The utilities quantified by a given agent's utility function might be utilities accruing directly to the agent – as throughout this chapter – or utilities accruing to other agents.

I will think of rational action in its narrow – sometimes called thin – sense to mean an action carried out because it was correctly regarded by the act's actor as the most beneficial action open to her or him, given the actor's preferences and general beliefs about the world. According to a broader – or presumably thicker – concept of rationality, a rational agent's preferences and beliefs must be rational, as well as the agent's action being rational in the light of given preferences and beliefs (Elster, 1983a; Macdonald and Pettit, 1981).

It goes without saying that full – or broad – or thick – rationality sets a stiff test: who will volunteer a list of all the beliefs it is rational to believe? It follows that a commitment to rational-choice analysis in the narrow sense does not entail a commitment to the full, or ultimate, rationality of the states of affairs under scrutiny from the narrow perspective.

Rational-choice explanation of human behaviour is a sub-species of intentional explanation, but this does not exclude its possible coexistence with other forms of non-intentional explanation. Suppose, for example, that a market system punishes sub-optimal behaviour (that is, behaviour that is irrational from the thin point of view) by driving irrational agents out of business. Then there might well be a functional explanation of why agents who survive in business are rational agents; part of which explanation would be a rational-choice explanation for the behaviour of rational agents. (I provide a slightly different example of composite explanation in the last section.)

In summary, rational-choice theory is wedded to the assumption of self-conscious optimisation, and is not wedded to

– particular dimensions of utility
– methodological individualism
– self-interested conduct
– the ultimate rationality of the social conditions to which the theory is applied
– explanatory exclusiveness

These remarks are made in spite of the impression left by Jon Elster in various places on several of these issues (for example Elster 1982; 1983b; 1985; 1989).

WHY APPLY RATIONAL CHOICE TO THE HOUSEHOLD?

There are at least three reasons for making the attempt to apply rational choice to the household.

First, rational-choice theory might give a true account of human motivation, or at least give a true account of one side of human motivation. So rational-choice theories might be true – or at least partly-true – theories.

Second, the application would unite the theory of the household with other theories inspired by rational-choice – such as theories of historical change, free market competition, class division and ethnic group interaction (Aston and Philpin, 1985; Roemer, 1982a; Banton, 1983; Carling, 1986).

Third, the theory belongs squarely within the power paradigm of social science, as opposed to the affect paradigm – it deals in opposing interests rather than common value systems. It seems therefore a particularly appropriate medium in which to explore the implications of the feminist adage that the personal is political – which implies *inter alia* that power relations pervade private life.

HOUSEHOLD PROPERTY RELATIONS

In order to analyse the household with the help of rational choice, we must first establish the character of the property relations which govern the disposition of household goods, for the incentives of actors to act – and hence the actions it is rational for actors to perform – will depend on the type of property relations that prevail. I will offer two specifications of household property relations, with corresponding models of household interaction.

In the Exchange Model, each of two (adult) actors is assumed to be able to produce two kinds of good – money and household use-values – which pass initially under the exclusive jurisdiction of the producer. Thus, actors produce money by working at a given wage rate in the public domain for a variable number of hours per week. (This is a proletarian household, with no property inheritance and no income from shares, building society accounts or investments in British Gas.[2]) And actors produce household use-values by performing housework with the same efficiency as one another, again for a variable number of hours per week.

These property relations obey a pure contribution principle (I own whatever my contributions deliver in the way of money and/or use-values) and are thoroughly privatised (I enjoy exclusive access to my money and my use-values). But this is not the end of the story, because actors are allowed to bargain with each other using their own money and/or use-values as bargaining chips. Indeed, a household will be established according to this model only if a mutually-advantageous deal (an exchange of use-values for money) can be concluded by the two parties on the basis of their initial private possessions of the respective goods.

In a second model, called Chicken (for reasons that will transpire) we consider just one good (either the provision of money or the provision of household use-values), and we imagine that the rule of distribution is a communal one – whatever is produced is shared, say equally, by the two (adult) members of a given two-person household.

Compared with the contributionist and privatised property relations of the Exchange Model, the Chicken model distributes benefit according to a pure needs principle (in proportion with needs if two equally needy adult individuals always receive equal shares) and with a public mode of goods provision.

The Exchange Model and the Chicken Model are located at the opposite poles of a continuum of property relations systems for households; the Exchange Model regards the household as analogous to a commodity exchange in a private ownership market economy, whereas Chicken depicts the household as a miniature communist republic.[3]

DOMESTIC EXCHANGE AND THE HOUSEHOLD DIVISION OF LABOUR

In order to generate behavioural predictions, we must specify actor's preferences as well as the property relations to which actors are subject. I assume subsistence preferences throughout: each actor must consume a fixed amount of money per week (say £k) and enjoy the fruits of a fixed amount of housework (say t hours). Actors will do anything to achieve these subsistence thresholds and do nothing to achieve anything beyond these thresholds (Roemer, 1988). But actors are also interested in minimising their aggregate weekly working time (in paid employment and/or housework) in order to reach their weekly subsistence levels. There is no intrinsic preference for either housework or paid employment; each is equally disliked.

Under all these assumptions, two actors will form a household if and only if each actor's aggregate weekly working-time is lower than the respective weekly working-times of the given actors living by themselves. It is now shown that such a mutually-advantageous deal will be struck if and only if the external wage rates of the two actors differ.

For suppose that there is a lower-earner (called L) and a higher-earner (called H). Then H is in a position to sub-contract with L for L to perform at least some of H's housework. If L does an extra amount of housework on H's behalf (say s hours) and H does an extra amount of wage working (yielding say £m in extra money above H's subsistence requirement), then the putative deal involves an exchange of s housework hours against £m money. This exchange is equivalent to a sub-contract for housework at a *shadow wage rate* of m/s £/hour; it is the rate that would be paid if the exchange which is implicit in the decision to form a household were made the subject of an explicit contract in a commodity market – as envisaged in the campaign of 'wages for housework'.

It is fairly obvious that such a deal will be in the interests of both parties if and only if the shadow wage for housework is (i) higher than L's external wage rate and (ii) lower than H's external wage rate. The first condition ensures that L prefers to substitute housework for wage work; the second condition ensures that H prefers to substitute wage work for housework. Under these circumstances, L will end up doing a greater proportion of the housework for the two adults considered as a unit, and H will end up doing a greater proportion of the wage-earning.

The household exchange is limited by the subsistence constraints as well as by the external wage rates. L will never require an amount of money from H greater than L's money requirement (that is, greater than £k); H will never require an amount of housework from L greater than H's housework requirement (that is, greater than t hours). It follows that formable households (that is, households preferred by both parties to separate living arrangements) are all those and only those contained in the shaded kite-shaped area of Figure 6.1.

Each point of the graph represents a particular household deal (a particular pair of values of m and s). The area of the kite is bounded by

1. the two rays from the origin (which represent the wage rate of the higher-earner H – the line with greater slope – and the wage rate of the lower-earner L – the line with the lower slope),
2. the vertical line representing the housework constraint at s = t and
3. the horizontal line representing the weekly income constraint at m = k.

Thus, all points in the kite involve deals in which (i) the shadow wage for housework is between the two external wage rates and (ii) the subsistence constraints are not exceeded. The kite does indeed contain all the formable households.

It is now possible to describe the different types of formable households according to the division of household labour they imply. Those in the interior of the kite (and along the two rays from the origin) are called symmetrical households (after Young and Willmott, 1973) in which both partners perform both paid work and housework; those on the vertical boundary of the kite are houseworker households (with L doing all the housework); those on the horizontal boundary are breadwinner households (with H doing all the wage-earning), while those at the apex are houseworker/breadwinner, or conventional house-

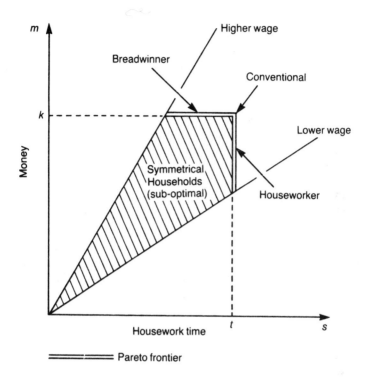

Figure 6.1   Domestic exchange and household division

holds in which there is a complete division of labour between the house-hold members (each partner does one and only one type of work).

The criterion for a formable household ensures that all points in the kite are preferred to separate living arrangements; technically they are called 'Pareto-preferred' (to launch into economists' jargon), in that they occupy a space in which both partners are better off together than living on their own. But it is also the case that some households in the kite are Pareto-preferred to other households in the kite. In particular, couples have a labour-time incentive to extend their division of labour until they arrive either on the vertical boundary of the kite, or on the horizontal boundary, or at the apex.

Thus, all points in the interior of the kite are Pareto-inferior to some points on the outward boundary of the kite, called the Pareto frontier. If we assume that the couple will always reach some Pareto-superior deal, then the interior of the kite will be evacuated, leaving households to form somewhere on the Pareto frontier of Figure 6.1.[4]

The Exchange Model therefore predicts that at least one of either paid work or housework will become the exclusive preserve of one of the household partners: there will be a domestic division of labour. (This is so much the worse for Young and Willmott's symmetrical family!)

The theory cannot however predict where exactly along the Pareto frontier the household will settle. Note that households to the north and west on the frontier as drawn in Figure 6.1 are better for the lower-earner L (the shadow wage received by L for housework is higher) whereas households to the south and east are better for the higher earner H (the shadow wage paid by H is lower).

This indeterminacy reflects the non-competitive, bargaining element in the Exchange Model. If, for example, there were a genuine market for housework (rather than a shadow market), and there were a Domestic Reserve Army of lower-paid people looking for domestic employment, then competitive pressures would push all households towards the Southernmost end of the frontier. If, on the other hand, there were an excess of high-earners competing for a scarce supply of houseworkers, the wage for housework would be bid up to the higher earner's wage level, corresponding to a determinate equilibrium at the opposite, northern and western, end of the frontier line.

DOMESTIC UNEQUAL EXCHANGE

We know that (i) a lower-earner living alone works longer overall than a higher-earner living alone, and that (ii) living together reduces each partner's aggregate working time; this after all is the motive for household formation (c.f. Humphries, 1977).

What is not so obvious is the additional fact that (iii) the lower-earner works longer overall than the higher-earner whenever they are living together; in any formable household, the lower-earner always performs an overload (to use a phrase from Pleck, 1985, p. 30)[5]

This fact is the basis of the contention that household formation implies Unequal Exchange. In particular, the existence of an antecedent wage differential causes a household to exist in which an inequality of working times persists. If we regard earning-power as an unequally distributed resource, then the unequal outcome of interaction would be eliminated by a suitable resource equalisation: namely, an appropriate equalisation of the external wage rates of the two parties.

Since the position of the higher-earner would deteriorate and the position of the lower-earner would improve under this equalising dispensation, it is possible to conclude that the higher-earner is taking advantage of the lower-earner in the unequal endowment status quo (c.f. Roemer, 1982a; 1982b).

Thus, the main findings of the Exchange Model are that

- a household will form if and only if there is an external wage differential between the two partners
- the higher-earner will take economic advantage of the lower-earner in any household that is formed.

GENDER AND EXPLOITATION

The presentation of the Exchange Model has been deliberately gender-blind. It is food for thought that one can easily generate quite a respectable set of household roles without reference to any phenomenon of gender difference.

Yet actors are not in reality immune to gender. So if we assume that people form households for emotional or sexual or procreative or conventional or even aesthetic reasons, rather than economic reasons, the Exchange Model slots into place as a model of the economic pressures to take on various roles within a household that has already joined together two adults along dimensions other than aggregate labour-time.

If attention is confined to cross-gender couples, the direction of the economic pressure will depend on the direction of the wage differential within the couple. The facts of this particular matter run down a depressingly one-way street. 1980 UK data indicates that the woman was the lower-earner and the man the higher-earner in at least 80 per cent of either actual or potential couples (Reid and Wormald, 1982; Norris, 1987).

Thus the Exchange Model is sufficient to predict that the woman would adopt the domestic role at least eight times out of ten. And in all these cases the man will take economic advantage of the woman, in the sense of gaining benefit from an unequal exchange.

If we wish to press home this indictment and claim further that the man is exploiting the woman, we must show that the exchange is unjust, as well as being unequal (Carling, 1987). Injustice can arise in general for one of three reasons: (i) because the antecedent wage differential is unjust in itself (if, for example, it is a consequence of gender discrimination in the external labour market); (ii) because the exchange transaction is coercive (if, for example, the woman's wage rate in the public domain is so low that she is effectively forced to contract with some higher-paid man to secure her subsistence); or (iii) because the outcome is unfair in itself (for instance in virtue of violating some end-state principle of justice such as welfare egalitarianism).[6]

If one or more of these adverse normative judgments is reached, then the Exchange Model establishes an exact parallel between the household division of labour and class divisions of the form addressed in the literature of Analytical Marxism (Roemer, 1982a; 1986; Wright, 1985). This supplies a strong subsidiary motive for presenting the Exchange Model in the above form.

Indeed, since the quantity which has emerged as the key statistic of the Exchange Model – the shadow wage for housework – figured prominently in the domestic labour debate of the 1970s (Beechey, 1987), the Exchange Model is a convenient vehicle for pursuing that important debate of the 1970s in the Analytical Marxist context of the 1980s and 1990s.

We now change tack from the private bargain of the Exchange Model to contemplate the public debacle of Chicken.

THE PROBLEM WITH EQUAL SHARES

If two individuals with equal needs share goods equally in the household, then there is a real problem about who will produce the good. For suppose that each of us knows that each of us needs the good so badly that, if it came to the crunch, each of us would be prepared to provide all of the good that both of us need. Then each of us has an interest in hanging back and waiting for the other person to produce the good – to play Chicken, in other words, over the act of producing the good.

Yet if both of us wait too long, we both go over the cliff (to borrow an image from *Rebel Without a Cause*). This means that if I believe your nerve will hold out longer than mine, then my rational response is to brake (or break) immediately, and to do all the work to produce the good for both of us. Whereas if I believe your nerve will give out first, my rational response is not to brake (or not to break) before you do, waiting confidently for you to do all the work to produce the good for both of us.

The Chicken game has several features of theoretical interest:

1. There are two equilibria in the game – either you do all the work and I do none, or I do all the work and you do none.
2. Each of these equilibria is evidently extremely inegalitarian from the distributional point of view. In particular, the maldistribution of effort is greater than anything that can occur in the Exchange Model.
3. It is impossible to determine which is the rational action to perform in a Chicken game: rational-choice theory is indeterminate in the face of Chicken. So it is impossible to know which (if either) of the two equilibria mentioned in (2) is going to occur.
4. The inegalitarian equilibria have arisen from a perfectly symmetrical structure of payoffs, which must imply that resources are equally distributed. The person who loses in the Chicken game does not do so because the opponent's resource position is superior, like the woman in the Exchange Model who loses out to her partner's superior earning-power. The loser in Chicken loses simply because the opponent has adopted winning behaviour by being prepared to hold out longer.

In summary, then, we have introduced an Exchange Model, based on a privatised conception of household property relations, offering a close analogy between household division and (analytical) Marxian class division, and an intriguing, but as yet indeterminate, Chicken Model, based on a conception of household goods as public property.

To what extent does either model fit the facts of household interaction?

CHICKEN AT LARGE

Perhaps the reader will be able to supply evidence for the fowl nature of domestic interaction from her or his own experience. At all events, once one is on the lookout for Chicken, examples of it seem to crop up all over the sociological literature of domestic life.

Here are some instructive self-reports, the first five from men and the last three from women:

> I come in sometimes and the place is a complete mess and I just sit amongst it. Other times I blow my top and get the children to clear everything, everywhere.

> It doesn't bother me whether the house is clean and tidy. Some-

times, though, I get annoyed if it's a mess of Lego and Action Men just where I want to sit down.

Helen does all the decorating, wall plugging, drilling. It's not that I can't do it, but I make out that I can't.

I do the shopping. I don't mind, I don't like it, but I do it. With Cathy working up in the city, there's nowhere for her to do any shopping. I do a lot of it when I'm working.

And from the same man:

I can do it [ironing], but I don't like it. I do muck a few things up, my wife's blouses and things like that. I used to stick a hot iron on them and that's goodbye to them (all from Ingham, 1984, pp. 47–59).

Ideally, everything should be shared but there are certain areas where I don't do as much, e.g. to do with keeping things ideally clean. I am prepared to leave things (Walczak, 1988, p. 103).

He doesn't do much. I get irritated at him at times. He's unaware that there are things to do. . . . He'd leave the paper on the couch but now he picks it up. He does this for a month, forgets, and then I have to remind him.

He tries to be helpful. He tries. He's a brilliant and successful lawyer. It's incredible how he smiles after he sponges off the table and there are still crumbs all over (both from Berk, 1985, p. 206)

The housework is my job, my responsibility. My husband does none. I frequently feel I have two jobs, especially at the end of term. I work so hard and then come home and have to start again. I begin to resent the demands put on me. I toyed with the idea of working part-time but I knew that I wouldn't be satisfied with that. My husband helping is not an option. There are times when he's sitting watching the telly and I'm out there in the kitchen and a bit frustrated about it all, but I don't do much about it (McRae, 1986, p. 136).

A thread running through these reports is a male attitude of *contrived insensitivity to domestic chaos*. If it is a fact about a man, or an impression skilfully created by him, that he is less bothered than a woman partner about the safety, warmth, cleanliness, health, hunger or comfort of the household members, then he has contrived to pre-commit himself against taking action in the Chicken Game. And if she is convinced that he will probably do nothing, then she is bound to do something, and so ends up with all the work of cleaning, caring, cooking, coping, and catering.

It seems a plausible further suggestion that gender socialisation is responsible for the differential tolerance thresholds to domestic chaos which trigger the woman's caring and coping reactions a moment before the man's.[7] Since a pure game of Chicken is balanced on a knife-edge between its two inegalitarian equilibria, it would only take the slightest influence of gender socialisation (in theory, an infinitesimal influence) to tip the balance in the household wholly against the woman. This might help to explain why the inequalities within households are so recalcitrant – they stem from a quirk in the public arrangements for the distribution of goods within each private household.

TESTING TIME FOR THE EXCHANGE MODEL

If there is less in the way of anecdotal evidence for the bargaining process inherent in the Exchange Model than there is for the existence of a Chicken-like mentality, this does not mean it is impossible to test the Exchange Model either against the Chicken Model or against the world.

Recall that the major prediction of the Exchange Model is that the lower earning woman partner will work longer overall. Is there evidence of overload? The answer is a qualified Yes. Women do tend to work (or have historically tended to work) longer time overall than men, taking account of both paid and domestic work (Reid, 1934; Meissner, 1975; Pleck, 1985, p. 30).

This body of evidence does not, however, serve the testing purpose very well, because it is equally consistent either with the Chicken model, or a third, straightforwardly sociological role model (according to which the conventional division of labour will occur regardless of economic incentive structures or systems of household property relations).

A more decisive test will involve cases in which the predictions of the various models diverge significantly. The general circumstance in which this occurs is when the direction of the correlation between wage and gender is reversed from that assumed hitherto. The Exchange Model predicts that wherever it is the woman who enjoys the higher wage (and preferential access to the public domain) there will be an utterly frictionless role reversal; the houseworker will be the househusband. Neither the Chicken model nor the sociological role model makes this prediction, because they both emphasise the 'stickiness' of the gender roles in each of the departments that together comprise the household game – the several departments of paid work, washing-up, child-care and so on.

The usual correlation between gender and pay will tend to be reversed when male unemployment occurs, especially in the context all too familiar in Thatcherite Britain of mass redundancy rather than individual misfortune. The result will be a sudden collapse in, and perhaps a virtual elimination of, the man's local earning-power. Leonard and Speakman's summary of the British research into the effects of unemployment is not encouraging to the Exchange Model:

> (The) studies . . . which have looked at the effects of redundancy, agree that unemployed husbands certainly do not take over the housework from their wives, enabling the women to try for jobs (except occasionally in the households where there are no children). Quite the reverse. Men's unemployment often actually increases their wives' work load, through the need to 'shop around' and 'make do and mend' on a much reduced budget, and through the need for wives to be present in the home, e.g. to cook a meal at midday, and for women friends not to be around when the husband is at home, thereby restricting women's day-time freedom of movement and association (Leonard and Speakman 1986, pp. 33 – 4).

A less traumatic case occurs when the background, qualifications or work experience of the woman give her a niche in the world of occupations superior to that of her domestic partner. Thanks to a fine study by Susan McRae (1986), something rather more detailed can be said of the case known as the Cross-Class Family.

THE CROSS-CLASS FAMILY

The wage rate data already suggests that cross-class married couples (in which the wife's occupation is unambiguously superior to her husband's) are thin on the ground, and Susan McRae took considerable pains to locate a sample of just 30 such couples.

Partly because the class scales used by McRae depended on status and conditions elements as well as pay elements, and partly because of the correlation between women's gender and low pay which persists throughout the class scale, it was not true of every couple in the sample that the wife's pay was higher than her husband's, despite the considerable disparity in the wife's and husband's class positions. In fact 'half of the wives earn higher incomes than their husbands, half do not'. (McRae, 1986, p. 95).

From collateral evidence in the book, it is possible to construct a list of 11 couples in which the wife's earning power is unambiguously higher than her husband's.[8] The Exchange Model can therefore be tested more loosely in the sample of 30 couples and more strictly in the sub-sample of 11. But this problem is perhaps not as serious as it might appear, for the simple reason that the Exchange Model performs almost equally poorly in both sample and sub-sample.

The Exchange Model makes a straightforward prediction: the lower-earning husband will always take on a preponderance of the domestic work. What was the result? In the 1980s, only one couple out of 11 showed anything that might plausibly be regarded as a reversal of the normal roles (and there are no other candidates in the remainder of the full sample, either).

Mrs Stone was an architect and Mr Stone was described as a downwardly mobile graduate who had held a succession of manual jobs before training to be a carpenter. Mr Stone was unique in the sample and rare in the world in staying at home to look after two pre-school children.

My wife refuses to be dependent upon anyone. It was clear when we married that, if I wanted children, I'd have to be prepared to stay at home and care for them. And I was – I am (McRae, 1986, p. 82).

Apart from the Stones, there were only two couples in the sub-sample of 11, and only six in the sample of 30, in which husbands took some share in the overall responsibility for domestic work, whereas the Exchange Model predicts that the husband would perform a preponderant share of housework in 11 cases out of 11 (and perhaps 30 out of 30).

Chicken fares a little better. There is clear evidence of Chicken strategies being pursued by the three men in the sub-sample (and one other in the full sample) whom McRae classifies as 'Refusing Husbands'.

More prominent in McRae's study is however another response – 'Wife-in-Control' – which involves a quite different way to play the game. Here there is such an aggressive pre-commitment of the wife to a strategy of activity, and of therefore becoming the victim from the distributional point of view, that the husband hardly gets a chance not to be the exploiter:

> It is too much, I get very tired. But a lot of it is my own fault. I'll be honest, I keep the work to myself. I've spoiled them (husband and children). I find it quicker and easier, without a lot of arguments, to do it myself. And that's how its gone. And it's wrong – I pay. But then, no one could do it the way I wanted it done. I'm very houseproud. It's my own fault. And if they do do it, I have to sort of bite my tongue and leave it for a day or two and then do it all over again (McRae, 1986, p. 137).

Is the Mrs Jason of this extract being irrational? Her testimony makes clear how difficult it may be to break the mould, and how much effort she would have to make to retrain her family. But she is also aware of having to retrain herself. As things stand, she seems to know as well as anyone that what she is doing is damaging to her own interests in several respects. But even if it is irrational, her response to the Chicken situation is readily understandable, and explicable partly as an attempt to maintain something of her conventional self-image as a wife and mother, intensified if anything by the somewhat counter-conventional nature of her employment in the public domain.

This superwoman response, in other words, might be an attempt to compensate for the partial role reversal in the public world with an exaggerated role performance at home (McRae, 1986, pp. 139–41). It is certainly very striking that as many as one-third of the wives in the full sample displayed this response, and it would be very interesting to know whether this is a higher proportion than in non cross-class families.

Summing up, we can say that the predictions of the Exchange Model are borne out in one case out of 11 (also one out of the full 30), the Chicken model in three cases out of 11 (four out of 30) and the superwoman version of the sociological role model in five cases out of 11 (10 out of 30).

The following conclusions emerge strongly from McRae's study:

1. The economic pressures described schematically in the Exchange Model very rarely translate themselves directly into changed behaviour, if the traditional gender roles are exerting a pressure in the opposite direction. This is a way of saying that the gender pressure is real or, in other words, that gender ideology is relatively autonomous.

2. Women's gender ideology tends to prevent women taking full econ-
    omic advantage of men, when women are in an economic position
    to do so. Quite often, it seems to result in the self-sacrificial (or
    is it self-preservative?) attempt to combine the role of career woman
    with the role of faultless wife and mother.
3. Men's gender ideology can sometimes tolerate domestic equality,
    but in the current state of play it rarely embraces domestic role
    reversal, even where the economic pressures foretell reversal.

A HISTORICAL REPRIEVE FOR THE EXCHANGE MODEL?

The conclusions of the previous section may well have convinced any
sociologically-minded reader (any who needed convincing) that
rational choice is not sufficient for an adequate theory of household
division. Indeed, it may have been so successful in this respect as to
undermine any conviction in the necessity of a rational-choice approach
the reader may have had, perhaps even acquired while reading the
earlier sections of the chapter. What use is a model whose empirical
performance is so unspectacular?

I plunged into the test of the Exchange Model on the Elsterian presupposition that rational-choice approaches offer plausible microfoundations for large-scale sociological phenomena (c.f. Levine *et al.*, 1987).
Perhaps this presupposition was wrong. Rational-choice theories may
not be very good at explaining the day-to-day operation of social entities like households, if only because ideological factors offer an autonomous source of resistance to the economic pressures pin-pointed by
rational-choice theories.

Over sufficient time, however, new ideologies arise and persist which
facilitate change in the direction demanded by the economic pressures.
Indeed, the ideologies may persist because they have this facilitative
effect, and this offers scope for the functional explanation of the ideological change by the economic pressure. The rational-choice approach
may thus be suited sometimes to illuminate the long-term evolution
of social entities, rather than explain their short-run operation. In this
case, rational choice would have supplied macrofoundations of social
change rather than microfoundations of social interaction.

I illustrate these ideas with an everyday story of industrial family
life derived from the Exchange Model.

Once upon a time, during the Industrial Revolution, women's and men's wages were low, and their commodity subsistence requirement (£k each) was higher than in their pre-industrial rural past. So wife and husband were both required to work outside the home, with women nevertheless performing all domestic labour. (In the early-industrial version of Figure 6.1, both rays from the origin intersect the Pareto frontier on its vertical segment; the kite shrinks to a triangular shape and all Pareto-optimal households are dual-earner houseworker households.)

Later in the century, some men's wages improved relative to all women's wages, so that the upper ray swung upwards (anti-clockwise), restoring the picture drawn in Figure 6.1. With this development, some male breadwinner households appeared on the newly-opened horizontal segment of the Pareto frontier. The non-wage-earning housewife came into being in the wake of a labour aristocracy and a later Victorian ideology of domesticity.

Moving into the next century, and perhaps originating in the USA, there arises a new tendency towards consumerism, and a consequent transfer of subsistence requirements from the domestic labour constraint (t) to the domestic income constraint (k) – in short, the commodity penetration of the household (Ehrenreich and Ehrenreich, 1979; Ewen, 1976).

The effect of an increase in k and a concomitant decrease in t is to move the apex of the kite in Figure 6.1 in a north-westerly direction (since the ratio k/t is increasing). If this movement goes far enough, the apex will cross the ray from the origin representing the man's higher wage (this occurs when the ratio k/t first becomes greater than the man's wage). The consequence is to close down the horizontal stretch of the Pareto frontier representing breadwinner households; dual-earning households once again become the norm, but at a much higher level of consumer spending (and a somewhat lower level of domestic labour) than was the case in the earlier throes of the Industrial Revolution.

According to such a sequence, a nineteenth century ideology of domesticity (complete with bread-winning husband) is replaced by a twentieth century ideology of household convenience (complete with wage-earning wife), although women are still performing all the labour in the home during both centuries (except for the occasional assistance of the Victorian breadwinner).

No doubt readers whose historical knowledge of these changes is much greater than my own can tell me how misguidedly simplistic this story is. I am impressed nevertheless that such a sparse model of domestic arrangements furnishes a story as close to history as this one seems perhaps to get. Maybe all is after all not lost for rational choice and household division.

Notes

1. The contents of this chapter abridges part of the argument in Carling (1991), Chapters 2, 7, 11 and 12.
2. Although the specific assumptions of the Exchange Model do not include the exact circumstances investigated in the chapters in this volume by Richard Wall, Gill Jones and Susan Hutson, the general principles will still apply (and see note 6).
3. In Chapter 10 of Carling (1991), I study a third model of household interaction – the Short Commons model – which spans the continuum of mixed needs–contributions principles connecting these two polar cases.
4. This behavioural assumption is the one adopted by cooperative game theory (as opposed to non-cooperative game theory).
5. The inevitability of lower-earner's overload is proved as follows:

    Let w_1 and w_2 be the external wage rates of the lower-earner and higher-earner respectively ($w_1 < w_2$). Then the conditions for household formation is

    $$w_1 < m/s < w_2$$

    where $m \leq k$; $s \leq t$. (These inequalities describe the kite-shaped area in Figure 6.1.)

    The lower earner's overload is given by

    $$Ov = [(t + k/w_1 - (m/w_1 - s)) - ((t + k/w_2 - (s - m/w_2))]$$

    which may be rearranged as:

    $$Ov = (k - m)(1/w_1 - 1/w_2) + 2(s - m/w_2).$$

    The first term on the right-hand side of this expression is non-negative (since $m \leq k$ and $w_1 < w_2$) and the second term is strictly positive (since $m/s < w_2$). Hence the overload is strictly positive. QED.
6. Refinements of this approach to the justice issue are discussed in Carling (1991), Section 7.3. Note that the existence of exploitation in either the inter-generational exchanges discussed by Wall or the adult-young person exchanges discussed by Jones and Hutson (this volume) will turn on two issues. The first question is the justice or otherwise of the antecedent resource distribution; for example, whether inheritance is justified (Steiner, 1987), and whether young persons should be given independent control of household resources. The second question is the standard of justice to be applied. This might, for example, be non-egalitarian in the case of relations between adults and young persons (adults arguably should contribute more to a household than young persons or children). In the latter case there might be unequal exchange without exploitation.

7.   This suggestion is elaborated and qualified in Carling (1991), Section 11.3. The connection between the Chicken game and public goods provision was first made in Taylor and Ward (1982); *cf.* Taylor (1987) and Ward (1987).
8.   The unambiguously higher-earning wives are those named Abbot, Allan, Barnes, Creighton, Harvey, Henley, James, Parker, Paton, Roberts and Stone.

7 The Differentiation of Households and Working Time Arrangements in West Germany[1]

Volker H. Schmidt

The 1980s have seen a rapid increase in the differentiation of working time arrangements throughout the public and the private sectors across Europe. The 'standard employment relationship' (a forty-hour, five-day working week, normally from Monday to Friday, an eight-hour working day, and a fixed daily working schedule), as it emerged during the 1950s and 1960s, no longer prevails. It is neither the dominant pattern of employment or even a normative fiction that can appropriately guide working time and social policy-making (Mückenberger, 1985). It has come under pressure from both employers and a rising number of employees who – although for different reasons – are demanding more flexibility. Two seemingly unrelated trends of socio-economic change have contributed to the questioning of the traditional working time structure.

On the one hand the employers have adopted production and employment strategies which were designed to give them more flexibility. This has been partly in reaction to the trades unions' working time reduction drives in the early 1980s, but more importantly has been a response to changes in the economic environment. The intensification of international competition, a growing demand from consumers for high quality and customised products, and the increase in market turbulence and volatility have exposed them to an unprecedented degree of uncertainty (Streeck, 1987). The application of computer-based technologies and the introduction of new management and production concepts such as 'flexible specialisation' (Piore and Sabel, 1984) are some of the strategies aimed at meeting these economic challenges and necessities.

In this process of economic and technical change, the restructuring of working time has played and continues to play a crucial role. New technologies, for instance, are often accompanied by a dramatic rise in capital intensity. Together with the rapid rate of equipment obsolescence in an era of accelerated technological innovation, this creates enormous pressure to maximise the utilisation of the new devices and, therefore, the working day (through increased shiftwork) and the working week (through increased work at the weekend). At the same time, many firms are trying to reduce labour costs by minimising the core labour force and resorting instead to irregular and relatively unprotected employment patterns for a growing segment of fringe-labour, such as part-time work, fixed-term contracts, and temporary work. The rationale behind these strategies is to escape having to pay social security contributions, to create a flexibility buffer against unstable and unpredictable demand, and to externalise the risks of uncertainty to sections of the labour force.

On the other hand, the time patterns and time needs of growing parts of the labour force are also becoming more heterogeneous. The standard employment relationship, an important component of which is the above-mentioned standardised working hours arrangement, was tailored to the needs of a male breadwinner and head of a conventional nuclear family-type household (Bosch *et al.*, 1988). In the last twenty years, however, the socio-cultural reality in which this arrangement operates has undergone dramatic changes which render obsolete the empirical and normative assumptions on which it is based. The traditional household, with the man bearing full responsibility for the family income, the woman being restricted to the role of homemaking, and one or more children present, is being supplanted by a variety of other household types and living arrangements (as is argued elsewhere in this volume by Crow and Hardey); more people are living alone, in single-parent households, or in dual earner (parent or non-parent) households, all of which are rising steadily in both absolute numbers and relative weight. Sustaining this trend towards increasing differentiation are, among other factors, the continuous influx of women into the labour market and the emergence of new cultural orientations towards work and lifestyle. They have contributed to the formation of preferences for discontinuous and less than full-time employment which are not easily reconciled with what the standard employment relationship presupposes as 'normal' patterns of labour market participation (Offé, 1990).

It is not surprising that the formal coincidence of employers' and employees' needs for some change in working time arrangements does not easily translate into substantive agreement over the terms and content of this change. The employers in many ways benefit from the employees' needs to coordinate both work and non-work responsibilities. Since employment patterns that deviate from the standard employment relationship are often poorly protected, employees are vulnerable to employers' strategies of lowering labour costs. Women, for instance, who request flexible working time arrangements, are frequently confronted with working conditions which are below standard in all relevant dimensions of the employment relationship. Such disadvantages, however, cannot be overcome by attempts at restandardising working time arrangements through general reductions in work hours, as favoured by trade union officials and some feminist writers (Kurz-Scherf, 1987). As in most advanced industrial societies, the West German social structure of the early 1990s is too individualised and fragmented for a strategy founded on the implicit notion of homogeneous class or gender interests to be a promising basis for working time reform.

The following discussion concentrates on these changes on the supply side of the labour market. Using recent empirical data, the next section documents some of the major changes that are taking place in the household structure in West Germany. It is then shown how these changes affect employees' (working) time needs and how they interact with the preferences of employers. The final step consists of some tentative thoughts on political consequences that may be drawn from this analysis. A working time model is sketched that would protect employees from unjust employment conditions and, at the same time, facilitate the realisation of their individual time needs.

HOUSEHOLD TYPES AND EMPLOYMENT PATTERNS

In 1986 the total number of households in West Germany was roughly 26 million. This statistic, however, groups together a variety of living conditions and arrangements that have much less in common than the use of one comprehensive term for all of them suggests. The extent to which the category 'household' signifies a homogeneous domestic unit is decreasing steadily; the conventional nuclear family – for long the prototype in conceptualisations of the household – is on the retreat (Hoffmann-Nowotny, 1988). Instead of one dominant pattern, we are observing a growing plurality of life-styles and living arrangements (Bertram and Bormann-Müller, 1988). This trend is well documented in recent empirical household data, and similar developments in Britain are discussed in other contributions to this volume.

Most remarkable is the rise in the number of people living alone or in two-person households that has occurred since the Second World War; single households grew from six per cent to 13 per cent and two-person households from 17 per cent to 24 per cent between 1950 and 1982 (Zapf *et al.*, 1987, p. 22). At the same time the proportion of households with five or more members has almost halved: it dropped from 32 per cent to 18 per cent in the same period. Taking a longer perspective, the change is even more dramatic. Around the turn of the century, more than 65 per cent of Germans lived in five-or-more person households; in the early 1980s, almost two thirds of the West German population lived in households containing two, three or four people, with proportions being equally divided between them (*ibid.*).

The differentiation of household types reflects major social, cultural and demographic changes. The increase in one-person households, for instance, is mainly due to a growing demographic imbalance in the population, caused by the coincidence of falling birth rates and rising life expectancies. A substantial portion of their members are the elderly, especially elderly women who outlive their spouses. However, another important factor contributing to the growth of single households is that more and more people deliberately choose to live alone. A disproportionate rise in the number of people living alone is being registered among those in the 25–45 year age range who have more than doubled their share in one-person households in only 16 years, from 12 per cent in 1969 to 24 per cent in 1985 (Meyer and Schulze, 1989, p. 16). Those who explicitly prefer living alone as an expression of personal independence have higher levels of educational qualifications than others of the same age, and this is particularly marked among the younger age groups (*ibid.*). As Bien *et al.* argue in Chapter 9 of this volume, young single-person householders in West Germany do not seem emotionally disadvantaged over those who live with others.

A second prime factor accounting for the differentiation of households and living arrangements must be seen in the changed circumstances of women's lives which both require and facilitate them taking on more responsibility for breadwinning. Four separate factors that play a part in motivating women to seek paid employment can be distinguished. Although in practice often inseparably intertwined, it is worth treating them as analytically distinct because of the different effects they potentially have on household structure as well as on intrahousehold processes. The four factors are:

(1) *The decline of conventional security-affording institutions.* Rising rates of divorce and family breakups increasingly make it necessary

for women to obtain an income independent of that earned by their potential or actual husbands. This is also reflected in new cultural norms and images concerning women's role in society: in principle they are now expected to provide for their own subsistence through paid work (Beck-Gernsheim, 1986). This applies to all women, married or unmarried, although to different degrees.

(2) *New options and dependencies.* With the accelerated dissolution of traditional, class-based social collectives and close knit communities since the early 1950s, the disintegration of homogeneous and solidaristic neighbourhoods, and the erosion of encompassing cultural and moral norms constraining the set of social roles open to the individual, more options became available to social actors, regardless of status or gender. As a consequence of this expansion of personal autonomy, people are obliged to make more choices on how to organise their lives. At the same time they are exposed to new dependencies. The ongoing individualisation of lifestyles and living arrangements leads to 'market dependency in all aspects of life' (Beck, 1986, p. 212). Households are much less self-provisioning now than they previously used to be. As a result, more goods and services must be bought. The welfare of households is thus crucially dependent upon the availability of (preferably high) external sources of income. This tendency is intensified through a permanent rise in the standards of living and consumption, or rather, in the aspirations and expectations concerning them. Hence the necessity for, or at least desirability of, more married women seeking paid employment. It facilitates the meeting of financial obligations and the realisation of costly domestic projects.

(3) *Identity.* This aspect must be understood in the context of growing uncertainty about women's social status. With the relative devaluation of housework, the shortening of the biographical phase of motherhood, and the disintegration of households out of stable communicative networks, employed work has become a source of self-esteem and social identity for many women: an 'intrinsically desirable' and status-conferring form of activity which is 'valued for the challenge (and) social contact . . . it affords and is therefore preferred to the alternative of unpaid and full-time family and household work' (Offé, 1990, p. 13).

(4) *Qualifications.* An upward shift has occurred in aspirations for a personal career, not just a paid job, amongst younger women, particu-

larly amongst the better educated younger women. Due to the reform and expansion of the educational system in the 1960s and 1970s, this group has grown significantly in recent years. For example, between 1960 and 1983 the proportion of female university students rose from 25 per cent to 43 per cent (Beck, 1986, p. 128). Considering that the total number of students has also multiplied in this period, this process becomes even more remarkable. The 'feminisation of education', as it has been referred to (Meyer and Schulze, 1989), has undoubtedly had a strong impact upon women's attitude towards work.

Taken together, these four factors may roughly explain the overall growth of women's labour market participation. Although in West Germany this has been slower than in many other OECD countries, women's participation rate has nevertheless increased as steadily there as elsewhere. By 1980 it had reached a level of 53 per cent, compared to 44 per cent in 1950 (Zapf *et al.*, 1987, p. 24). However, the employment behaviour of women, their work commitment and degree of labour market participation as indicated by hours spent in paid work per week are much less uniform than those of men. They differ substantially between age groups, according to levels of qualification, and they are subject to more change over the life course of the individual woman. It is worth keeping this in mind for the discussion of the relation between women's employment behaviour and household differentiation.

What, then, are the effects of their labour market participation on household structure? First, there has obviously been a decrease in the number of *traditional*, single-earner nuclear family-type households. The rise in the labour force participation rate of married women has been especially striking: between 1950 and 1980 their participation rate has nearly doubled, from 26 per cent to 48 per cent (Zapf, *et al.*, 1987, p. 24).

As a corollary, *dual-earner* households have been rapidly spreading. They include the total number of households with both partners, married or unmarried, having paid jobs, full-time or part-time. According to a recent representative survey, slightly more than one third of employees are currently living in dual earner households (Groß *et al.*, 1989, p. 155).

Following a suggestion by Gowler and Legge (1982), a further distinction can be drawn between three subtypes of dual earner households, according to the employment patterns practised by the respective couples. The first type is *non-career*, and comprises couples in which both partners have jobs, rather than careers. In them, the woman's income is often indispensable for the family budget, because her partner's earnings are too low to cover all expenses. This pattern is typical of couples where both partners belong to the low or unskilled segments of the labour force. The second pattern is that of a *one career* family, where one partner, usually the man, pursues full-time employment and has a career. Here, the main motive for the wives to seek paid employment is probably the wish to add to their husband's income in order to make higher consumption levels affordable.

The employment behaviour followed by women belonging to either of these two subcategories is roughly in accord with what Yeandle (1984) calls the dominant pattern of female employment. This, she claims, is typical of married women with children. They enter full-time employment immediately after school or college, remain in it during early marriage, and leave the labour force when they expect their first child. After the child-rearing period a majority return to participation in the labour market, sometimes as a full-time, but more frequently as a part-time employee and often of lower occupational status than before having children. This group is likely to become larger over time as relatively more young mothers re-enter the labour market earlier after childbirth and between births. In the early 1980s, nearly half of all mothers with one child below the age of eighteen, and 40 per cent of those with two children, were employed in West Germany (Grimm, 1985, p. 292).

Another pattern of female employment that can be expected to gain considerable weight in the near future is that practised by women living in the third type of dual earner households, which Gowler and Legge call *dual career*. Here, both partners have a career and pursue full-time employment, before and after the birth of children. With the rapid expansion of higher education in the last twenty years, this pattern has been spreading continuously. It is found in married as well as in unmarried couples, but it is more pronounced among the latter. Younger, well-educated and work-committed women increasingly cohabit, not least to enhance their bargaining position in the negotiation of domestic chores with a partner (Meyer and Schulze, 1989). Studies of the organisation of work within the household suggest that, among unmarried dual career couples, responsibilities for homemaking tend to be much more equally divided than among the corresponding group of married couples. Hence the preference of many younger women who espouse egalitarian values for this type of living arrangement.

A final category contributing to the growing differentiation of living arrangements are *single-parent* households with young children. Between 1976 and 1985 their proportion rose from nine per cent to 13 per cent of all West German households. An overwhelming majority of single parents (85 per cent) are women, but men's share in this group is gradually becoming larger since the number of single fathers has increased disproportionately in recent years (Neubauer, 1988, p. 26). The bulk of the growth in single-parent households can be attributed to two trends. First, the rising rate of family breakups: 45 per cent of single parents are divorced, and another 16 per cent live separated from their spouses. Secondly, the growing incidence of extra-marital births: 18 per cent of single parents are unmarried. More than half of single mothers are employed (Meyer and Schulze, 1989, p. 17).

Brief as this review has been, it nonetheless substantiates in broad outlines the above claim that household structure in West Germany has become increasingly differentiated and diverse. We now turn to the question of how this affects employee's working-time needs.

SOCIAL DIFFERENTIATION AND WORKING TIME NEEDS

The diversity of household forms is only one empirical example of a general characteristic of modern societies: their differentiation into functionally specialised sub-systems of social action. The individual experiences a 'pluralisation of lifeworlds' (Berger *et al.*, 1973), that is, a tendency to be connected with and participate in a potentially unlimited number of distinct social spheres, with the single spheres being decoupled in relation to one another and operating on the basis of their own, systems-specific, or, as Luhmann (1986) prefers to say, 'self-referential' logics of action. This entails a continuous confrontation with a variety of role expectations and rationalities which are often inconsistent and even incompatible. With respect to the organisation of time, a further problem arises: the sub-systems and institutions relevant to the individual not only adopt different logics of action, but they also follow different time patterns which stem from their respective internal priorities and external environmental references. These time patterns cannot be controlled or modified individually: they must be respected by whoever wants to participate in any of the sub-systems. At the same time they tend to be highly disintegrated and desynchronised. Hence the 'multiplication of social times' (Brose *et al.*, 1987), resulting in a set of coordination problems.

These problems are not new but they have gained in prominence in the last two decades. With the emergence of 'optional society' (Dovring and Dovring, 1971) – due to the 'decline of traditional commitments, routines, facticities, and expectations' (Offé, 1987, p. 3) on the one hand, and to a radical shift in material living conditions since the 1950s on the other – more people have gained access to more social spheres and sub-systems than ever before. Empirically this is reflected, first and foremost, in women's growing labour market participation, and in the ensuing erosion of dominant living arrangements as described in the previous section. No single life-sphere guarantees a secure and fulfilling social existence any longer; multiple-sphere inclusion and participation have become the norm across all social categories. Second, the ongoing socio-cultural change results in the deinstitutionalisation and temporalisation of the life course. To the extent that the biography of the individual is released from seemingly fixed routines determined by social class and gender, it becomes instead a matter of personal choice. This is reflected in the individualisation of lifestyles and in the increased likelihood of shifts occurring in personal life-priorities with the succession of biographical phases.

From this analysis, two conclusions can be drawn concerning the relationship between the differentiation of life-patterns and the formation of working time needs. First, the more people get involved in more than one sphere of social action, the less they can adapt their entire time organisation to the imperatives of one dominating sphere, namely work. In a growing number of dual earner families and partnerships, for instance, 'two self-constructed biographies' (Beck-Gernsheim, 1986) have to be coordinated and synchronised. This requires not only that each partner be prepared to have regard for the other's external responsibilities, but also if possible that they find objective conditions of employment which allow their different schedules to be made compatible. If both partners are subject to strictly unalterable but asynchronous working time regimes, they may hardly get a chance to meet each other. Coordination problems also stem from the need to obey the on and off times of other relevant organisations. For any employees who cannot delegate routine responsibilities to friends or relatives, the opening hours of shops or nursery schools become immensely important parameters of their time management; if working time arrangements are fixed and preclude any adaptations, any unexpected events beyond personal control such as illnesses of children can threaten people's whole daily organisation. It is impossible, however, to make material rules for new arrangements which would better suit the time needs of all employees. The spectrum of time-related interests, generated by the differentiation of living conditions and life-styles, is too wide to be met by one paradigmatic employment pattern. All they have in common is their deviation from what the standard employment relationship, referred to above, presupposes as normal forms of work.

Secondly, in addition to their diversity between individuals, time needs are also likely to vary with different stages of the life cycle. This is especially true of women but it applies to men as well, although to a lesser degree. After childbirth, for instance, women may want to leave the labour force for an extended period at home and return to it later, full-time or part-time, depending on the support they receive in the domestic role. Others may just want to reduce their hours spent in paid work, but, once more, only temporarily. The time needs and personal preferences at the beginning of a career may differ substantially from those after the realisation of major personal projects, or from those in the years before retirement. Life activities other than those related to work may for a time demand more attention than would be possible with full-time employment.

Again, such needs have no common denominator apart from their incompatibility with the standard employment relationship, which has become too narrow a corset to accommodate the more fluid life plans of increasing parts of the labour force (Hinrichs, 1990). The available empirical data on working time preferences provide ample evidence in support of this postulate. All pertinent studies published in the 1980s report growing levels of discomfort among the employed with their current working time situation. At the same time, none of these studies found a common pattern in which the stated preferences for change would converge (Landenberger, 1983; Engfer *et al.*, 1984; Groß *et al.*, 1989).

PATTERNS OF FLEXIBLE WORKING TIME

From what has been said so far, one might get the impression that the West German working time structure is relatively rigid and inflexible. This is not the case, or more precisely, not the whole truth. If one defines as flexible all working time patterns which are irregular in the sense that they deviate, in length or organisation, from the standard employment relationship, then working time arrangements in the Federal Republic are indeed characterised by a great deal of flexibility:

by 1989 the proportion of employees conforming to the conventional standard had fallen to less than a quarter. Most other employees were engaged in some type of non-regular working time pattern, be it through overtime, short-time work, shift or night work, work at the weekend, flexitime, or part-time work (Groß *et al.*, 1989).

Flexibility, then, has many forms. It is evident that its impact on the lives of employees is not necessarily to their advantage or in accord with their needs and preferences. Moreover, such employee flexibility is not always strictly voluntary. Overtime, for instance, can be required by employers and often it is not even paid for. Work at unsocial hours (especially shift and night work) is extremely unpopular and exposes affected workers to above average health risks. A majority of them would prefer other working hours and conditions, but their labour market position does not allow them to opt out, since in most industries shiftwork and nightwork are characteristic of occupational categories with comparatively low bargaining power (Schmidt, 1988). At the same time, many employees who explicitly request more temporal flexibility for themselves by seeking working time arrangements which do not interfere with their non-work duties and activities, are either denied them totally or confronted with extremely unfavourable working conditions. Flexitime and part-time work are cases in point here.

Flexitime enables employees to vary their daily starting and finishing times as well as, within certain limits, their daily hours, so long as they complete the total number of hours required per week or per month. The proportion of employees working formal flexitime arrangements is relatively high in West Germany (19 per cent) compared to Britain, where it is so low it barely registers in survey responses (Marsh, 1991). It is also rising steadily in West Germany and is very popular among all employee groups; 39 per cent of employees with fixed schedules would prefer flexitime (Groß *et al.*, 1989). Nonetheless, employers are hesitant in extending its application beyond the higher and middle ranks. They tend to treat it as a gratification for executives and white collar employees from which manual and low-skilled workers are excluded (Wiesenthal, 1987).

Part-time work, on the other hand, has remained almost exclusively the domain of married women, who are using it as a strategy for combining family life with paid employment: 94 per cent of part-timers are women, with four-fifths being married (Büchtemann and Schupp, 1986, pp. 10, 45). The price they have to pay for this strategy can be very high, both in terms of employment conditions and social security. The supply of part-time jobs is largely restricted to low-skill and low-

grade occupations in areas like retailing, personal service, and so forth.
Employees in higher occupational positions, such as professionals or
managers, are commonly denied the opportunity to work part-time,
or threatened with a loss in status and with the risk that a later request
to return to full-time employment will be refused (Hoff and Scholz,
1985). Most part-time jobs are therefore badly paid and of low status
with little work autonomy and responsibility. Workers in such jobs
are poorly protected and likely to be the first to be laid off in an
economic downturn. And they forego almost all promotional prospects
and many of the customary fringe benefits to which full-time employees
are entitled.

Part-timers also face a number of serious disadvantages in the social
security system. Despite the dramatic changes which have occurred
in living arrangements and actual employment patterns, the standard
employment relationship remains the key reference point for social
and labour-market policy. Since benefits are tied to the duration of
employment and to the level of former earnings and contributions,
the system is so designed as to privilege a traditional male-oriented
employment behaviour, that is, continuous and year-round full-time
work throughout the employment biography. All those who do not
wish or are unable to meet these conditions are discriminated against.
This is especially true for the growing number of employees, mostly
female, in the 'precarious' part-time jobs which fall below the thresholds for compulsory social insurance contributions which qualify
them for benefits. Currently, this threshold is set at 17 hours per week
for unemployment insurance, and 15 hours for health insurance; furthermore, those who work less than 10 hours per week are not even
entitled to sick pay.[2]

For many employers, hiring such unprotected labour has become
part of an explicit strategy to lower labour costs. Many of the affected
women, on the other hand, have no choice but to accept sub-standard
conditions because they do not have the bargaining power to negotiate
more comfortable forms of flexible working time regimes for themselves. Not surprisingly, they are far from content with these conditions.
This is clearly reflected in the data on working time preferences referred
to in the previous section: most part-timers, including those currently
employed in 'precarious' jobs, as well as most of those full-time
employees who would rather work part-time (provided they find appropriate jobs), prefer weekly hours within the range of 25–30 hours,
that is, employment conditions affording at least minimum standards
of social security (Groß *et al.*, 1989).

It is obvious, then, that the content of what employers and employees understand by flexibility differs sharply. Yet the disadvantages encountered by women who request flexible working time arrangements cannot solely be attributed to the employer's reluctance to offer them attractive employment conditions. Just as important in this context are the relevant social institutions which have not sufficiently responded to the socio-economic and cultural changes in their environments. In favouring a conventional, male-oriented employment behaviour, they are contributing to the cementing of gender divisions within the household. Since the household division of labour is connected to the conditions of employment, women's subordinate position in the marketplace makes it difficult for them to overcome their partner's resistance to equal housework. In the previous chapter, Alan Carling discussed the extent to which the decision by individuals to form partnerships could be viewed as a rational response to relative wage rates. But the employer is an important third player in these games. Women end up being losers in a three-actor-game in which employers justify their unwillingness to pay them equally on the grounds of a historically obsolete household model in which a woman's income is something just added on to that of the male breadwinner. This discrimination in turn can be exploited by their male partners and labour market competitors as a legitimation for assigning them the role of the sole 'houseworker' because women's career opportunities and income prospects are comparatively worse. As long as key labour market and social security institutions continue to discriminate against the non-linear and less than full-time employment patterns typical of women, this situation is unlikely to change.

SOME SUGGESTIONS FOR POLITICAL REFORM

Historically, the normal working day and week, both key elements of the standard employment relationship, have been important concepts to improve the quality of working life in industrial societies. Standardised working time arrangements, by setting upper and lower limits on the normal length of work hours, and by requiring their even distribution over the course of the day and week, have reduced the employers' disposal of the workers' time and, indeed, life chances. They have contributed to the formation of socially validated expectations concerning the minimal standards of a 'family income' to which all full-time employees are seen as entitled. And they have drawn a clear distinction between working and non-working time, thus restricting employers' grip on the employees' own time.

But at the same time they have always had a gender bias, discriminating against the 'deviant' employment patterns typically, but not exclusively, followed by women. The empirical data on the differentiation of living arrangements and employment conditions, cited above, indicate that such patterns are hardly marginal phenomena any more; rather than deviating from 'normality', they are becoming the empirical norm. In response to the many disadvantages that have been associated with such jobs in the past, two suggestions have been made for working time reform, one aiming at the restandardisation of working time arrangements through massive general reductions in work hours, the other at an enhancement of the individual employee's position in the bargaining over the precise temporal conditions of employment. The former, which is favoured by some unionist and feminist writers, is exemplified by the idea of a six-hour working day for all (Kurz-Scherf, 1987). The latter, which was first discussed in 'green' circles, has been labelled as 'optional working time policy' (Wiesenthal, 1986). This second approach appears to be the more promising one, and it does so basically for two reasons. First, the needs for more flexibility are real and ought to be taken seriously. Second, and just as important, the heterogeneity and specificity of these needs at the individual level make it extremely difficult, if not impossible, to find a common pattern that suits them all. On both grounds standardised models are inadequate. The concluding remarks shall therefore be devoted to a brief discussion of the logic and the most basic elements of optional working time policies.

Models of optional working time involve a shift from a substantive to a procedural mode of regulation. In contrast to conventional working time policies, they are less concerned with the fixing of material rules that translate into concrete norms and conditions for the temporal organisation of work. Rather, their emphasis lies with the institutionalisation of meta-rules that define the terms and conditions of negotiations between employers and employees. More specifically, their advocates suggest that all employees be granted, through legislation and/or collective agreements, risk-free opportunities for less-than-full-time work and for temporary interruptions of employment. Such options, if devised properly, are said to result in more individual time autonomy without leading to a loss in collective rationality.

Concerning individual autonomy, instead of one-sidedly demanding that the employees accommodate themselves to the needs of the organisation, working time conditions must be so designed as to take account of their responsibilities and interests as well. Rights to work less than 'normal' hours or to withdraw from the labour market for an extended period of time can be thought of as an equivalent to the employers' right to require overtime. In view of the coordination problems faced by growing parts of the labour force, and of the socially and economically indispensable 'back-up' functions, performed by non-work life-spheres, such rights are highly legitimate. Formal procedures must be established that allow the employees to put their own time preferences on the table and that give them a realistic chance of realising them, even if they run counter to the employer's interests. At the same time such procedures must, at least to some extent, allow employees to refuse conditions which do not suit them. Positive examples of a 'right to work lesser hours' include:

- options for a partial or complete *release from work*, be it through the providing of opportunities for temporary moves from full-time to part-time work, or through the granting of possibilities to block commitments and free whole days, weeks or months for the employees' own disposal.
- options for extended *leave of absence*, either as unpaid sabbaticals if used for personal projects, or as partly remunerated leave (for instance, through tax allowances) if used for socially desirable activities outside the labour market.
- the right to take *free shifts*, as compensation for overtime, at times that suit the employees.

In contrast to existing regulations, the granting of such options should not be tied to specific life-situations or occasions, such as the birth of children in the case of parental leave. Nor should entitlement be restricted to one gender, as in some collective agreements offering women the opportunity to take a family break or to reduce their work commitment during the family phase. Purpose-indifference and gender-neutrality, on the other hand, would normalise the realisation of such options in three welcomed ways. First, more people would actually make use of them, thus contributing to an easing of the labour market situation under conditions of high unemployment rates. Second and related, it would be less plausible to treat them as 'deviations' from normality, legitimating some substandard conditions in other aspects of the employment relationship. And third, men would find it harder to resist their fair share in domestic chores.

In order to make the realisation of such options a viable strategy of combining work and non-work interests and responsibilities, at least three additional requirements must be met.

1. The first condition is that equal treatment be secured in all non-temporal aspects of the employment relationship, including job protection, opportunities for career advancement, fringe benefits, paid holidays, sick pay, and so forth.
2. Options to work less than normal hours or to interrupt paid employment for a time can be used as chosen strategies only if they are reversible, that is, if they allow an unimpeded movement in and out of the labour market and if the temporary 'opting' for part-time work does not preclude a later return to full-time work.
3. Upper and lower limits of the permissible length of work hours remain important to protect employees from excess demands by employers. Lower limits are necessary to guarantee the material subsistence of part-time workers and to keep them beyond the insurance thresholds. And upper limits of the daily and weekly length of hours are important to allow for sufficient recreation times and to distinguish between normal and overtime hours.

CONCLUSION: A BRIEF SOCIOLOGICAL COMMENT

The above can be viewed as an adequate response, in one specific policy area, to a general problem observed in multiple variants in all modern welfare states: labour market institutions and systems of welfare provision are typically based on empirical as well as normative assumptions of what constitutes social 'normality'. They are built around what are perceived to be the standard examples of family life (Lewis, 1989; Crow and Hardy, this volume; Collins, this volume), housing needs (Watson, 1989) and employment behaviour (Mückenberger, 1985), automatically favouring those who conform to the behavioural assumptions and expectations underlying them, and disadvantaging those who don't. To some extent, such normalisation may be unavoidable. Indeed, in matters of resource allocation and of redistribution, it may well be justified: it would hardly make sense to consider all potential recipients and beneficiaries of goods or transfers as equally eligible and 'deserving' (Elster, 1989b). However, in modern societies, no authorities or institutions exist that are capable of defining – or indeed are entitled to define – universally binding standards of living and behaviour, on the basis of which clear-cut boundaries can be drawn between different categories of citizens and grades of deservedness. All policy measures established at any given point in time are contingent upon specific conditions and interpretations, hence contestable and subject to change. Hence, and because of the degree of pluralism and differentiation of living patterns that has actually been reached in most advanced industrial societies, the appropriate goal of social policy-making should be to devise institutions which 'allow otherness to be' (Connolly, 1988, p. 375), rather than pressing all deviations and forms of 'otherness' under the imperatives of normalisation. Optional working time models are an example of a policy following precisely this logic.

Notes

1. The author wishes to thank Sara Arber, Cathie Marsh, Claus Offe, and Udo Staber for valuable comments and suggestions on an earlier draft. The contribution draws extensively on a chapter, co-authored with Helmut Wiesenthal, which was written as part of a study on the relationship between the implementation of new technologies and the restructuring of working time arrangements (Berger, Schmidt and Wiesenthal, 1991). The study was funded by the labour ministry of Northrhine Westfalia as part of its program 'Mensch und Technik – Sozialverträgliche Technikgestaltung'.
2. Similar regulations are – with similar results – applied in most countries of the European Community. For a recent account of the British situation see Hakim (1989).

8 Diversity and Ambiguity Among Lone-Parent Households in Modern Britain

Graham Crow and Michael Hardey

Lone-parent households constitute an increasingly important group in British society. Although precise estimates of their number vary, there are certainly well over a million such households, and the number is rising. One in eight dependent children currently live in one-parent families, and these family types make up one in six of all families with dependent children – a proportion which has doubled in the space of less than two decades. Of all households, eight per cent are headed by a lone-parent (over 90 per cent of whom are lone mothers), and nine per cent of the general population live in lone-parent households (Haskey, 1989b; OPCS, 1989c). The number of people who live in a lone-parent household at some stage can only be guessed at on the basis of existing data, but the figure is undoubtedly high (Rimmer, 1983).

In addition to their growing numerical significance, lone-parent households are important because of certain structural characteristics of the group. For example, their poverty represents a major challenge to social policy (Millar, 1989). Unlike childless single-person house-holders (Bien, this volume), their aloneness works to exclude them from much conventional, couple-centred social life (Elliot, 1986). On the basis of this adverse economic and social situation, Field (1989) has argued that single-parent families, together with the long-term unem-ployed and pensioners, are among the most deprived sections of society.

The continued clustering of lone-parent households at the disadvan-taged end of the social structure has confounded earlier optimism regarding their status. Chester (1977) based his claim that the situation of one-parent families was improving on their growing visibility, on greater tolerance in society, on wider economic opportunities, and on more favourable treatment in public policy. Such assessments have proved at best premature. Social changes such as the growth of separ-ation and divorce as routes into lone parenthood have undoubtedly worked to undermine old stereotypes of 'unmarried mothers', but the material divisions between lone-parent households and other household types (in particular two-parent households) remain pronounced. Lone-parent households are still subject to a degree of social and economic marginalisation which policy measures have done little to alleviate, and may even have exacerbated.

This chapter is concerned to investigate why a group as significant as lone-parent households has not secured the improvement in its situation which the growth in its numbers led commentators to expect. We suggest that part of the answer reflects the diversity of lone-parent households which limits their collective strength, while the blurred boundary surrounding lone parenthood creates ambiguities relating to identity and action as lone parents. This diversity and ambiguity found amongst lone parents also presents difficulties for social policy which have as yet been unresolved, and the chapter concludes by considering these issues.

THE EVOLVING CATEGORY OF 'LONE-PARENT HOUSEHOLDS'

For a long time the common situation of lone parents went unrecognised, not least in official thinking, and it is only in the last three decades that the categories 'lone-parent households' and 'one-parent families' have come into common usage. Townsend notes that, as late as the 1960s, 'there was, significantly, no collective name for, and no official estimate of the numbers of, one-parent families' (1979, p. 754), and that establishing the case for common treatment of one-parent families was a long struggle. Thus, while the Finer Report (DHSS, 1974) stands as something of a watershed by recommending the introduction of a new, non-contributory benefit that was to be available to all lone parents (the Guaranteed Maintenance Allowance), it had to be preceded by extensive argument over the unfairness and unworkability of previous classifications (Smart, 1984). The Report acknowledged the force of the case against the highly generalised, imprecise and emotive term 'broken homes', and recognised as illogical the different treatment of widows and other single parents.

The term 'one-parent family' promised in addition to avoid the stigma attached to alternatives (such as 'unmarried mother' and 'unsupported mother') which conveyed a sense of deviance from a two-parent norm. This factor also contributed to the decision of the National

Council for the Unmarried Mother and her Child to change its name in 1973 to the National Council for One Parent Families (Macintyre, 1977). More recently 'lone-parent family' has come to be preferred to 'one-parent family' by some writers (Millar, 1989), although 'lone-parent household' is arguably a more precise term sociologically speaking, since many lone-parent families involve a parent who is absent from the household, not living under the same roof, but who is involved in 'family' relationships to some extent (Harris, 1983; Rimmer, 1983). Illustrating this point, O'Brien identifies the lone fathers of her study as single parents by virtue of the fact that although their children's mothers may be involved in some way as a non-custodial parent, it is they who have 'major responsibility for care of the children' (1987, p. 225). Similarly, Hipgrave describes lone fathers as 'the sole major parent' (1982, p. 173).

Further alternatives include 'the sole supporter' (Yudkin and Holme, 1963, p. 68), 'single-handed parents' (Blaxter, 1990, p. 228), 'solo parenthood' (Elliott, 1986, p. 152), and 'the 'one-parent family' type household' (Close, 1985, p. 16), each with its own nuances, and all adding to the general uncertainty over terminology. What matters most, however, is that lone parents head a separate 'income unit' (Townsend, 1979, p. 756); single-parent families are functioning households whose organisation rests on a different pattern of work to that found in two-parent families (Graham, 1984). Single parents are, as a category, 'obliged to adopt a distinctive household work strategy' (R. Pahl, 1984, p. 225).

The evolving category of single-parent families reflected a growing awareness of the disadvantaged position and particular needs common to such families, a development which challenged established conceptions. Negative stereotypes of lone parents can be traced back several centuries (Page, 1984). The general treatment of lone mothers under the Poor Law was notably punitive (Wilson, 1977), although over time the distinctions drawn between them were liable to change, altering the relative positions of widows and others, for example. Unmarried mothers were at one stage divided into two broad types, 'the young innocent who needed sensitive help and the depraved or mentally defective who required punishment or incarceration' (Ginsburg, 1979, p. 82), with such classifications being open to further sub-division (Page, 1984).

Essentially these distinctions were variations on the deserving vs undeserving poor theme. Those lone mothers falling into the latter category were seen as having more in common with other members of 'the social problem group' (where social dependency was rolled together with characteristics such as insanity and inebriety) than they did with their more sympathetically-treated deserving fellows (Lewis, 1986). Even the liberal Beveridge proposals of the 1940s retained an element of this distinction by discriminating between those lone parents 'at fault' in creating their situation and those not (Millar, 1989). Unmarried mothers were still seen as essentially 'pathological'.

These moralistic distinctions between different types of lone parents broke down in the 1960s under the weight of social change, with increasing numbers of lone-parent households, and growing criticism of existing policy arrangements by both pressure groups (such as the campaigning group Gingerbread) and social researchers (such as Wynn, 1964). Typical of the latter is the following passage from a study of working mothers:

> The difficulties and distresses facing the widowed, divorced or deserted wife, or the unmarried mother, will vary enormously, but in the long run, unless they are fortunate enough to possess a private income or to have the financial support of their families, or to make or complete a family by marriage or remarriage, they will all be faced with the common problem of making ends meet on inadequate or no statutory allowances (Yudkin and Holme, 1963, p. 69).

The presence of common problems amongst lone parents meant that it made little sense to discriminate between them for welfare purposes. Wynn's policy conclusion was to 'raise the standards of all lone mothers and their children at least to the modest level of the widows' (1972, p. 237). Ideally, social security schemes would treat fatherless families 'simply and equitably' (Marsden, 1973, p. 4).

Yet lone-parent households are not a homogeneous or unified group, and it is an oversimplification to treat them as such. As Rimmer notes, 'In many ways the term "one parent family" is a convenient but misleading shorthand for a complex variety of family situations' (1983, p. 12), between which important lines of division exist. Earlier and more judgmental terms such as 'deserted wives', 'fatherless families', 'incomplete families' and 'broken homes' may have given way to less value-laden language, but even apparently neutral distinctions between different types of lone parent have significant implications.

The contrasting assumptions made about lone fathers and lone mothers, with the former being seen as less capable carers and the latter placing a lower priority on taking paid work, are well documented (George and Wilding, 1972; O'Brien, 1987). Further, Ginsburg (1979) has argued that the old distinction between deserving and undeserving poor continues to apply to widows and other lone parents respectively. Rightly or wrongly, certain groups of lone parents are more likely than others to be seen as having chosen lone parenthood, as being responsible for their situation, and this has a bearing on both their treatment in the formal welfare system and the extent of informal aid and assistance sought and forthcoming from kin.

A clearer sense of the common needs of lone-parent households has not produced a 'simple and equitable' scheme through which welfare support is organised. There are marked differences in lone-parent households' housing situations, for example, with over half of all widowed mothers being owner-occupiers while 93 per cent of never married lone mothers are tenants (Haskey, 1989b). More generally, Field (1989) argues that one of the main divisions currently emerging is that between lone mothers locked into long-term dependency on welfare benefits and others who pass through lone parenthood for briefer periods.

In part these divisions reflect the difficulties of defining lone-parent households for the purposes of formulating social policy. The Finer Report adopted as its working definition of a single-parent family 'a family in which there is an adult and dependent child or children, one parent or partner is absent (for whatever reason), there is no reasonable prospect of his or her return within a fairly short period and there is no effective parent substitute' (DHSS, 1974, p. 39). Graham (1984) has argued that such definitions may lose sight of several important groups of lone parents, including those with sharing arrangements which disguise their situation (such as those living with parents), and those whose children are taken into care, about whom insufficient is known.

In addition, there are definitional problems raised by the fact that lone parenthood is 'a shifting experience' (Jackson, 1982, p. 163) which needs to be understood dynamically. The boundary line around lone parenthood is in practice far from clear-cut, and definitions may fail to convey the often confused nature of the transitions into and out of lone parenthood at certain points, such as where lone parenthood blurs into cohabitation and the point at which children cease being dependent. The problematic nature of the boundary around the category of lone-parent households has thrown up awkward cases fairly consistently. These include the situation where women seeking protection from violent husbands experience difficulty in establishing their claim to housing assistance (Brailey, 1985) or financial support (J. Pahl, 1984), and that where a mother's cohabitation with a new partner does not necessarily imply his economic support of her (Popay *et al.*, 1983).

More routinely (in a bureaucratic sense), there is a genuine problem in answering Jackson's question about single-parent families, 'How long or formally does a family have to be split up in order to qualify?' (1982, p. 175) and the related issue of how long a new parent needs to be around before the label no longer applies. There have long been suspicions on the part of officials that some 'deserted' wives may be in collusion with their absent husbands, as a means of improving their eligibility for benefits – the practice of 'collusive desertion' (Ginsburg 1979) – raising doubts about their status as lone parents. More generally the Finer Report observed that 'it is often very difficult to distinguish between temporary separations and marriages that have finally broken down' (DHSS, 1974, p. 1).

Similarly, the point of exit from lone parenthood is often hard to specify precisely. Donnison (1982), for example, notes that three-quarters of the eight thousand cases of benefits being withdrawn on grounds of cohabitation which came before the Supplementary Benefits Commission in the 1970s related to women with dependent children. He found that the procedures inevitably involved arbitrary decisions on where to draw the line concerning what counted as 'lone parent-hood', confirming the view that the single-parent family's social situation is 'full of ambiguities' (Oakley, 1976, p. 70).

Having outlined the evolution of the category of lone-parent households, we now turn to consider evidence relating to the experience of lone parenthood. The argument is supported by quotations derived from in-depth interviews conducted by one of the authors, Michael Hardey, among a sample of 60 lone parents from Birmingham, London and the home counties. The interviews were conducted in 1988 with lone parents who had been living on their own for at least a year. Although not formally representative, the sample included individuals from across the range of circumstances to be found amongst lone parents.

THE BLURRED BOUNDARY AROUND THE CATEGORY OF 'LONE-PARENT HOUSEHOLDS'

Following Leete (1978) and Haskey (1986) it is possible to portray diagramatically the various routes into and out of lone parenthood (Figure 8.1). Of the routes into lone parenthood, the death of a partner and births to single mothers are more or less clear-cut changes, but the ending of marriage through separation (and possibly divorce) and the ending of cohabitation are much more ambiguous processes. Simi-

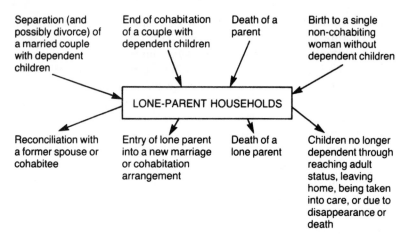

Figure 8.1 Routes into and out of lone parenthood

larly the routes out of lone parenthood (marriage or remarriage, reconciliation, cohabitation, children growing up and leaving home, children being taken into care, and the death of the lone parent or child) embody a range of transitions, some sudden and simple, others prolonged and complicated.

The blurred nature of some routes into lone parenthood is not a new discovery. For example, Illsley and Thompson's study of 'broken homes' noted that 'Parental death produces a clear-cut situation and the date of the break can easily be specified. Separation and divorce, on the other hand, are usually only the final stages of a long drawn-out process' (1961, p. 36). Given that most lone-parent households are created by separation and/or divorce, with 60 per cent of lone mothers falling into this category (OPCS, 1989c), closer consideration of these blurred transitions promises to illuminate the problems faced in estimating the number of lone-parent households and also to aid understanding of the diversity of lone parents' experiences and identities.

Difficulties of classifying cases were thrown up regularly in Illsley and Thompson's research by the irregularity of people's behaviour as they moved towards divorce. Sometimes the couple 'continued to live together until the formal break occurred, sometimes one or other partner left the home several times' (1961, p. 36). In such circumstances, precise definitions may be inapplicable; a terminating relationship is often better understood as a process rather than an event (Maclean, 1987). The reality of becoming a lone parent, with all its confusion and ambiguity, resists attempts to impose onto it tidy classification (J. Pahl, 1984).

It is certainly the case that many individuals experience the move into lone parenthood as a lengthy transition. Hart has described the process of marital breakdown as a status passage, and suggests that 'the precise point at which a person recognises complete dissociation from his [or her] partner in life is often hard to define. "Being divorced" is better thought of as *becoming* something than as occupying a fixed social position with well demarcated boundaries in time' (1976, p. 103, emphasis in original). The question of when a marriage ends may have several answers, with those of the individuals involved quite possibly identifying times or periods long before official recognition is granted. The difference between the 'objective' and 'subjective' definitions of the situation came out in Hart's respondents who 'said that they had "felt divorced" months before a judge ratified their feelings' (1976, p. 106). Other research has found it more accurate to think of a terminating marriage's 'dead period' in terms of years (Ambrose *et al.*, 1983).

There is in addition nothing to prevent the wishes and perceptions of two people separating being quite at variance as they renegotiate their relationship. Vaughan's account of relationships coming apart treats it as typical that 'uncoupling' is 'a tale of two transitions: one that begins before the other' (1988, p. 6). Within these transitions there may be particular 'turning points' (Burgoyne, 1984, p. 12) that stand out, but they follow the build up of difficulties over a considerable period. For the non-initiator, the transition may not be complete at the point of divorce, and the subjective feeling of being married may continue for some time after.

As one lone mother in Hardey's research who had been divorced for two years said,

> I think it takes a time to come to terms with being a single mother.
> In my case I've only accepted that's what I am in the past year.
> I suppose before I always thought we might get back together
> but when he got married I had to give that up. I felt very bad
> at the time, but now I think it was the best thing that could happen
> because it made me come to terms with my life.

Another divorced lone mother spoke of it taking the greater part of two years before she 'started to surface. I had to come to terms with being a lone parent, you know, accept it as a positive thing'. This ties in with Ebaugh's comments on divorce as an example of 'the process of role exit', where she describes the intermediate stage between being married and being divorced as a type of 'vacuum' (1988, p. 144) in which the individual is neither married nor divorced.

Other routes into lone parenthood can also contain an intermediate stage of indeterminacy, even when they appear clear-cut at first sight. One single mother experienced the disadvantages of lone parenthood early when she was told by her landlord to leave her flat before her child was born: 'I had this nice little place but someone must have told the landlord I was expecting. . . . I was a good tenant but it was made very clear to me that I would have to go'. In another way, a widower from Birmingham had experienced some of the practical aspects of lone fatherhood before his wife had died, as her illness made her incapable of contributing to the running of the household:

> My wife had got problems and it was the sort of problem where most of the time she was alright, but then the illness or whatever you want to call it would start and she'd be absolutely hopeless. . . . I began being a single father from almost the start. . . . So when she passed on it was nothing new to me to be on my own with a young child.

Becoming a lone parent is also likely to have an impact on the income available to the household. The dealings which individuals have with officialdom may have an important part to play in shaping their new identity. One respondent's story of her interaction with the Department of Social Security brings out this point well:

> I explained about myself to the woman and she said, 'Oh, you're a single parent then?' I hadn't really thought of myself like that before. . . . She kept on about 'people like you', you know, single parents. I think that changed my outlook because it was like having an official stamp say that you were not an ordinary person but a single parent.

This lone parent's negative experiences of official treatment echoes other research findings (see, for example, Collins's chapter in this volume). In general, lone parents are 'singled out for more grudging and inferior assistance, and subject to more official controls over their credentials and honesty' (Lawson, 1987, pp. 93–4).

With the passage of time other interactions could generate more positive images of single parenthood, as was the case for the divorced woman who joined Gingerbread and found it 'very good because I've got lots of friends who are also in my situation and you can see that it's quite O.K. to be a single mum'. Another respondent spoke of reorganising her life so that she could get herself 'established as a lone parent', wanting to see how she and her child managed in the absence of her ex-husband. As time goes on, lone parents learn to develop a range of coping strategies through which they can come to be 'better off poorer' (Graham, 1987, p. 235). Even though the level of household income is almost certain to drop following separation or divorce, single mothers may have greater access to and control over household income than they had when married/cohabiting, and this may make them wary of the idea of entering a new relationship.

Further ways exist in which lone parenthood may come to be compared favourably with marriage. It may, for example, bring greater independence in the organisation of home life and leisure time, at least for lone mothers (Sharpe, 1984), although the difference is not always obvious to outsiders:

> It's what makes single parents different. We have to explain ourselves whereas couples are just seen as normal. You know the reaction: 'Oh dear, I'm sure you will find a nice partner soon', that kind of thing, as if you can't manage without one. I'll tell you, I'm a bloody sight better off than many women who are married and have to run around after the husband as well as the kids.

Nor is it an immediate change for people coming to terms with lone parenthood; one of Green and Hebron's (1988) respondents spoke of it taking over four years to build up a new social life as a lone parent. The general point to draw out here is that lone parenthood is not an easy status to adapt to. In the transitional period there is no automatic association or identification with other lone parents, social isolation being the more likely outcome.

Less is known about the processes involved in the movement out of lone parenthood than is known about becoming a lone parent, but similar points apply about the boundary around the category of lone parents being blurred. In Burgoyne and Clark's study of stepfamilies, in some instances 'the end of one relationship overlapped with the beginning of another', while others who had not initiated the ending of their first marriage went through 'a distinct stage of demarriage' (1984, pp. 70, 67). The 'ambiguities of the state of demarriage' (*ibid.*, p. 81) contributed to the pressures to remarry, but most of the couples in the study cohabited before getting married again, and in some of these cases it was difficult to identify a precise moment at which cohabitation began.

It is also worth noting that moving out of lone parenthood does not necessarily improve people's positions. It is quite common to find arrangements made whereby a divorced mother and children stay on in what was formerly the marital home until the children become adults, although such agreements came more grudgingly in some cases than in others. Two contrasting situations illustrate the point. One lone mother felt that her ex-husband had

> been very good. He wanted us to stay in the house even though it is really too big for the three of us. He felt that it was important that the children should keep the home and environment they were used to.

She was under much less pressure than the lone mother who said

> Technically we can live here until the children leave home after which the house has to be sold. My ex resents us staying here and now that he has remarried and is living abroad he can be very awkward when it comes to maintenance and things.

Either way, however, lone parents in this situation face downward mobility in the housing market following their exit from lone parenthood. The same is true for tenants of local authorities, which place single-person households further down their list of priorities than single-parent families, although both groups are vulnerable to homelessness (Watson with Austerberry, 1986).

OPPORTUNITIES, CONSTRAINTS AND STRATEGIES WITHIN LONE PARENTHOOD

In terms of their material situation and their subjective experiences, lone-parent households are neither a homogeneous social group nor, given the blurred boundary that surrounds them, a type of people easily distinguished from others. Striving to establish a unitary category of one-parent families rather than distinguishing between widows, separated and divorced mothers, single mothers, and lone fathers, served the important purpose of highlighting the existence of common problems amongst lone parents, whatever their route into lone parenthood, but it has not solved those problems. In Jackson's view, 'the naming of it [the one-parent family] as a social phenomenon has enlarged our knowledge, mildly increased our action and generally created a characteristically misleading stereotype' (1982, p. 175).

That a negative stereotype of lone-parent households exists is evident in a whole range of fields, including the criminal justice system (Carlen, 1988) and public housing allocation, where single mothers and their children (particularly those from ethnic minorities) are 'frequently described as "problem families"' (Karn and Henderson, 1983, p. 78). Yet lone-parent households are too sizeable a section of the population to be ignored, and too complex a group to have their situation explained in simple terms of either individual responsibility and choice or personal misfortune, although analysis is frequently conducted on this level. There is, for example, an extensive debate about whether young single women in disadvantaged situations may use motherhood as a way of improving their housing prospects by increasing their eligibility for local authority tenancy. The evidence on this is at best inconclusive, however (Holme, 1985; Clark, 1989). More generally, while it is clear that the description 'single mothers by choice' fits some lone parents well (Renvoize, 1985), it is 'unlikely that very many one-parent households will be created out of choice or preference' (Close, 1985, p. 16). Collins, in Chapter 10, shows that the rate of births outside of marriage correlates highly with various indicators of poverty and social distress in Britain.

There is, of course, no clear-cut dividing line between those cases where lone parenthood is 'an active choice' (Jackson, 1982, p. 176), such as those women leaving violent husbands, and those where it is involuntary, for example through bereavement. Pahl argues that 'It is surely wrong to assume that all young unmarried mothers are in that position by mistake' (R. Pahl, 1984, p. 329), while Cashmore takes the discussion further by noting that although some 15 per cent of lone parents may be considered to have entered their situation freely, 'the voluntary one parent family is rarely a planned phenomenon. People don't assess their futures and weigh up the strengths and weaknesses of having children and rearing them alone' (1985, p. 199). The debate about choice, in other words, needs to be set in the broader context of the structures of opportunity and constraint within which choices take place, and the ways in which those structures shift over time.

The nature of the choice about becoming a lone parent has undoubtedly changed significantly since the nineteenth century when 'the options for the single, pregnant woman were few' (Lewis 1984, p. 64), as is indicated by the widespread practices of infanticide and informal adoption. More recently, the issue of choice was raised in the Finer Report in relation to the discussion of lone mothers becoming more independent through taking up paid work. The view expressed was in the tradition of laudably liberal sentiment, if rather superficial in its sociological analysis: 'lone parents should have a free and effective choice whether or not to take up paid employment. The decision is one which lone parents must make for themselves. . . . Our concern is to see that the choice is a real one' (DHSS, 1974, p. 17).

Deacon and Bradshaw have pointed out that the great obstacles to implementing the Finer Report's proposals, through which it was hoped greater choice could be introduced for lone parents, were essentially two: the cost of the measures, and 'the problem of equity with married people. . . . These problems of cost and equity have effectively blocked any substantial development of non means-tested benefits for single parents' (1983, p. 179). The means-testing of the one-parent benefit available on top of child benefit resulted in a situation whereby 'in the mid 1980s it was only claimed by around a half of those entitled' (Alcock, 1987, p. 101). Similar arguments applied earlier this century, at the end of the First World War, when attempts to take one-parent families out of the ambit of the Poor Law failed on grounds of cost and fear of increased illegitimacy (Lewis, 1984). The conventional wisdom is that welfare provision should not be seen to favour alternative household types to the two-parent married family, compared to which one-parent families are treated as somehow deviant, special cases (Oakley, 1976; Smart, 1984).

However, there are limits to how far people behave in a calculating way about something as emotionally significant as their marital status. For most of Burgoyne and Clark's respondents,

> The passage from first marriage to demarriage to remarriage, whilst punctuated in some cases by numerous contacts with the public structures of the law and welfare agencies, was typically seen as a private trauma, something to be negotiated personally and to be come to terms with individually (1984, p. 75).

Similarly, the calculations which lone parents make about taking up paid employment are not narrowly economic. In addition to the system of benefits being so complex, it is very difficult to work out precisely the costs and rewards of working (Beechey and Perkins, 1987). In general, paid work represents independence and offers a potential route out of poverty for single mothers (Sharpe, 1984; Gordon, 1990).

Further, it is not at all clear on what basis the comparison between lone-parent households and two-parent households is most appropriately conducted. The comparison which separated or divorced lone parents make with their former married state is not a narrowly economic one, but also refers to issues such as autonomy (Hardey, 1989). The single mothers in Sharpe's study are portrayed as being 'happier alone' (1984, p. 205), while lone motherhood does not necessarily lead to greater social isolation than that of married women, at least in the longer term (Green and Hebron, 1988). And, provided that material circumstances are held constant in comparisons between lone- and two-parent households, expectations of children's welfare being un-favourable in lone-parent households are not necessarily borne out (Kruk and Wolkind, 1983; see also Illsley and Thompson, 1961). Put another way, it is the poverty of the lone-parent household which is primarily responsible for the difficulties and restrictions on choices encountered, and poverty is not unique to lone-parent households. It is this poverty which is the central question for social policy relating to lone-parent households to address.

It is, of course, correct to observe that social policymakers are rarely ahead of their times, but it does not follow from this that lone-parent households will necessarily see an improvement in their situation in the future, even with continued growth in their numbers. Similarly, lone-parent households do not necessarily stand to benefit from the fact that several of the points of entry into and exit from lone parent-hood are blurred. Goodin and Le Grand have argued that where boundary problems exist, selective benefits will have a tendency to become more widely available because in difficult, marginal cases there is a 'bias towards generosity' (1987, pp. 109–10). While it is undeniable that marginal cases inevitably throw up problems for systems of welfare administration, it is far from clear that benefits always become more widely available. In the case of lone parents, there has not been a levelling up of their conditions, either within the broad category of lone-parent households or between lone-parent households and adja-cent household types which they blur into. Instead, lone-parent house-holds are confronted by a system of support which has been described as 'fragmented' and 'woefully inadequate' (Rimmer and Wicks, 1984, p. 39).

CONCLUSION

It is becoming increasingly clear that a key aspect of improving the situation of lone parents lies in the promotion of measures to facilitate their participation in the labour market (Millar, 1989). Already, signifi-cant numbers of lone parents manage to combine bringing up children with employment, but the majority experience the absence of adequate and affordable child-care facilities as a serious obstacle to this route to greater independence and would benefit from more extensive nursery provision, after-school care and parental leave. Such difficulties are not unique to lone parents, but they are problems to which lone parents are particularly prone.

The evolution of the broad category of lone-parent household has served to draw attention to the presence of common problems faced by lone parents which arise out of their structurally disadvantaged position in the housing and labour markets. The diversity of routes into lone parenthood and the blurred nature of the boundary around the category of lone parent households have proved to be obstacles to social policy makers in the past, but it does not follow that common problems necessitate common solutions, particularly if the Finer Report's point about choice is to be taken seriously. Just as two-parent households have devised a range of strategies for coping with the competing demands of child-care and work, so too have lone-parent households, and extending choice requires that such options are increased, not foreclosed. To the extent that this is achieved, lone-parent households are set to become more heterogeneous yet.

9 Social Networks of Single-person Households

Walter Bien, Jan Marbach and
Robert Templeton

INTRODUCTION

The household and the family are different social entities. The family is a socio-biological unit constituted by relations between parents and children. Households, on the other hand, are socio-economic units consisting of people who dwell and manage their everyday life together. Despite these obvious differences, historians and researchers of the family have often confused the household with the nuclear family. This point was discussed by Marsh and Arber in the introduction to this volume; they showed how hard it was to document real social trends about family and household composition in the UK because of the inconsistent and overlapping way in which these two key terms had often been defined. Furthermore, in the previous chapter we have just seen what confusion has arisen over the category of 'lone parenthood' when the object of discussion is usually more properly single-parent households.

This confusion can also be seen from the way in which the official census data in the Federal Republic of Germany (FRG) defines and counts families. In general, as in the UK, only children who live in their parents' households are included in the official count of families in the FRG. Couples whose children have moved-out of their households are counted as childless married couples. Children who live in the parental household are only counted as household members if they are unmarried, regardless of age. Divorced people whose children live with their former spouse appear as 'standing alone without children'.

All three situations just identified are common forms of family relations, and most individuals in such situations would see people outside their household as members of their family. Yet, because they do not fit the definition of the nuclear family used by the census bureau, they are not categorised as such in official counts. Defining the family in this manner results in the family members outside of the target household being neglected and unidentified. In turn, census results appear to reinforce the idea that the family is an isolated, household-bound unit.

In shifting the unit of analysis away from the household, historians have discovered a modified or extended family that was kin-based, but was not limited to co-residence within households nor to nuclear kin (Demos, 1970; Goode, 1963; Greven, 1970; Hareven, 1982). In the nineteenth century, the nuclear family/household was only a part of a larger network in the USA and the UK; it was extended outside the household by a network of kinship ties (Anderson, 1971; Greven, 1970; Hareven, 1984; Yans-McLaughlin, 1972). These historical findings were confirmed for families in the 1950s and 1960s by sociological research into support systems of the nuclear family (Litwak, 1960a, 1960b; Sussman, 1959, 1965; Sussman and Burchinal, 1962). The same question has not been adequately addressed for the modern period. Do people who live alone nowadays still have access to a family network that exists outside of their house?

THE PROBLEM

In the household-bound definition of the family, as applied by the census bureau in the FRG, people who live alone, or in single-person households (singles), are defined as isolated. This has an interesting implication. When one broadens this view to the societal level, the increase in the number and percentage of people who choose to live alone may suggest that the whole society is becoming more atomistic. Between 1957 and 1989, for example, the percentage of households consisting of people living alone has increased from 18 per cent to 35 per cent (see Figure 9.1). Over a third of households in the FRG now comprise a type that traditionally has been viewed as the epitome of loneliness and isolation. This chapter attempts to address an important question: are they alone in any sociologically meaningful sense?

The stereotype of loneliness comes from the image of an older person who lives alone. The composition of elderly households in the FRG is similar to that in the UK as outlined by Arber and Ginn in their chapter in this book. The ratio of women to men increases dramatically in later life (see Figure 9.2); it moves away from unity after the age of 60, by 80 it is double and over 90 it is approaching quadruple. As a corollary, the percentage of women in the total population who are widows also increases considerably (see Figure 9.3).

Furthermore, the social networks of older people are smaller and

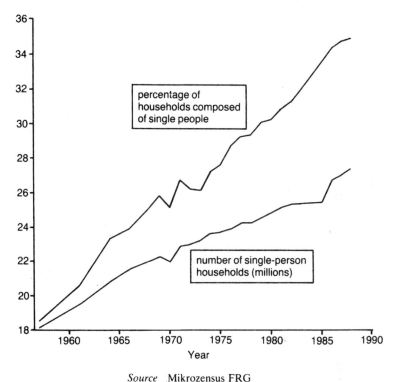

Source Mikrozensus FRG

Figure 9.1   Single-person households, 1957–88, in Federal Republic of Germany

involve lower contact frequency than is typical for younger people. This is the result of several factors. First, it is difficult for older people to generate new social networks after the loss of a spouse. There is a tendency for people who have been bereaved to lessen contact with others (Spiegel, 1977; Glick *et al.*, 1974). Second, family and friends may avoid the widowed person for a variety of reasons (Spiegel, 1977; Glick *et al.*, 1974). Third, the bereaved person tends to lose contact with married couples that were friends of the couple before the bereavement (Glick *et al.*, 1974). Thus, the loss of a spouse may have a long-term negative effect on the social networks of older people and, without new contacts or friendships, widows and widowers are likely to become more alone (Blau, 1973). Conjugal bereavement may rate as the most momentous thing that can affect the social networks of older people.

This chapter does not seek to call into question the robustness of

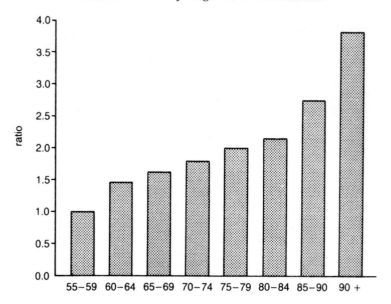

Source Census 1987 of the Federal Republic of Germany

Figure 9.2   Ratio of number of women to men, by age group

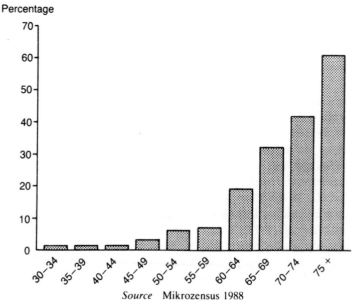

Source Mikrozensus 1988

Figure 9.3   Percentage of women who are widows, by age group
Source   DJI Survey 1988

these studies which suggest genuine social isolation among the elderly. But what about younger people who live alone? They are a mixed group, comprising those who have not (yet) found a spouse and those whose partnerships have failed, occasionally through bereavement but much more commonly through divorce or separation. Can anything of a general nature be said about this group, and if so what? In particular, do they conform to the same stereotype of isolation of those who live alone? To answer these questions, this chapter focuses on the social networks of younger people residing in single-person households.

The current analysis focuses on the social networks of people between the ages of 18 and 55. The central question is: are such people living in single-person households really alone or is their apparent isolation a sociological artefact, resulting from operational definitions of households and families?

DATA AND METHODS

The data reported in this chapter stem from the project 'Change and Development of Family Life Patterns' which is sponsored by the Department of Youth, Family, Women and Health of the Federal Government of Germany and carried out by the Deutsches Jugendinstitut based in Munich (Bertram, *et al.*, 1986).[1] The project included a survey with a representative random sample of the adult population of the FRG.

The sample was drawn from two different sources. The first was a random sample of individuals drawn from the official residential registration lists; these are lists of persons resident at particular addresses which exist for all regions of the FRG. 3011 interviews were secured by this method from a corrected gross number of 4849 addresses (that is after elimination of incorrect addresses, deceased target interviewees and residents who were repeatedly unavailable); this represented a response rate of 62 per cent. A second random sample of 6931 interviews was collected using a random route procedure based on households. There was a corrected gross number of 10924 households, so the response rate to the second, random route, sample amounted to 63 per cent.

One part of the survey attempted to establish the social networks in which the respondents were implicated. The method used to uncover the social networks was that of multiple name generators and name interpreters (Burt, 1984; Fischer, 1982). In one half of the questions, respondents were asked to name the people who played an important role in their life in fulfilling significant tasks or functions. Three of these tasks reflected the essentials of family life as defined by Max Weber: shared catering (item 2 in the list below), emotional intimacy (3) and shared leisure time (6). Another three functions (1, 4, 5) dealt with transactions in the broader context of the core family. Members of the respondent's household, when they existed, were usually named in the first six questions, but some respondents did not name them in answer to these questions. Five more questions (7–11) therefore collected information specifically about household members and close relatives (children and parents). Information on spouse or partner was provided in other parts of the questionnaire, and so did not need to be asked about specifically. The final name generator (12) was designed to extract from the respondents the people who they perceived to be members of their family. Many of the names given in answer to question 12 were people who had been named in answer to other questions, but sometimes the question elicited other names which had not yet been given.

In summary, the following name-eliciting questions were asked:

Name Generators: Tasks

1. With whom do you discuss personal matters?
2. With whom do you have your dinner regularly?
3. To whom do you have a close emotional relationship?
4. Who sometimes or regularly gives you financial aid?
5. To whom do you sometimes or regularly give financial aid?
6. With whom do you spend most of your leisure time?

Name Generators: Kinship

7. Please name your parents.
8. Please name the parents of your spouse or partner.
9. Please name your children.
10. Which of the people listed above live in your household? Please name the people living in your household who are not on your list yet.
11. Do you have a second household? If so, please name the people who are not on your list and live in this household.

Name Generators: Defined Family

12. Which people on your list do you recognise as members of your family? If there are other people you recognise as members of your family, please name them too.

For each of the people who were named in answer to any of these twelve questions, further items of information were noted: their sex, their relationship to the respondent, the distance which they lived from the household of the respondent, the frequency of contact, and their age (the last item only being obtained about non-kin). The structure of the network data is presented in Table 9.1; it shows the answers given by a hypothetical survey respondent who named seven people in total in answer to the twelve generators listed above.

To compare the representativeness of this dataset with official statistics, a special analysis of 1988 census data was performed by the Zentrum für Umfragen, Methoden und Analysen (ZUMA) in Mannheim. These census data come from the 'Mikrozensus', a periodically repeated survey of a one per cent sample of the population of the FRG (N = 600 000), conducted by the Federal Statistical Office.

RESULTS

Household Structure

The 1988 Microzensus can be used as a validating source to examine the household composition in the FRG around the time of the survey (see Table 9.2). Thirty five percent of all households in 1988 were single-person households. The second column of the tables shows the distribution of individuals rather than households. It demonstrates that people living in single-person households made up 16 per cent of the population (equivalent to 9.5 million people). A further four per cent of the population lived in non-kin households and 80 per cent lived in households containing kin members. As noted above, the main focus of this chapter is people between the ages of 18 to 55. Over the years, this age group has formed a variable proportion of the total number of people living in single-person households, fluctuating between one-third and one-half of all single households. In 1988, this group made up 48 per cent of single households or 17 per cent of all households. Table 9.3 compares the household distribution for this specific age group among the respondents to the Mikrozensus of 1988 and among

Table 9.1   Example of a matrix of network persons for a respondent who named seven persons

Persons named	Name generators 1–6	7–12	Sex	Name interpreters Relation	Distance	Frequency	Age
P1	100111	000101	1	A	A	A	–
P2	101100	001001	2	C	E	C	–
P3	000111	001101	1	C	G	D	–
P4	000100	010001	1	G	C	B	–
P5	010000	100001	2	G	C	C	–
P6	100001	000000	2	R	C	B	42
P7	001000	000000	1	R	C	D	27

Key   1 = yes
0 = no
Age requested for non-kin only

Relation
A = Spouse/partner
B = Ex-spouse
C = Own child
D = Partner's child
E = Foster child
F = Child in law
G = Own parent
H = Parent-in-law
 I = Own sibling
J = Sibling-in-law
K = Grandparent (own and partner's)
L = Grandchild (own and partner's)
M = Other kin
N = Friend
O = Workmate
P = Member of voluntary organisation
Q = Neighbour
R = Other persons

Distance
A = Same household
B = Same house
C = Neighborhood
D = Same quarter
E = Same town, more than 15 minutes by foot
F = Another town, less than 1 hour away
G = Further away

Frequency of contact
A = Daily
B = Several times a week
C = Once a week
D = Once a month
E = Several times a year
F = More seldom
G = Never

the 10000 respondents to the DJI survey. The data in this table confirms that the sample drawn for this survey was extremely close in household structure to the most robust official estimate available.

Size of Network

The first and central way to approach the question of whether people living in single-person households were more isolated is to find out if their networks were significantly smaller than the networks of people living with others in the household. An important finding emerged:

Table 9.2 Household configuration, FRG 1988

Household types	Households (thousands)	%	Members of households* (thousands)	%
Overall	27,403		61,613	
Single person	9,563	35	9,563	16
Others:	17,840	65	52,051	84
direct line kin				
one generation	6,134	34	12,265	23
two generations	10,207	57	35,490	68
three and more generations	399	2	1,957	4
other kin	179	1	390	1
non kin	920	5	1,949	4

*children are included

Source Mikrozensus 1988 (see Pöschl, 1989).

Table 9.3 Household configuration for age 18–55 (column percentages)

	Mikrozensus	*Survey DJI*
Single person	12	11
Direct line, 1–3 generations	83	81
Other kin	1	1
Non kin	4	7

Sources Mikrozensus 1988 (Pöschl 1989); DJI Survey 1988; Bertram et al., 1986.

the average network size for single householders was not very different from that for all people: 5.4 compared to 6.7 overall.

Functions Performed by Network Members

A tally was next performed of the number of different ways in which the network members related to the respondent; the number of relationships (as shown in column 5 of Table 9.1) mentioned by each respondent was counted. A clear difference emerged between single-person households and all households: the average number was 21 relationships per network in the whole sample but only 11 among single-person households. So people living alone, although they had similarly sized networks to the average person, did not have the range of relationships which were typical throughout the FRG as a whole.

But on its own this is not important. The significant issue is whether there were any differences in the numbers of people mentioned in answer to the twelve questions listed above. Table 9.4 shows the breakdown of the number of people named. As expected, for single-person households the numbers in response to each question were on average smaller. But it would be misleading to describe these single-person householders as people who had no family; typically they had between two and three other family members. This name-generating procedure revealed people considered as family by the respondents who would have remained hidden in procedures which restrict the definition of the family to those who co-reside in the household.

Table 9.4   Average number of named people undertaking different tasks (per each 100 respondents in the whole sample and single householder sample)

	Whole sample	*Single person households*
Tasks:		
discussing personal problems	182	176
having regular meals together	208	54
having strong emotional		
relationship	243	170
getting financial aid	34	24
giving financial aid	33	20
sharing most of leisure time	234	163
Kin:		
parents	134	129
parents-in-law	101	52
children	132	35
household members	210	0
girl or boy friend	84	36
Defined family	368	260

Source   DJI Survey 1988

When it comes to tasks (the first six rows of Table 9.4), it is significant that, apart from eating a regular meal together, the differences between single-person householders and the whole sample in answer to the questions about family-type tasks were generally small. The number of people available to discuss personal problems with, for example, was virtually identical. The single householders, just as the whole sample, typically named more than one person with whom they could speak about personal problems, with whom they had a close emotional relationship and with whom they shared leisure time. Furthermore, half the respondents had someone with whom they had regular meals, despite the fact that they lived on their own.

It is not surprising that single householders had fewer named people in family and kin relationships. But the fact that one in three had someone they described as a girlfriend, boyfriend or partner is another indicator that a substantial number of these single householders had very close networks outside the household.

Distance and Contact Frequency

Having established that single-person householders managed to achieve similar sorts of family functions to those living with others, we now need to consider how easy it was for them to achieve this. The first two columns of Table 9.5 presents the percentage of named people who resided in the immediate neighbourhood of the respondents' house or closer for each relation category. Thus we discover, for instance, that seven per cent of single householders but 79 per cent of people who lived with others had children living at least in their immediate neighbourhood. There were clear and radical differences between the two groups in the distance which they lived from their kin. However, if we consider the bottom five rows of Table 9.5, we see that the differences between the two groups in the distance they lived from friends, workmates and so on were very small; indeed, there were *more* single-person householders who socialised in clubs in their immediate neighbourhood.

Columns 3 and 4 of Table 9.5 show the frequency with which the members of the sample had contact with these various types of kin and friends. In general, the differences between single householders and others were not as marked as the sheer distances might lead one to suppose; single householders travelled further than others to have contact with their kin. For example, only 16 per cent of single householders had parents in their neighbourhood, compared to 33 per cent of those living with others. However, 40 per cent of them managed to see these parents at least once during the week, whereas the contact frequency of the others was only 49 per cent. Moreover, the frequency with which single householders met with friends and other non-kin was generally the same as those who lived with others.

Thus, single-person householders had smaller networks than the whole population. They travelled further and had contact with family less often than people who lived with others. But most of the apparent

Table 9.5   Distances and contact frequencies between respondents and different relation categories by household type (cell percentages)

| | Distance: In the neighborhood or closer | | Contact frequency: Once a week or more often | | | |
	Single-person households %	People living with others %	Single-person households %	People living with others %	N1	N2
Partner or spouse	13.7	90.7	82.5	97.0	395	7584
Own child	7.0	79.3	24.1	84.9	199	5883
Partner's child	0.0	54.6	25.0	64.1	12	284
Parents	16.1	33.1	40.3	49.3	831	7151
Parents-in-law	6.7	17.1	13.4	29.2	299	5559
Siblings	9.1	24.1	21.6	33.9	485	3326
Siblings-in-law	5.3	10.6	31.6	20.1	19	735
Grandparents	13.2	32.8	21.7	43.4	106	756
Grandchildren	20.0	28.0	50.0	61.9	30	289
Other kin	5.5	15.5	17.7	25.9	164	1313
Friends	10.6	13.7	46.1	45.4	640	3163
Workmates	9.1	9.6	83.0	84.7	88	353
Club members	14.3	9.9	35.7	48.4	14	91
Neighbours	82.4	89.4	70.6	69.9	17	123
Other persons	9.3	23.8	31.5	43.4	54	265

Key   N1: single-person households
N2: people living with others

Source   DJI Survey 1988

singles were not really 'singles' as such, in the sense of being socially isolated. Rather, they had well-performing social networks that were not very different in terms of outcome from the average network.

Only if people had no kin, no people performing tasks for or with them, and no-one they considered as a member of their family, should one consider them as genuinely socially isolated. In the DJI sample, very few indeed fell into this category: 47 (0.5 per cent) people did not name anyone as kin, 46 (0.5 per cent) people did not name anyone performing tasks, 225 (2.3 per cent) people did not name anyone as a family member, and only 13 (0.1 per cent) people did not name anyone in all three cases. The conclusion is obvious: these individuals were not socially isolated and should not be treated as such.

Close Density Networks

To obtain a clear summary picture of the situation of single-person householders, we constructed a set diagram (a Venn diagram) as shown in Figure 9.4. It presents the average composition of the close relation, ego-centred network of a person living in a single-person household. It shows the overlap of kin, people performing shared tasks and members who were part of the respondent's defined family. The numbers inside the circles show the typical number of people who fell in various categories of respondents' networks. For example, the number of people named as kin are shown as:

0.8 persons Kin only
1.2 persons Kin ∩ Defined family
0.6 persons Kin ∩ Shared tasks
<u>1.3</u> persons Kin ∩ Shared tasks ∩ Defined family
3.9 total number of persons named as Kin.

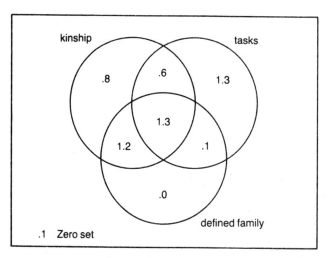

Source   DJI Survey 1988

Figure 9.4   Set diagram: average network composition of single-person households

We use these sets to build an ego-centred definition of the family, or 'dense family network'. We are defining here the members of the dense family network as those people with whom ego realises family life. In other words, this is our attempt to define the family from the point of view of ego: with whom does ego interact ('shared tasks')?, who does ego define as her family ('defined family')?, and who are ego's kin?

Our set definition of the dense family network is:

Kin ∩ Shared tasks (kin who share tasks)
Kin ∩ Defined family (kin who are defined as being part of the family)
Defined family ∩ Shared tasks (people defined as family members who share tasks)
Defined family ∩ Kin ∩ Shared tasks (people defined as family members who are kin and who share tasks).

Therefore, according to our definition above, there are on average 3.2 (= 0.6 + 1.2 + 0.1 + 1.3) persons in the dense family network of people living in a single-person household.

By contrast, Figure 9.5 presents a Venn diagram of the average ego-centred network of *all* people in our survey (N=9985), in the same terms of kinship, shared tasks and defined family. The dense family network of people in this group is 4.6 people, 1.4 more people than in the dense family networks of single persons. The largest difference between these two groups is found in the 'core' set: Defined family ∩ Kin ∩ Shared tasks, 1.3.

In comparing these groups more closely, we found three main differences. First, there was a difference in the total number of persons who were named in each set:

Kinship		Shared Tasks		Defined Family	
Single Person	Whole Sample	Single Person	Whole Sample	Single Person	Whole Sample
3.86	5.71	3.30	3.97	2.60	4.08

In general, single-person householders named smaller sets of people. The difference was smallest within tasks (0.67) and largest in terms of kinship sets (1.85).

Secondly, if we compare the percentages of people named that fell outside of any intersecting sets, then there were clear differences between single-person householders and the whole population with regard to people named for tasks: only 20 per cent named by the whole

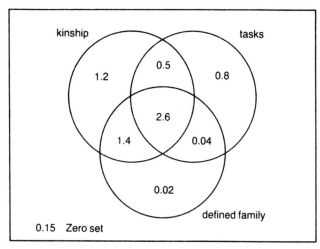

Source   DJI Survey 1988

Figure 9.5   Set diagram: average network composition of whole sample

population for tasks did not intersect at all, whereas for single-person householders, 39 per cent named for tasks did not intersect at all. Thus, single-person householders shared tasks with more people outside the dense family network.

Third, looking in the dense family networks for both single householders and the whole population, we found a higher percentage of named persons in the core, but a lower percentage of named persons in the two-fold intersections (Defined Family ∩ Shared Tasks, Kinship ∩ Defined Family) for the whole population. In general, the level of intersection was lower for the single-person householders than the whole population.

In sum, people living alone in households named fewer people as either kin or as belonging to their perceived family, but in terms of percentages, they integrated them to an equal extent as the whole population into their dense family network. On the other hand, they named nearly an equal number of people who shared tasks with them, but integrated them less in their dense family network. Although people living in single-person households had smaller dense family networks, their overall social networks did not suffer because they shared more tasks with people outside of the dense family network than the whole population.

DISCUSSION

People under 55 who live alone have social networks nearly similar in size, density and frequency of contact to their counterparts who live in multiple-person households. Why is this so? Unlike the older group, younger people have more opportunities to generate and maintain their social networks, even when they live alone. Living alone for older people may be the result of losing a lifelong companion. By contrast, younger people may live alone until they find someone to be their partner. Or they may have made a positive decision to leave a partnership to live alone. Hence, the enforced loneliness that the older group faces is something that the younger group does not have to deal with at such a frequency for many years.

Furthermore, the ease with which young people make friends or acquaintances make them unlikely to stay isolated. As Ziegler (1983) has demonstrated using representative survey data from the FRG, friendship choices are strongly influenced by age: people prefer their age peers and seek to reduce age distance. However, the preferences for age peers itself varies systematically across different age groups, with the youngest age group showing the strongest preference for its peers while at the same time also having greater chance of being chosen as friends by older people. In light of this sort of evidence, it is not surprising that younger people, even when they live alone, are not as isolated.

So living alone does not automatically denote that a person is isolated in a sociologically meaningful sense. It might express a transient status passage between leaving the parents' home and founding a new family. On the other hand, as McLanahan *et al.*, (1981) demonstrated for single parent families, living in a household alone after a divorce is often a means to replace a dissatisfying marital relationship with a broader network or alternative relations. This may be the family of origin or a circle of new friends and acquaintances or an alternative conjugal relationship. In any case, the status of living alone in a household does not indicate social isolation.

Examining only the simple demographic figures on household composition then fails to provide an exact picture of the situation of living alone. People who live alone between the ages of 18 and 55 are not as isolated as a common stereotype of single-person householders might suggest. Instead, the networks of this younger group in the Federal Republic of Germany have been shown to be similar to the rest of the population.

While similar research remains to be conducted in Britain, it seems possible that similar findings would emerge. It is important for future researchers to realise that examining household composition figures alone will not provide an exact picture of the situation which the official statistical category purports to represent. Behind such categories, a bundle of different configurations often lie hidden. In the future, family research should only use these official statistical categories as the starting point of a more sophisticated analysis. Such analysis should, wherever possible, involve investigation of the real social networks and social interactions of the people studied.

Note

1. The head of the project was Professor Dr. H. Bertram. The project involved a collaborative team of researchers: the person responsible for data storage – D. Bender; data preparation and methods – C. Alt; for social networks – Dr. W. Bien, J. Marbach and Dr. E. Schlemmer; for biographical data – Dr. A. Tölke and H. Löhr; for social inequality and attitudes – Professor Dr. H. Bertram and C. Dannenbeck; for the economic situation of families – A. Weidacher; for separation of gender roles – B. Keddi and G. Seidenspinner; for dwelling and infrastructure – H-U. Müller; for health and stress – K. Späth.

10 Upholding the Nuclear Family: A Study of Unmarried Parents and Domestic Courts

Rosemary Collins

The conventional nuclear family, consisting of a co-residing husband, wife and children, has been on the decline since the 1960s, as other chapters in this book have ably documented. Change in the 1980s has been particularly rapid. At the beginning of the decade, 12 per cent of births were outside marriage (OPCS 1986). By the end of the decade, the figure had risen to 27 per cent (OPCS 1990a). During the same period, families headed by a single person rose by about 20 per cent from 840,000 to well over a million (OPCS 1989c).

These trends pose a challenge to our systems of social insurance and welfare. The above changes in the 1980s were accompanied by a large increase in state expenditure on single parent families. By 1989, three-quarters of a million such families depended on state benefit, compared to only 318 000 families in 1979 (*ibid.*). Expenditure on unmarried parents accounted for about a third of all single-parent benefits and was the fastest-rising element of social security spending during the 1980s. Between 1979 and 1988 the number of divorced and separated women on benefit increased by 88 per cent while the number of unmarried mothers on benefit rose by 225 per cent (National Audit Office 1990).

During this period, the British government tried to find ways of reducing expenditure on unmarried mothers and, in line with an overall policy of reducing welfare provision, has increasingly put pressure on natural fathers to pay maintenance.

Using data from an E.S.R.C. funded research project,[1] this chapter examines the legal system in England and Wales as it applied in 1988 for making unmarried fathers pay maintenance. The research was carried out for two reasons. First, little, if anything, was known about the effectiveness of the legislation for providing financial support for children born outside marriage. Secondly, it was important to provide

174

a comparative base for monitoring impending new legislation brought in under the Family Law Reform Act 1987. As we shall see, the findings expose the inadequacies of maintenance payments for the support of children born outside marriage. They show that the legal system largely failed to improve the economic position of such children because most of the fathers concerned were poor. The legal process was underpinned by traditional notions of gender roles and neo-conservative values of increased parental responsibility which served to discourage the autonomous development of single parent households. The research also studied custody and access issues through focussing on the use made of the relevant legislation by unmarried fathers. The findings show that the conjugal family form and attendant division of labour was the dominant model used by the courts when decisions about custody and access were made and that due recognition was not given to the diversity of single parent households.

In an earlier chapter, Crow and Hardey drew attention to the stigma attached to the term 'unmarried mother', which conveys a sense of deviance from a two-parent norm, and noted that 'lone-parent household' was a more precise term. While concurring with Crow and Hardey on this point, the term 'unmarried mother' is retained here because, for the period during which the research was carried out, legislation dealt separately with separated or divorced parents and unmarried parents.

At the time of the research (1988), the Affiliation Proceedings Act 1957 covered all applications made by unmarried mothers to get support for their children. Under the terms of this act, mothers could apply to the courts to obtain financial support from the father of their children. If the father had never provided any such support, applications could only be made on behalf of children under the age of three. If fathers had made some payments, mothers could apply up to the time of the child's sixteenth birthday. Paternity had to be proved and the mother's evidence corroborated (Collins 1989). Proceedings took place in the magistrates' court – the lower tier of the English civil justice system. The Social Security Act of 1986 tightened up the state's powers to take proceedings against fathers whose former partners were living on state benefit, with the purpose of reclaiming some of the benefit paid from liable fathers.

Custody and access applications made by unmarried parents continued to be covered by the Guardianship of Minors Act 1971. Unlike the legislation on maintenance, this act could also be used by divorced or separated parents. The jurisdiction extended to the magistrates and county courts. When the research was undertaken, unmarried parents had greater legal equality with other categories of single parents for care of and contact with their children than for financial provision.

Before turning to the research findings, it is appropriate first to consider demographic trends in the formation of unmarried parent households. The aim is to demonstrate that one of the main structural characteristics of unmarried parents is poverty. We can then turn to discussing the implementation and outcome of the legal process, in light of this knowledge.

BIRTHS OUTSIDE MARRIAGE IN ENGLAND AND WALES

In the last quarter of the twentieth century, there has been a shift at the ideological level in the norms surrounding sexual behaviour and its relationship to marriage. The percentage of women marrying when pregnant dropped significantly from 25 per cent in 1977 to 12 per cent in 1987 (OPCS 1989d). Cohabitation became increasingly common – a change for all single women aged 18–49 from 11 per cent cohabiting in 1979 to 19 per cent cohabiting in 1987 (Haskey and Kiernan 1989). Cohabitation and births outside marriage were associated. In 1988, 70 per cent of births outside marriage were jointly registered by both parents (OPCS 1989a) and the conclusion drawn from the OPCS report was that at least half the children born outside marriage had parents living together at the time of the child's birth (*ibid.*). However, statistics on the duration of the unions have not been available to date.

The number of births outside marriage in England and Wales during the 1980s was one of the highest in Western industrial societies, second only to Denmark and Sweden (OPCS 1990b). High rates in the Scandinavian countries have been associated with low teenage fertility rates and long term cohabitation. The rate in the U.K. was the same as in the U.S.A. in the mid-1980s although the occurrence of births in the U.S.A. was different from the Scandinavian countries. Births outside marriage in the U.S.A. predominated among low income and ethnic minority groups (Garfinkel 1988). By 1989, 62 per cent of babies born to black mothers in the U.S.A. were extra-marital compared to 16 per cent of babies born to white mothers (U.S. Bureau of the Census 1989). Never-married black mothers were highly dependent on state support (*ibid.*), and constituted one of the poorest sectors of society (Garfinkel 1988).

While some parents in both countries may have actively chosen cohabitation and parenthood outside marriage, it seems likely that 'single parents by choice' applies to only a minority of such families (Crow and Hardey, this volume). Crow and Hardey argue that "the debate about choice . . . needs to be set in the broader context of the structures of opportunity and constraint within which choices take place, and the ways in which those structures shift over time" (p. 153).

Indeed, official statistics indicate that the relationship between extramarital births and indicators of the structure of economic disadvantage in England and Wales conforms to the American pattern. Figures on the rate of births outside marriage, unemployment and crime for thirty-three of the thirty-eight police force areas in England and Wales are presented in Table 10.1. There is a systematic and strong relationship between these variables (all significant at 1 per cent level): areas with high rates of birth outside marriage also had high levels of economic disadvantage and high crime rates.

If finer grain areas are inspected (data not shown here), extra-marital births can be seen to peak in certain major towns and cities. Outside London, the highest rates of such births were recorded in Nottingham at 44 per cent of all live births, Manchester – 43 per cent, Knowsley – 41 per cent Liverpool – 39 per cent, Middlesbrough – 39 per cent and Hull – 36 per cent. These births all took place in counties with extremely high crime and unemployment rates.

Others have shown that there is a link between high unemployment, crime and economic disadvantage (Winyard, 1987; Box, 1987). Winyard, for example, has shown that poverty is concentrated in decaying inner-city areas such as those found in Liverpool and in the council estates built to solve the inner-city problem. Box has shown that all research on crime and deviance has found a correlation between high crime rates and economic deprivation.

But this link with the birth rate is not so well appreciated. The data in Table 10.1 suggests an association between births outside marriage in urban industrial areas and a lack of economic resources among the parents concerned. These aggregate data hint that systems for making liable natural fathers pay maintenance may do little to improve the finances of families headed by unmarried parents if there is not enough money to redistribute from fathers to children. The research findings discussed below indeed confirm that it is unmarried parents with limited economic resources and opportunities whom the legal

Table 10.1   Extra-marital birth rates, unemployment rates and crime rates
for police force areas in England and Wales, 1987

Police force area	% births outside marriage	% unemployed	% found guilty or cautioned for indictable offences
Avon and Somerset	19	9	1.02
Bedfordshire	18	9	1.12
Cambridgeshire	17	8	1.08
Cheshire	22	12	1.16
Cleveland	32	20	1.81
Cumbria	20	10	1.31
Derbyshire	21	12	1.06
Devon and Cornwall	20	14	1.00
Dorset	18	9	0.84
Durham	25	16	1.24
Essex	18	10	0.87
Gloucestershire	19	8	1.00
Greater Manchester	31	14	1.71
Hampshire	19	9	1.10
Hertfordshire	16	6	0.92
Humberside	28	15	1.51
Kent	20	11	0.93
Lancashire	25	13	1.24
Leicestershire	21	9	1.12
Lincolnshire	20	12	1.24
Merseyside	34	20	1.32
Metropolitan Police District	–	–	1.36
Greater London	27	10	–
Norfolk	21	12	1.00
Northamptonshire	23	9	1.05
Northumbria	17	15	1.50
North Yorkshire	17	10	1.00
Nottinghamshire	29	12	1.65
South Yorkshire	26	17	1.51
Staffordshire	20	11	1.00
Suffolk	17	8	1.00
Sussex	16	8	0.85
Warwickshire	19	10	0.90
West Midlands	27	15	1.50
West Yorkshire	26	12	1.60
Wiltshire	16	8	1.06
WALES	23	15	1.30
ENGLAND	23	10	1.21

Rank order correlations   % births outside marriage with % unemployed: 0.82
                            % births outside marriage with % offenders: 0.72
Proportions of unemployment in Surrey were not available. Differences between police
force and county area boundaries meant that Thames Valley and West Mercia police
force areas had to be excluded from the calculations.

Sources   Key Population and Fertility Statistics 1987: Table 4.1; *Employment Gazette,
July 1987: Criminal Statistics in England and Wales, 1987*: Table 7.21, p. 162.

process channels into the responsibilities and roles associated with the conventional nuclear family and that many natural fathers are unable to meet the financial duties associated with the husband-provider role.

THE NOTTINGHAM AND BRISTOL STUDY OF UNMARRIED PARENTS AND DOMESTIC COURTS

Prior to this study, little, if anything, was known about how far the relevant legislation achieved its stated purpose of making provision for financial support, custody of and access to children born outside marriage. Similarly, little was known about how unmarried parents were dealt with by the courts (Collins 1989). The aims of the research were to provide quantitative information on maintenance orders and on the financial and domestic circumstances of the parents concerned, to examine the significance of maintenance orders for supporting children, to examine the use made of the relevant legislation by unmarried parents seeking custody of and access to their children and to examine how parents are dealt with by the court system.

The two sample cities, Nottingham and Bristol, were chosen because of the contrast in their rates of birth outside marriage and different use of the courts by unmarried parents. Nottingham had one of the highest rates of births outside marriage in England and Wales and the highest proportion of maintenance applications from unmarried mothers (information provided by the Home Office). Bristol had lower rates on both counts. Its lower use of the magistrates' court was similar to that of other towns and cities in southern England (Murch 1987).

The fieldwork fell into two parts: a court files study and court observation. It was conducted in the first six months of 1989 in the two magistrates and two county courts in Nottingham and Bristol. Research on unmarried parents and domestic courts was carried out by the author and Alison Macleod in Nottingham and Bristol in 1989.

All magistrates and county court files for 1988 (the last full calendar year before repeal of the Affiliation Proceedings Act 1957) relating to unmarried parents' custody, access and maintenance applications were studied. The findings are based on 384 relevant files from the magistrates' courts (257 Nottingham files and 127 Bristol files) and 74 files from the county courts (35 Nottingham files and 38 Bristol files) – a total of 458 cases. The magistrates' courts cases covered maintenance, custody and access. There were 295 maintenance applications and 192 applications for custody and access. All the county court cases were for custody and access. Forty-two per cent of these custody cases were accompanied by applications for domestic violence injunctions and 26 per cent were for the return of children who had been snatched by their fathers.

Maintenance, custody and access cases were observed by Collins and Macleod in the magistrates' courts to examine how the courts operated in practice and how unmarried parents were dealt with by the courts. Nearly a hundred cases were observed in the sample courts and systematic schedules were used to record the observations. The cases included some in which fathers applied for custody.

SOCIO-ECONOMIC CHARACTERISTICS OF THE MAGISTRATES' COURTS SAMPLE

Despite the high percentage of children born outside marriage, few unmarried parents use courts for financial relief. In 1988, for example, only 12 per cent of unmarried mothers who received state benefit had ex-partners who were officially recorded as paying maintenance (National Audit Office 1990). This figure confirms that few unmarried mothers take legal action against the father. As all maintenance is deducted from state benefit, there is no financial incentive for mothers on state benefit to go to court. Some mothers may not wish to name the father if the relationship has been coloured by conflict and violence and some may want to make a clean break, preferring not to have maintenance and access ties.

The research discovered that courts were most often used by previously cohabiting parents whose relationships had broken down. Nearly all the county court sample parents – 89 per cent – had lived together. Information on whether the magistrates' court sample parents had cohabited was recorded for only 60 per cent of the sample but 72 per cent of this sub-group had cohabited for an average time of one to three years. The pattern of cohabitation was identical in Nottingham and Bristol.

Former cohabitees may have been using the court because the applicants modelled themselves on the traditional conjugal family in which the father takes the main responsibility for financial support and the mother takes the main responsibility for the children. When the family unit breaks up, the mother's responsibility for children and housework remain while the financial support from the father alters. Mothers may then take legal action to try to continue the father's financial involvement. The situation is analogous to maintenance for divorcing and separating couples. Delphy (1976: 83) has argued that in divorce, as in marriage, child-care is carried out by women gratuitously and the husband is exempted from this charge. On divorce, the financial support of the children which had been previously shared by the couple or assumed by the husband alone is 'assumed predominantly or exclusively by the woman':

> All the situations in which children exist and are cared for, have similar characteristics and are different forms of one and the same institution, which could be called X. The situation of the unmarried mother can be taken to be its extreme form and at the same time its most typical form, since the basic dyad is the mother and child. Marriage could be seen as one of the possible forms of X in which the basic couple is joined by a man who temporarily participates in the financial upkeep of the child and in return appropriates the woman's labour power (Delphy 1976: 85).

Delphy's view is that women's responsibility for child-care, which exists in and outside of marriage, can be defined as 'the collective exploitation of women by men and . . . the collective exemption of men from the cost of reproduction' (*ibid.*: 86). Following Delphy, previously cohabiting women may go to court for maintenance because their relationship with the father has been characterised by economic dependency.

Furthermore, when cohabitation breaks down, an unemployed or low paid woman has to claim state benefit for herself and her child. The policy of the Department of Social Security is to contact the father with a view to obtaining maintenance, although at the time of this study they would not press a mother to name him (DSS, SB20, April 1988). However, the 1986 Efficiency Scrutiny carried out by the Department estimated that not requiring unmarried mothers to name the fathers resulted in an inability to recover up to £16 million a year (National Audit Office 1990: 22). Consequently, the Department subsequently revised the forms given to unmarried mothers to emphasise more the importance of arranging maintenance rather than the mother's right not to name the father (*ibid.*). Previously cohabiting women may be under more pressure to name the father than never-cohabiting women because they have shared a home openly. Action taken by the Department of Social Security is an indicator of state imposition of the conjugal family form, with its unequal division of domestic responsibilities, on unmarried parents.

Although the financial position of previously cohabiting women may
have worsened after the relationship had broken down, the court files
data reveal that most of the fathers were low paid or unemployed.
Table 10.2 shows that proportionately three times as many men appearing at maintenance hearings were unemployed in the sample cities than
in England. Men's average earnings were more than £4500 lower than
the national average.

Table 10.2   Employment status of fathers in the Magistrates' Court sample

	Sample fathers	Average for whole of England
Unemployed men	27%	10%
Average earnings of employed men	£7629	£12 220
N of sample fathers	(384)	

Sources   *Employment Gazette*, July 1987; *Regional Trends*, vol. 23, (1988)

A similar picture of economic disadvantage emerged for the mothers.
Three quarters were on state benefit, typically living on £64 a week
or less. Earnings of the employed minority were very low, averaging
£4800 per annum. The pattern of disadvantage for both mothers and
fathers was reflected in their living arrangements. Although few in
the sample were younger than twenty, more lived with their own parents
than in any other type of accommodation – 32 per cent of the mothers
and 37 per cent of the fathers. Townsend has argued (1979: 180) that
shared housing between families is regarded as a sign of poverty and
housing stress.

Lone parents live in a diversity of family situations, which change
over the life course (Crow and Hardey, this volume). Our research
showed that many sample parents had children by other partners –
42 per cent of the fathers for whom the information was recorded
(N = 65) and 36 per cent of the mothers (N = 64). These parents were
involved in more complex and wide ranging family patterns. The
research findings highlight the issue raised by Crow and Hardey that
lone parent households are not a homogeneous or unified group. The
legal process treats all families headed by an unmarried parent as a
variant of the conjugal family: this approach obscures the range of
family situations that exist.

MAINTENANCE ORDERS AND DECISION MAKING IN THE MAGISTRATES' COURT

The research aimed to show the range in the amounts ordered for maintenance, correlate the order with fathers' incomes, investigate how decisions about the amount were made in the absence of a national formula and to examine whether and how an order improved the financial position of the child.

Table 10.3 shows that the majority of the orders made in the sample courts in 1988 were for amounts of between £10 and £15 per week. The mean order in Nottingham was £11 per week and in Bristol, £14 per week. A fifth of the Nottingham orders were for nominal amounts only (that is, 5p per annum). The amount of the order is decided by a panel of three magistrates on the basis of oral evidence presented to the court about the fathers' and mothers' domestic circumstances. A number of factors came into play in the magistrates' decision, including the father's income and expenditure, debts, the amount agreed by the parties before going to court and the magistrates' own views about the amount of money needed to support a child. As Smart (1984) has shown, typical moral dilemmas facing magistrates include deciding whether economic hardship should be evenly spread among all households affected by the order and whether mothers should go out to work. In cases where fathers have two families to support, a decision has to be made about whether the principle of a man's primary duty to his first family should be upheld to the detriment of his second family. The maintenance award must also not be so high that it creates a disincentive to work.

In practice, the courts either reached their decision by listening to

Table 10.3   Amount of maintenance order in Nottingham and Bristol in 1988 (column percentages)

Amount per week	Nottingham men	Bristol men
Nominal	22	7
£1–5	9	10
£6–9	5	13
£10–15	50	44
£16–19	1	3
£20–25	8	8
Over £25	5	15
N of fathers	(222)	(82)

the evidence and then announcing a figure that the father should pay or by agreeing to a consent order. A consent order is one in which the parents have made an agreement about the amount prior to the hearing which is then ratified by the magistrates at court. Consent orders save time and appear to award the child an amount that the mother agrees is realistic, yet they can be made on the basis of ignorance of the relevant facts and ignorance of whether consent was arrived at by 'undue influence' (Ingleby 1984).

The picture is complicated further by the intervention of the Department of Social Security in the pre-court decision on a consent order. Maintenance cases can be heard at court as a result of the Department of Social Security discussing possible action with the parents. At least four of the fifteen consent orders observed in court were made on the basis of DSS advice to fathers that they should increase the amount of the payments that they were already paying to the mother.

The orders, whether made on the basis of magistrates deciding the amount or ratifying consent orders, were in the range of 7 per cent to 19 per cent of the fathers' weekly income. The percentage would be expected to vary in line with outgoings (housing, heating, other dependants, debts and so on) but the amount was not systematically related.

This can be illustrated by three cases observed in Nottingham. In Case A the father earned £180 net per week. He did not appear in court and an order for £20 per week was made on the basis of a letter he sent stating his willingness to pay this amount. In Case B, the father earned £130 net. The bench made no enquiries about his weekly expenditure and he was ordered to pay £25. In Case C the father, also earning £130, was ordered to pay £22 following advice from the Department of Social Security. The fact that orders were in a relatively tight percentage range suggests that magistrates were influenced more by the father's ability to pay than by the income needs of the mother and child. In Case A for example, the mother was supporting three children (two by a former partner), while in cases B and C the mothers had one child to support.

The consent orders based on advice from the Department of Social Security ranged from £15 to £25 a week. These figures suggest that parents were being advised to consent to amounts which maximised the private contribution to public provision, whatever the cost to the father, as the high amounts ordered were above the state allowance for a dependent child in 1988.

Commenting on government policy, Novak (1988: 200) points out that the social security system has been used by the government to 'play a major part in the creation of a more coercive social policy and a more authoritarian state'. In support of this line of argument, Smart (1984: 199) has noted that 'the nature of the work of the domestic courts and the courts' structural location between the individual and the DHSS inevitably means that the courts are operating more or less as collection agencies for the state'.

EFFECTIVENESS OF MAINTENANCE ORDERS FOR SUPPORTING CHILDREN

A maintenance order only benefits a child if it is paid. When the mother is supported by the state, a maintenance order has no advantages at all for the child because it is deducted directly from benefit. The research examined the frequency of payments made to the children of the employed mothers in the sample because they were the only group who were in a position to gain. The maintenance files of the employed mothers in the Nottingham sample (N = 43) were re-examined towards the end of 1989 to discover how many orders were still being paid. Ten of the employed mothers had unemployed former partners who had made no contribution since the order was granted. Only thirteen of the thirty-three remaining mothers had orders which had not fallen into arrears when the records were rechecked. In other words, only 6 per cent of 222 Nottingham mothers who applied for maintenance in 1988 appeared to be in receipt of orders a year later which had contributed towards the economic resources available to their children.

The onus for paying maintenance rests on the father, unless courts order that payments are deducted directly from wages by employers. When the research was carried out, a significant proportion of maintenance orders for all single parents in England and Wales fell into arrears.

In Nottingham Magistrates' Court, for example, there were four times as many proceedings for enforcement of maintenance in 1988 than for original orders[2]. This extremely high ratio calls into question the effectiveness of the entire maintenance order system. It is doubtful whether the court costs in establishing and attempting to enforce the system are balanced either by the benefits which actually reach the mother or even by the amounts repaid to the Department of Social Security. Only about a third of the men whose payments fell into arrears, for instance, paid off the amount owed to the mothers and children. The court remitted arrears in 20 per cent of the cases and reduced or suspended the order in the remaining cases. The figures from Nottingham indicate that as many as two-thirds of men in arrears were unable to pay when enforcement proceedings were taken out. This suggests that the earlier court decision on the amount of the order did not take into consideration the long term effects of surviving on a low income.

In short, the financial gain for unmarried mothers going to court is minimal and the system is largely ineffective. The irregularity of payments from fathers means that the recovery of maintenance by social security is very small. In 1988, for instance, £1.85 billion was paid to lone parents in state benefits but only £155 million was recovered from liable relatives (National Audit Office 1990). The court process itself is expensive and the Legal Aid fund bears the legal costs for most parents.

Increasingly, the legal process has taken on a symbolic function with regard to unmarried families. It serves to reproduce the gender inequalities present within the conjugal family by drawing unmarried parents into marriage-like relationships in which fathers take financial responsibility and mothers take responsibility for caring. The low awards confirm women's economic dependence on men and the state. As Delphy notes:

> the courts ratify the exclusive responsibility of women for child-care both by positive actions . . . assigning a low allowance for the children; and by negative action, failing to ensure the payment of the allowance (1976, p. 83).

Effective systems for making fathers pay, such as the Australian Child Support scheme, which claimed a success rate of over 60 per cent in payment received by the end of 1989 (Wicks, 1990), are based on a more equal division of financial responsibility for children between parents than the system operating in England and Wales in the 1980s. Such systems can offer positive gains to custodial parents whose partners earn average or above average wages, but do little to help poorer parents (Collins, 1992). As births outside marriage peak in economically disadvantaged areas of England and Wales, the deprivation experienced by the sample families is likely to be replicated among many other families headed by unmarried parents. As Crow and Hardey argued in chapter 8, poverty is the central question to be addressed in social policy relating to lone-parent households. The government plans for introducing a Child Support Agency in the U.K. have not been matched by comprehensive policies aimed at lifting single parents out of the poverty trap. Until such policies are introduced, unmarried parent families will continue to reap few rewards from maintenance orders.

CUSTODY AND ACCESS ORDERS IN THE MAGISTRATES' AND COUNTY COURTS

The lack of information on the legal arrangements made for children when cohabitation ends is a blind spot in sociological studies on the effects of family breakdown on children. It is not clear, for instance, whether the legal outcome of cohabitation ending places children in a similar situation to the children of divorced parents. Little is known about the circumstances in which growing numbers of unmarried fathers apply for custody and access, especially in cases where children have not lived with their fathers.

Our research focused on court practice in custody and access cases, noting in particular the use made of the different courts and the processes by which agreements were reached and orders made. Accordingly, we examined the data to uncover the background circumstances behind the applications. Magistrates' court and county court applications were distinct in character, it transpired, in that more complex cases were heard in the county court. In all, 104 applications were made for fathers to have access to their children. Most were made by the fathers themselves, but fourteen mothers in Nottingham also applied on behalf of the father. An interesting difference arose between magistrates[1] practice in the two courts, however. In Nottingham, the magistrates clearly viewed access as the norm, and were inclined to offer it verbally even when it had not been formally requested. Nineteen orders were for defined access only and nine applications were refused. But in Bristol, one third of access applications were turned down and a half (8) of the orders granted were for defined access.

The court files show that applications in Nottingham were generally made to confirm the status quo (two-thirds of the fathers who applied already had contact with their children). Conversely, in Bristol applications were generally made when the parents were in dispute about access taking place. Table 10.4 shows that the majority of the fathers who applied for custody were granted custody orders. Twenty of the applicants had the children living with them at the time of the application and all the orders made were with the mothers' pre-trial consent. Half of the fathers awarded custody were recorded on the files as sharing their homes with other women (wives, mothers, new partners or relatives), suggesting that custody by the father might really mean another women taking responsibility for housework and childcare.

Table 10.4   Applications for access and custody and orders granted in the Magistrates' Courts

	Formal applications	Orders eventually granted
Applications for access:		
Nottingham	78	121
Bristol	26	16
Total	104	137
Applications for custody:		
Nottingham	18	14
Bristol	11	11
Total	29	25

The smaller number of more complex cases taken to county court, however, were markedly different from the magistrates' court cases. Characteristically, the children in county court cases were living disrupted lives overshadowed by parental conflict and fear. In two-thirds of the county court cases, there was a history of molestation or child snatching. Thirty-five per cent of the fathers had criminal records, more than half involving crimes of violence. One in ten of the mothers were also allegedly involved in crime. Although a few families in the magistrates courts had similar problems, the county court pattern was more consistent and more extreme.

The outcomes of applications for access and custody at county courts (shown in Table 10.5) differed from the magistrates' courts (as in Table 10.4), but, interestingly, the judges seemed readier to offer and grant access, despite the difficult family circumstances, than were the magistrates, in both cities. In Bristol, all the fathers who applied for access in the county court were granted it and in Nottingham 83 per cent of the fathers were granted access. Furthermore, five reasonable access orders were made in Nottingham at the same time as orders excluding the father from the home because of domestic violence.

The greater readiness of judges to award access and custody, even to difficult fathers, when compared to magistrates, may stem from their

Table 10.5 Applications for access and custody and orders granted in the county courts

	Formal applications	Orders eventually granted
Fathers applying for access:		
Nottingham	2	29
Bristol	9	9
Total	11	38
Fathers applying for custody:		
Nottingham	10	3
Bristol	7	5
Total	17	8

experience with divorce cases (all of which have to go to county court). These data suggest that judges in the courts studied appear to believe that access by the father is nearly always in the child's best interest, even when the father has a history of violent or irrational behaviour.

The evidence suggests that some mothers may not share this belief. The court files indicate that some of the mothers were fearful of the fathers' continuing involvement. The following quotations from the written evidence of two of the mothers illustrates typical behaviour of violent men in the sample:

Jack is terrified of his father but Jason is still a bit young. He never hits Jason too hard. He threatened to knife me if I did not hand the baby back. He said it would be worth doing four years.

His visits occur either in the early morning or late at night. Generally, he either stands looking through the letter box or at the back window looking in. I have become afraid to go out of the house.

However, it is important to set the number of fathers' applications for access or custody in the context of the overall number of applications either unmarried parent made with respect to a child in magistrates and county courts.

The findings show that although cohabitation had taken place in most cases that came to court, the fathers of the children involved were less likely than the divorced fathers to have an access order. When parents divorce, 'access to the child is the norm; refusal will not be lightly undertaken' and 'the welfare of the child imparts a *prima facie* presumption that access is in the child's interests' (Maidment 1984). However, only a third of all applications in the four sample courts were from fathers seeking custody and access and less than half were granted orders. More often than not, then, fathers do not get access. Whether the child is disadvantaged by being denied access to a father, or potentially threatened by access to a violent father is the key issue that both magistrates and county courts are trying to grapple with, yet the policy debates surrounding unmarried parenthood remain focused on the financial aspect.

DISCUSSION

The legal response to unmarried parents is to treat them as a variant of the dominant conjugal family form. Yet children experience scant economic gain from litigation, few attempts are made to establish their wishes and feelings about continuing contact with the absent parent and access orders may be awarded inappropriately in some cases.

The law remains focussed on two issues – the legal obligation of the biological father to maintain and the resolution of custody and access disputes. As long as this bifurcated approach continues, courts will remain dominated by the idea that the only successful type of family is the one which conforms to, or attempts to match, the nuclear family stereotype.

Since the research was conducted, the government has taken steps to increase the determination with which natural fathers should be pursued to assist with maintenance payments. The Affiliation Proceedings Act 1957 was repealed in 1989 and replaced with the Family Law Reform Act 1987. This Act made it easier for mothers to apply for maintenance by abolishing the three year old age bar and by extending hearings to the county court level. It also enabled custodial fathers to apply for maintenance from mothers. In 1990, social policy changes were instigated to make all liable fathers pay and measures were introduced to strengthen the system for tracing an absent father. Legislation was passed allowing the Inland Revenue to reveal employment details and addresses of liable fathers to social security offices. Courts were subsequently empowered to make orders deducting maintenance directly from wages when appropriate. In July 1990, the government announced plans for a new system of enforcing maintenance. Payments would be set by a national formula and collected by a Child Support

Agency. The Child Support Act received the Royal Assent in 1991, with the intention that the system would come into operation after the next general election in the U.K.

The research reported in this chapter would suggest that such initiatives, while possibly increasing the pressure on an already hard-pressed sector of the community, are most unlikely to produce any substantial benefits either for the single parent with custody or for the public purse.

Notes

1. The research was funded by the ESRC, Grant No 000231347. I am grateful to them for their support. The research was co-directed by Rosemary Collins and Alison Macleod. I am grateful to Alison for all her work on the project and for her invaluable contribution to joint articles currently in preparation. The statistical analysis was ably conducted by Michael Little of the Dartington Social Research Unit, University of Bristol.
2. These figures include orders for previously married partners as well as never married partners and also include county court orders enforced in the magistrates' court.

Bibliography

ABRAMS, M. (1978) *Beyond Three Score Years and Ten. A first report on a survey of the elderly* (London: Age Concern).

ACKER, J. (1989) 'The problem with patriarchy', *Sociology*, vol. 23, no. 2, pp. 235–40.

ALCOCK, P. (1987) *Poverty and State Support* (London: Longman).

ALLATT, P. and YEANDLE, S. (1986) 'It's not fair, is it? Youth unemployment, family relations and the social contract', in (eds.) S. Allen, et al. *The Experience of Unemployment* (London: Macmillan).

AMBROSE, P., HARPER, J. and PEMBERTON, R. (1983) *Surviving Divorce* (Brighton: Wheatsheaf).

ANDERSON, M. (1971) *Family Structure in Nineteenth-Century Lancashire* (Cambridge: Cambridge University Press).

ANDERSON, M. (1977) 'The impact on the family relationships of the elderly of changes since Victorian times in government income-maintenance provisions', in E. Shanas and M. B. Sussman (eds.), *Family Bureaucracy and the Elderly* (Durham, N. C.: Duke University Press).

ANDERSON, M. (1988) 'Households, families and individuals: some preliminary results from the national sample of the 1851 census of Great Britain', *Continuity and Change*, vol. 3, pp. 421–38.

ANDERSON, M., COLLINS, B. and STOTT, C. (1977) 'The national sample from the 1851 census of Great Britain', *Urban History Yearbook*, pp. 55-9.

ARBER, S. (1990) 'Opening the 'black box': inequalities in women's health', in P. Abbott and G. Payne (eds.) *New Directions in the Sociology of Health* (Brighton: Falmer Press), pp. 37–56.

ARBER, S. (1991) 'Class, paid employment and family roles: making sense of structural disadvantage, gender and health status', *Social Science and Medicine*, vol. 32, no. 4, pp. 425–36.

ARBER, S., GILBERT, G. N. and EVANDROU, M. (1988) 'Gender, household composition and receipt of domiciliary services by the elderly disabled', *Journal of Social Policy*, vol. 17, no. 2, pp. 153–175.

ARBER, S. and GILBERT, G. N. (1989a) 'Transitions in caring: gender, life course and care of the elderly' in B. Bytheway, T. Keil, P. Allatt, A. Bryman (eds.), *Becoming and Being Old: Sociological Approaches to Later Life* (London: Sage) pp. 72–92.

ARBER, S. and GILBERT, G. N. (1989b) 'Men: the forgotten carers' *Sociology*, vol. 23, no. 1, pp. 111–118.

ARBER, S. and GILBERT, G. N. (eds.) (1991) *Women and Working Lives: Divisions and Change* (London: Macmillan).

ARBER, S. and GINN, J. (1991) 'The invisibility of age: gender and class in later life', *Sociological Review*, vol. 39, no. 2, pp. 260–91.

ASTON, T. H. and PHILPIN, C. E. (eds.) (1985) *The Brenner Debate* (Cambridge: Cambridge University Press).

ATKINSON, J. (1971) *A Handbook for Interviewers*, Social Survey Division, OPCS (London: HMSO).

BANTON, M. (1983) *Racial and Ethnic Competition* (Cambridge: Cambridge University Press).
BECK, U. (1986) *Risikogesellschaft* (Frankfurt: Suhrkamp).
BECK-GERNSHEIM, E. (1986) 'Von der Liebe zur Beziehung?', in J. Berger (ed.), *Die Moderne: Kontinuitäten und Zäsuren* (Göttingen: Schwartz) pp. 209–233.
BECKER, G. S. (1981) *A Treatise on the Family* (Cambridge, Mass.: Harvard University Press).
BEECHEY, V. (1987) *Unequal Work* (London: Verso).
BEECHEY, V. and PERKINS, T. (1987) *A Matter of Hours* (Cambridge: Polity).
BERGER, P. A. (1986) *Entstrukturierte Klassengesellschaft* (Opladen: Westdeutscher Verlag).
BERGER, P. L., BERGER, S. and KELLNER, H. (1973) *The Homeless Mind* (New York: Random House).
BERGER, U., SCHMIDT, V. H. and WIESENTHAL, H. (1991) *Neue Technologien – verschenkte Gelegenheiten?* (Opladen: Westdeutscher Verlag).
BERK, S. F. (1985) *The Gender Factory* (New York: Plenum Press).
BERK, R. A. and BERK, S. F. (1983) 'Supply-side sociology of the family: the challenge of the New Home Economics', *Annual Review of Sociology*, 9, pp. 375–95.
BERTRAM, H., BARTHELMES, J., BAYER, H., BURGER, D., BURGER, A., GILLE, M., KEDDI, B.,MARBACH, J., MÜLLER H. U., SANDER, E., SEIDENSPINNER,, G., WEIDACHER, A. (1986) 'Entwicklung und Erprobung eines Forschungskonzepts zur kontinuierlichen Beobachtung von Familien', Zwischenbericht 1985—1986 (Munich: German Youth Institute (DJI)) working paper 0-001.
BERTRAM, H. and BORMANN-MÜELLER, R. (1988) 'Individualisierung und Pluralisierung familialer Lebensformen', *Aus Politik und Zeitgeschichte* B13/88, pp. 14–22.
BIEGEL, D. E. and BLUM. A. eds. (1990) *Aging and Caregiving. Theory Research and Policy* (Beverly Hills: Sage).
BLAU, Z. S. (1973) *Old Age in a Changing Society* (New York: Franklin Watts).
BLAXTER, M. (1990) *Health and Lifestyles* (London: Routledge).
BOOTH, C. (1894, 1980) *The Aged Poor in England and Wales* (London; New York: Garland Publishing).
BOSCH, G., ENGELHARDT, N., HERMANN, K., KURZ-SCHERF, I. and SEIFERT, H. (1988) *Arbeitszeitverkürzung im Betrieb* (Köln: Bund).
BOX, S. (1987) *Recession, Crime and Punishment* (London: Macmillan).
BOYD, M. and PRYOR, E. T. (1988) 'The cluttered nest: the living arrangements of young Canadian adults', paper presented as a joint session of the annual meetings of the Canadian Population Society and the Canadian Sociological and Anthropological Associations, Windsor, Ontario.
BRAILEY, M. (1985) 'Making the break' in N. Johnson (ed.) *Marital Violence* (London: Routledge and Kegan Paul), pp. 26–39.
BRAITHWAITE, V. A. (1990) *Bound to Care* (Sydney: Allen and Unwin).
BRANNEN, J. and WILSON, G. (1987) *Give and Take In Families* (London: Allen & Unwin).

BROSE, H.-G., SCHULZE-BÖING, M. and WOLRAB-SAHR, M. (1987) 'Wie normal ist Prekarität, wie normal ist die Normalität', in J. Friedrichs (ed.), *Technik und Sozialer Wandel* (Opladen: Westdeutscher Verlag) pp. 111–114.

BROWN, G. W. (1973) 'The mental hospital as an institution', *Social Science and Medicine*, vol 7, pp. 407–424.

BÜCHTEMANN, F. and SCHUPP, J. (1986) 'Zur Sozio-Ökonomie der Teilzeitbeschäftigung in der Bundesrepublik Deutschland', Discussion paper IIM/LMP 86–15, Wissenschaftszentrum Berlin.

BURGOYNE, J. (1984) *Breaking Even* (Harmondsworth: Penguin).

BURGOYNE, J. and CLARK, D. (1984) *Making a Go of It* (London: Routledge and Kegan Paul).

BURROWS, R. and MARSH, C. (eds.) (1991) *Consumption and Class: Divisions and Change* (London: Macmillan).

BURT, R. S. (1984) 'Network items and the General Social Survey', *Social Networks*, vol. 6, pp. 293–339.

CARLEN, P. (1988) *Women, Crime and Poverty* (Milton Keynes: Open University Press).

CARLING, A. (1986) 'Rational choice Marxism', *New Left Review*, no. 160, pp. 24–62.

CARLIN, G. A. (1987) 'Exploitation, extortion and oppression', *Political Studies*, vol. XXXV, no. 2, pp. 173–88.

CARLING, A. (1991) *Social Division* (London: Verso).

CASHMORE, E. E. (1985) *Having To* (London: Unwin).

CENTRAL STATISTICAL OFFICE (1979) *Social Trends*, 9 (London: HMSO).

CENTRAL STATISTICAL OFFICE (1983) *Social Trends*, 13 (London: HMSO).

CHERLIN, A. and FURSTENBERG, F. F. Jr (1988) 'The changing European family: lessons for the American reader', *Journal of Family Issues*, vol. 9, no. 3, pp. 291–7.

CHESTER, R. (1977) 'The one-parent family' in R. Chester and J. Peel (eds.) *Equalities and Inequalities in Family Life* (London: Academic Press) pp. 149–61.

CLARK, E. (1989) *Young Single Mothers Today* (London: National Council For One Parent Families).

CLOSE, P. (1985) 'Family form and economic production', in P. Close and R. COLLINS (eds.) *Family and Economy in Modern Society* (Basingstoke: Macmillan) pp. 9–48.

COLLINS, R. (1989) 'Illegitimacy, inequality and the law in England and Wales' in P. Close (ed.) *Family Divisions and Inequalities in Modern Society* (London: Macmillan).

COLLINS, R. (1992) 'Pursuing errant fathers: A comparative study of maintenance systems in England, Australia and the U.S.A.' in P. Close (ed.) *The State and Caring* (London: Macmillan).

CONNIDIS, I. A. (1989) *Family Ties and Aging* (Toronto: Butterworths).

CONNOLLY, W. E. (1988) *Political Theory and Modernity* (Oxford: Basil Blackwell).

CORR, H. and JAMIESON, L. (1989) 'Earning your keep: the politics of independence', mimeo, Department of Sociology, University of Edinburgh.

CORRIGAN, P. (1989) 'Gender and the gift: the case of the family clothing economy', *Sociology*, vol. 23, no. 4, pp. 513–34.

COURTNEY, G. (1989) *Youth Cohort Study: Report on cohort 1, sweep 1* (Sheffield: Manpower Services Commission), Publication No 41.

CRIMINAL STATISTICS IN ENGLAND AND WALES 1987 (1988) (London: HMSO).

CRYSTAL, S. (1982) *America's Old Age Crisis: Public Policy and the Two Worlds of Aging* (New York: Basic Books).

DALLEY, G. (1988) *Ideologies of Caring: Rethinking Community and Collectivism* (Basingstoke: Macmillan Education).

DANT, T. (1990) 'Agency and ageing: the resources and powers of persons', paper presented to the British Sociological Association Annual Conference, University of Surrey, April.

DEACON, A. and BRADSHAW, J. (1983) *Reserved for the Poor* (Oxford: Martin Robertson).

DELPHY, C. (1976) 'Continuities and discontinuities in marriage and divorce', in D. Leonard Barker and S. Allen (eds.), *Sexual Divisions and Society: Process and Change*, (London: Tavistock).

DELPHY, C. (1977) *The Main Enemy: A Materalist Analysis of Women's Oppression* (London: WRCC Publications).

DEMOS, J.A. (1970) *A Little Commonwealth: Family Life in Plymouth Colony* (New York: Oxford University Press).

DEPARTMENT OF HEALTH (1989) *Caring for People. Community Care in the Next Decade and Beyond*, Cmnd 849 (London: HMSO).

DEPARTMENT OF HEALTH AND SOCIAL SECURITY (1974) Report of the Committee on One-Parent Families (London: HMSO).

DEPARTMENT OF HEALTH AND SOCIAL SECURITY (1981) *Growing Older*, Cmnd. 8173 (London: HMSO).

DEPARTMENT OF HEALTH AND SOCIAL SECURITY (1988) *Guide to Income Support*, Leaflet SB20, April (London: HMSO).

DOBASH, R. E. and DOBASH, R. (1980) *Violence against Wives: A Case against Patriarchy* (London: Open Books).

DONNISON, D. (1982) *The Politics of Poverty* (Oxford: Martin Robertson).

DOVRING, F. and DOVRING, K. (1971) *The Optional Society* (The Hague: Nijhoff).

EASTERLIN, R. (1987) *Birth and Fortune: The Impact of Numbers on Personal Welfare* (London and Chicago: University of Chicago Press).

EBAUGH, H. (1988) *Becoming an Ex.* (Chicago: University of Chicago Press).

EHRENREICH, B. and EHRENREICH, J. (1979) 'The professional-managerial class', in Pat Walker (ed.), *Between Labour and Capital* (Hassocks Sussex: Harvester) pp. 5–48.

ELLIOT, F. R. (1986) *The Family* (Basingstoke: Macmillan).

ELSTER, J. (1982) 'Marxism, functionalism and game theory: the case for methodological individualism', *Theory and Society*, vol. 11, no. 4, pp. 453–81.

ELSTER, J. (1983a) *Sour Grapes* (Cambridge: Cambridge University Press).

196   *Bibliography*

ELSTER, J. (1983b) *Explaining Technical Change* (Cambridge: Cambridge University Press).
ELSTER, J. (1985) *Making Sense of Marx* (Cambridge: Cambridge University Press).
ELSTER, J. (1989) *The Cement of Society* (Cambridge: Cambridge University Press).
ENGFER, U., HINRICHS, K., OFFE, C. and WIESENTHAL, H. (1984) 'Arbeitszeitsituation und Arbeitszeitverkürzung in der Sicht der Beschäftigten', in C. Offe (ed.), *Arbeitsgesellschaft* (Frankfurt: Campus) pp. 167–204.
EQUAL OPPORTUNITIES COMMISSION (1980) *The Experience of Caring for Elderly and Handicapped Dependants* (Manchester: Equal Opportunities Commission).
EQUAL OPPORTUNITIES COMMISSION (1982) *Caring for the Elderly and Handicapped: Community Care Policies and Women's Lives* (Manchester: Equal Opportunities Commission).
ERICKSON, R. (1984) 'Social class of men, women and families', *Sociology*, vol. 18, no. 4, pp. 500–14.
ERMISCH, J. (1990) *Fewer Babies, Longer Lives* (York: Joseph Rowntree Memorial Trust).
EWEN, S. (1976) *Captains of Consciousness* (New York: McGraw Hill).
FIELD, F. (1989) *Losing Out* (Oxford: Basil Blackwell).
FINCH, J. (1987) 'Family obligations and the life course', in A. Bryman, W. R. Bytheway, P. Allatt and T. Keil (eds.), *Rethinking the Life Cycle* (London: Macmillan).
FINCH, J. (1989) *Family Obligations and Social Change* (Cambridge: Polity Press).
FINCH, J. and MASON J. (1990a) 'Filial obligations and kin support for elderly people', *Ageing and Society*, vol. 10, no. 2, pp. 151–75.
FINCH, J. and MASON, J. (1990b), 'Divorce, remarriage and family obligations', *Sociological Review*, vol. 38, no. 2, pp. 219–46.
FINKELHOR, D. *et al.* (eds.) (1983) *The Dark Side of Families: Current Family Violence Research* (Beverly Hills: Sage).
FISCHER, C. S., (1982) *To Dwell Among Friends. Personal Networks in Town and City* (Chicago and London: University of Chicago Press).
FOSTER, P. (1990) 'Community care and the frail elderly', paper presented to the Social Policy Association Annual Conference, July, University of Bath, mimeo.
FRIES, J. (1980) 'Aging, natural death and the compression of morbidity', *New England J. Medicine*, vol. 303, no. 3, pp. 130–5.
FRIES, J. (1989) 'Reduction of the national morbidity', in S. Lewis (ed.), *Aging and Health* (Michigan: Lewis Publishers) pp. 3–22.
FURLONG, A. and COONEY, G. H. (1990) 'Getting on their bikes: teenagers leaving home in Scotland', *Journal of Social Policy*, vol. 19, no. 4, pp. 535–51.
FYFE, A. (1989) *Child Labour* (Cambridge: Cambridge Polity Press).
GAMBETTA, D. (1987) *Were They Pushed or Did They Jump?: Individual Decision Mechanisms in Education* (Cambridge University Press).
GARDINER, J. (1976) 'Women's domestic labour', *New Left Review*, vol. 99, pp. 47–58.

GARFINKEL, I. (1988) 'The evolution of child support policy', *Focus*, p. 11.

GEORGE, V. and WILDING, P. (1972) *Motherless Families* (London: Routledge & Kegan Paul).

GERSHUNY, J. (1982) 'Household work strategies', paper presented at the International Sociological Association conference in Mexico City; mimeo, Nuffield College, Oxford.

GILBERT, G. N., BURROWS, R. and POLLERT, A. (eds.) (1991) *Fordism and Flexibiity: Divisions and Change* (London: Macmillan).

GINN, J. and ARBER, S. (1991) 'Gender, class and income inequality in late life', *British Journal of Sociology*, vol. 42, no. 3, pp. 369–96.

GINSBURG, N. (1979) *Class, Capital and Social Policy* (London and Basingstoke: Macmillan).

GLICK, I. O, WEISS, R. S. and PARKES, C. M. (1974) *The First Year of Bereavement* (New York: John Wiley and Sons).

GOFFMAN, E. (1963) *Asylums*, (Harmondsworth: Penguin).

GOLDTHORPE, J. (1983) 'Women and class analysis: in defence of the conventional view', *Sociology*, vol. 17, no. 4, pp. 465–488.

GOODE, W. (1963) *World Revolution and Family Patterns* (New York: Oxford University Press).

GOODIN, R. and LE GRAND, J. (1987) *Not Only The Poor* (London: Allen & Unwin).

GORDON, C. (1988) 'The myth of family care. The elderly in the early 1930s', LSE Centre for Economic and Related Disciplines, Discussion Paper 29.

GORDON, T. (1990) *Feminist Mothers* (Basingstoke: Macmillan).

GOWLER, D. and LEGGE, K. (1982) 'Dual-worker families', in R.N. Rapoport., M.P. Fogarty and R. Rapoport, (eds.), *Families in Britain* (London: Routledge & Kegan Paul), pp. 138–158.

GRAHAM, H. (1983) 'Caring: A labour of love', in J. Finch and D. Groves, (eds.), *A Labour of Love: Women, Work and Caring* (London: Routledge & Kegan Paul).

GRAHAM, H. (1984) *Women, Health and the Family* (Brighton: Wheatsheaf).

GRAHAM, H. (1987) 'Women's poverty and caring', in C. Glendinning and J. Millar (eds.), *Women and Poverty in Britain* (Brighton: Wheatsheaf) pp. 221–40.

GRAY, P. G. and BELTRAM, A. (1950) 'The housing requirements of special groups. Older people. An inquiry carried out in Hamilton in 1950 for the Department of Health for Scotland', *The Social Survey*, Report 162.

GREEN, E. and HEBRON, S. (1988) 'Leisure and male partners', in E. Wimbush and M. Talbot (eds.), *Relative Freedoms* (Milton Keynes: Open University Press) pp. 37–47.

GREEN, H. (1988) *Informal Carers*, OPCS Series GHS, no. 15, Supplement A, OPCS (London: HMSO).

GREEN, H. (1990) 'Survey of informal carers: Measurement problems', *Survey Methodology Bulletin*, no. 26, OPCS, pp. 17–25.

GREVEN, P. (1970) *Four Generations: Population, Land and Family in Colonial Andover, Massachusetts* (Ithaca, New York: Cornell University Press).

GRIFFITHS REPORT (1988) *Community Care: Agenda for Action* (London: HMSO).

GRIMM, S. (1985) 'Aktuelle Entwicklungstendenzen familialer und schu-
lischer Sozialisation in der Bundesrepublik Deutschland', in S. Hradil (ed.),
Sozialstruktur im Umbruch (Opladen: Westdeutscher Verlag) pp. 287–304.

GROß, H., THOBEN, C. and BAUER, F. (1989) Arbeitszeit '89 (Düsseldorf:
MAGS Nordrhein-Westfahlen (ed.)).

HAKIM, C. (1980) 'Census reports as documentary evidence: the census com-
mentaries 1801–1951', *Sociological Review*, vol. 28, no. 3, pp. 551–80.

HAKIM, C. (1989): 'Workforce restructuring, social insurance coverage and
the black economy', *Journal of Social Policy*, vol. 18, no. 4, pp. 471–503.

HARDEY, M. (1989) 'Lone parents and the home', in G. Allan and G. Crow
(eds.). *Home and Family* (Basingstoke: Macmillan) pp. 122–40.

HAREVEN, T. (1982) *Family Time and Industrial Time* (New York: Cambridge
University Press).

HAREVEN, T. (1984) 'Themes in the historical development of the family',
in R. D. Parke (ed.), *Review of Child Development Research, vol. 7, The
Family* (Chicago and London: University of Chicago Press) pp. 137–78.

HARRIS, C. C. (1983) *The Family and Industrial Society* (London: George
Allen & Unwin).

HART, N. (1976) *When Marriage Ends* (London: Tavistock).

HASKEY, J. (1986) 'One-parent families in Great Britain', *Population Trends,*
vol. 45 (London: HMSO), pp. 5-13.

HASKEY, J. (1989a) 'Current prospects for the proportion of marriages ending
in divorce', *Population Trends*, vol. 55 (London: HMSO).

HASKEY, J. (1989b) 'One-parent families and their children in Great Britain'
Population Trends, vol. 55 (London: HMSO) pp. 27–33.

HASKEY, J. and KIERNAN, K. (1989) 'Cohabitation in Great Britain –
characteristics and estimated numbers of cohabiting partners', *Population
Trends,* vol. 58 (London: HMSO), pp. 23–32.

HINRICHS, K. (1990) 'Irregular employment patterns and the loose net of
social security: some findings on the West German case' (Bremen: Centre
for Social Policy Research) ZeS-Working Paper, 7/90.

HIPGRAVE, T. (1982) 'Lone fatherhood', in L. McKee and M. O'Brien (eds.)
The Father Figure (London: Tavistock) pp. 171–83.

HOEM, B. and HOEM, J. M. (1988) 'The Swedish family: aspects of contemporary developments', *Journal of Family Issues*, vol. 9 no. 3, pp. 397–424.

HOFF, A. and SCHOLZ, J. (1985) 'Späte Väter, arrivierte Umsteiger und
andere Männer an der Peripherie der Arbeitsgesellschaft', in T. Schmid (ed.),
Das Ende der starren Zeit (Berlin: Wagenbach) pp. 72–96.

HOFFMANN-NOWOTNY, H.-J. (1988) 'Ehe und Familie in der modernen
Gesellschaft, *Aus politik und Zeitgeschichte'*, B13/88, pp. 3–13.

HOLME, A. (1985) *Housing and Young Families* (London: Routledge & Kegan
Paul).

HOWES, D. (1984) 'Residential mobility and family separation in retirement',
Kings College London, Department of Geography Occasional Paper, 22.

HOWIESON, C. (1990) 'Beyond the gate: work experience and part-time work
among secondary-school pupils in Scotland', *British Journal of Education
and Work*, vol. 3, no. 3, pp. 49–61.

HUMPHRIES, J. (1977) 'Class struggle and the persistence of the working
class family', *Cambridge Journal of Economics*, vol.1, no.3, pp. 241–58.

HUNT, A. (1978) *The Elderly at Home. A Study of People Aged Sixty-Five and Over and Living in the Community in England in 1976* (London: OPCS Social Survey Division).

HUNT, E. H. (1989) 'Paupers and pensioners: past and present', *Ageing and Society*, vol. 9, pp. 407–30.

HUTSON, S. and JENKINS, R. (1989) *Taking the Strain* (Milton Keynes: Open University Press).

ILLSLEY, R. and THOMPSON, B. (1961) 'Women from broken homes', *Sociological Review*, vol.9, pp. 27–54.

INGHAM, M. (1984) *Men* (London: Century Publishing).

INGLEBY, R. (1984) 'Consent orders', *New Law Journal*, p. 1024.

JACKSON, B. (1982) 'Single-parent families', in R.N. Rapoport, M.P. Fogarty and R. Rapoport (eds.) *Families in Britain* (London: Routledge & Kegan Paul), pp. 159–77.

JAMIESON, L. and TOYNBEE, C. (1990) 'Shifting patterns of parental authority 1900–1980', in H. Carr and L. Jamieson (eds.), *Politics of Everyday Life: Continuity and Change in Work and the Family* (Basingstoke: Macmillan).

JENKIN, P. (1977) Speech to 1977 Conservative Party Conference, quoted by A. Cooke and B. Campbell, *Sweet Freedom* (London: Pan Books, 1982).

JOHNSON, P. AND WEBB, S. (1989) 'Counting people with low incomes: the impact of recent changes in offical statistics', Institute of Fiscal Studies Commentary, No. 14, London.

JONES, D. C. (1934) *The Social Survey of Merseyside*, vol. III (Liverpool: University Press of Liverpool).

JONES, G. (1987) 'Leaving the parental home: an analysis of early housing careers', *Journal of Social Policy*, vol. 16, no. 1, pp. 49–74.

JONES, G. (1988) 'Integrating process and structure in the concept of youth: a case for secondary analysis', *Sociological Review*, vol. 36, no. 4, pp. 706–32.

JONES, G. (1990) *Household Formation among Young Adults in Scotland*, Discussion Paper, 2 (Edinburgh: Scottish Homes).

JONES, G. (1991) 'The cost of living in the parental home', *Youth and Policy*, vol. 32, pp. 19–29.

KARN, V. and HENDERSON, J. (1983) 'Housing atypical households', in A.W. Franklin (ed.), *Family Matters* (Oxford: Pergamon) pp. 71–86.

KIERNAN, K. (1988) 'The British family', *Journal of Family Issues*, vol. 9 no. 3, pp. 298–316.

KIERNAN, K. and WICKS, M. (1990) *Family Change and Future Policy* (London: Family Policy Studies Centre).

KRUK, S. and WOLKIND, S. (1983) 'Single mothers and their children', in N. Madge (ed.), *Families at Risk* (London: Heinemann) pp. 119–40.

KURZ-SCHERF, I. (1987) 'Der 6-Stunden-Tag', in I. Kurz-Scherf and G. Breil (eds.), *Wem gehört die Zeit?* (Hamburg: VSA) pp. 300–305.

LACZKO, F., DALE, A., ARBER, S. and GILBERT, G. N. (1988) 'Early retirement in a period of high unemployment', *Journal of Social Policy*, vol. 17, no. 3, pp. 313–33.

LAING, R. D. and COOPER, D. G. (1964) *Reason and Violence: a Decade of Sartre's Philosophy, 1950–1960* (London: Tavistock).

LAING, R. D. and ESTERSON, A. (1964) *Sanity, Madness and the Family* (London: Tavistock).

LANDENBERGER, M. (1983) 'Arbeitszeitwünsche', Discussion Paper IIM/ LMP, 83–17 (Wissenschaftszentrum Berlin).

LASLETT, P. (1965) *The World we have Lost* (London: Methuen).

LASLETT, P. (1972) 'Introduction', in P. Laslett and R. Wall (eds.), *Household and Family in Past Time* (Cambridge: Cambridge University Press) pp. 1–89.

LAWSON, R. (1987) 'Social security and the division of welfare', in G. Causer (ed.), *Inside British Society* (Brighton: Wheatsheaf) pp. 77–97.

LEETE, R. (1978) 'One-parent families', *Population Trends*, vol. 13, pp. 4–9.

LEEUWEN, M. H. D. VAN (1986) 'Poor relief and paupers in pre-industrial Amsterdam c. 1800–1850', European University Colloquium Papers, Work and family in pre-industrial Europe (DOCIUE 26/86, Col.20).

LEONARD, D. (1980) *Sex and Generation* (London: Tavistock Publications).

LEONARD, D. and SPEAKMAN, M. A. (1986) 'Women in the family: companions or caretakers?', in V. Beechey and E. Whitelegg (eds.), *Women in Britain Today* (Milton Keynes: Open University Press) pp. 8–77.

LE PLAY, F. (1855, 1877–9) *Les ouvriers Europeens* (1st edition Paris; 2nd edition Tours: Alfred Mame et fils).

LEVINE, A., SOPER, E. and WRIGHT, E. O. (1987) 'The limits of micro explanation', *New Left Review*, no. 162, pp. 67–84.

LEWIS, J. (1984) *Women in England 1870–1950* (Brighton: Wheatsheaf).

LEWIS, J. (1986) 'Anxieties about the family', in M. Richards and P. Light (eds.), *Children of Social Worlds* (Cambridge: Polity) pp. 31–54.

LEWIS, J. and MEREDITH, B. (1988) *Daughters Who Care: Daughters Caring for Mothers at Home* (London: Routledge).

LEWIS, J. (1989) 'Lone parent families: politics and economics', *Journal of Social Policy*, vol. 18, no. 4, pp. 595–600.

LEYBOURNE, G. G. and WHITE, K. (1940) *Education and the Birth-rate: A Social Dilemma* (London: Jonathan Cape).

LIDDIARD, M. and HUTSON, S. (1990) 'Youth homelessness in Wales', in C. Wallace and M. Cross (eds), *Youth in Transition: the Sociology of Youth and Youth Policy* (London: Macmillan).

LITWAK, E. (1960a) 'Occupational mobility and extended family cohesion', *American Sociological Review*, vol. 25, pp. 9–21.

LITWAK, E. (1960b) 'Geographic mobility and extended family cohesion', *American Sociological Review*, vol. 25, pp. 385–394.

LUHMANN, N. (1986) *Ökologische Kommunikation* (Opladen: Westdeutscher Verlag).

MACDONALD, G. and PETTIT, P. (1981) *Semantics and Social Science* (London: Routledge & Kegan Paul).

MACFARLANE, A. (1978) *The Origins of English Individualism: The Family, Property and Social Transition* (Oxford: Basil Blackwell).

MACINTYRE, S. (1977) *Single and Pregnant* (London: Croom Helm).

McKEE, L. (1987) 'Households during unemployment: the resourcefulness of the unemployed', in J. Brannen and G. Wilson (eds.), *Give and Take in Families: Studies in Resource Distribution* (London: Allen & Unwin) pp. 96–116.

McLANAHAN, S. S., WEDMEYER, N. V. and ADELBERG, T. (1981)

'Network structure, social support and psychological well-being in the single-parent family', *Journal of Marriage and the Family*, vol. 43, pp. 601–12.

MACLEAN, M. (1987) 'Households after divorce', in J. Brannen and G. Wilson (eds.), *Give and Take in Families* (London: Allen & Unwin) pp. 42–55.

MACLENNAN, E., FITZ, J. and SULLIVAN, J. (1985) *Working Children* (London: Low Pay Unit).

McRAE, S. (1986) *Cross-Class Families* (Oxford: Clarendon Press).

MAIDMENT, S. (1984) *Child Custody and Divorce: The Law in Social Context* (London: Croom Helm).

MARSDEN, D. (1973) *Mothers Alone* (Harmondsworth: Penguin).

MARSDEN, D. and ABRAMS. S (1987) '"Liberators", "companions", "intruders" and "cuckoos in the nest": A sociology of caring relationships over the life cycle', in P. Allatt, T. Keil, A. Bryman and B. Bytheway (eds.), *Women and the Life Cycle* (London: Macmillan) pp. 192–207.

MARSH, C. (1986) 'Social class and occupation', in R. Burgess (ed.), *Key Variables in Social Investigation* (London: Routledge & Kegan Paul) pp. 123–52.

MARSH, C. (1991) *Hours of Work of Women and Men in Britain*, Equal Opportunities Commission (London: HMSO).

MEISSNER, M., HUMPHREYS, E. W., MEISS, S. and SCHEU, W. J. (1975) 'No exit for wives', *Canadian Review of Sociology and Anthropology*, vol. 12, no. 4, pp. 424–39.

MEYER, S. and SCHULZE, E. (1989) *Balancen des Glücks.* (München: Beck).

MILLAR, J. (1989) *Poverty and the Lone-parent Family* (Aldershot: Avebury).

MILLETT, K. (1969) *Sexual Politics* (New York: Doubleday).

MORRIS, L. (1990) *The Workings of the Household: A US-UK Comparison* (Cambridge: Polity Press).

MÜCKENBERGER, U. (1985) 'Die Krise des Normalarbeitsverhältnisses', *Zeitschrift für Sozialreform*, vol. 7, pp. 415–434, and vol. 8, pp. 457–475.

MURCH, M. (1987) *The Overlapping Family Jurisdiction of Magistrates' Courts and County Courts* (Bristol: Socio-Legal Centre for Family Studies, University of Bristol).

NALSON, J. S. (1968) *Mobility of Farm Families. A study of occupational and residential mobility in an upland area of England* (Manchester: Manchester University Press).

NATIONAL AUDIT OFFICE (1990) *Department of Social Security: Support for Lone Parent Families* (London: HMSO).

NEUBAUER, E. (1988) *Alleinerziehende Mütter und Väter – Eine Analyse der Gesamtsituation* (Stuttgart: Schriftenreihe des BMJFFG 170).

NISSEL, M. and BONNERJEA, L. (1982) *Family Care of the Handicapped Elderly: Who Pays?* (London: Policy Studies Institute).

NORRIS, P. (1987) *Politics and Sexual Equality* (Brighton: Wheatsheaf).

NOVAK, T. (1988) *Poverty and the State* (Milton Keynes: Open University Press).

NUFFIELD FOUNDATION (1947) *Old People. Report of a Survey Committee on the Problems of Ageing and the Care of Old People* (London: Nuffield Foundation).

OAKLEY, A. (1976) *Housewife* (Harmondsworth: Penguin).

OAKLEY, A. and OAKLEY, R. (1979) 'Sexism in official statistics', in J.

Irvine, I. Miles and J. Evans (eds.), *Demystifying Social Statistics* (London: Pluto Press) 172–198.

O'BRIEN, M. (1987) 'Patterns of kinship and friendship among lone fathers', in C. Lewis and M. O'Brien (eds.), *Reassessing Fatherhood*, (London: Sage) pp. 225–45.

OFFE, C. (1987) 'The Utopia of the zero-option', *Praxis International*, vol. 7, no. 1, pp. 1–24.

OFFE, C. (1990) 'Smooth consolidation in the West German welfare state' (Bremen: Centre for Social Policy Reserach) ZeS-Working Paper, 4/90.

OFFICE OF POPULATION CENSUSES AND SURVEYS. (1974) *Census of England and Wales, 1971: National Report* (London: HMSO).

OFFICE OF POPULATION CENSUSES AND SURVEYS (1986) OPCS Monitor FMI 86/2 (London: Government Statistical Service).

OFFICE OF POPULATION CENSUSES AND SURVEYS (1987) *General Household Survey, 1985* (London: HMSO).

OFFICE OF POPULATION CENSUSES AND SURVEYS (1988) *Marriage and Divorce Statistics, 1987* (London: HMSO).

OFFICE OF POPULATION CENSUSES AND SURVEYS (1989a) *Key Population and Fertility Statistics*, 1988 ((London: HMSO).

OFFICE OF POPULATION CENSUSES AND SURVEYS (1989b) *The General Household Survey, 1986* (London: HMSO).

OFFICE OF POPULATION CENSUSES AND SURVEYS (1989c) *OPCS Monitor*, SS 89/1 (London: Government Statistical Service).

OFFICE OF POPULATION CENSUSES AND SURVEYS (1989d) *Population Trends*, vol. 57 (London: HMSO).

OFFICE OF POPULATION CENSUSES AND SURVEYS (1990a) *Population Trends*, vol. 60 (London: HMSO).

OFFICE OF POPULATION CENSUSES AND SURVEYS (1990b) *Population Trends*, vol. 61 (London: HMSO).

OUVRIERS DES DEUX MONDES (1857–99) 1st and 2nd series.

PAGE, R. (1984) *Stigma* (London: Routledge & Kegan Paul).

PAHL, J. (1984) 'The allocation of money within the household', in M. Freeman (ed.), *State, Law and the Family* (London: Tavistock) pp. 36–50.

PAHL, J. (1989) *Money and Marriage* (London: Macmillan).

PAHL, R. E. (1984) *Divisions of Labour* (Oxford: Basil Blackwell).

PARKER, G. (1989) *A Study of Non-Elderly Spouse Carers* (University of York: Social Policy Research Unit).

PARSONS, T. (1949) 'The social structure of the family', in R. N. Ashen (ed.), *The Family* (New York, Hayner) pp. 241–74.

PENHALE, B. (1990) 'Households, families and fertility', *Longitudinal Study User Guide, no. 1*, May.

PIORE, M. J. and SABEL, C. F. (1984) *The Second Industrial Divide* (New York: Basic Books).

PLECK, J. H. (1985) *Working Wives/Working Husbands* (Beverley Hills: Sage).

POPAY, J., RIMMER, L. and ROSSITER, C. (1983) *One Parent Families* (London: Study Commission on the Family).

PÖSCHL, H. (1989) 'Formen des Zusammenlebens 1988', *Wirtschaft und Statistik*, vol. 10, pp. 627–34.

QURESHI, H. and WALKER, A. (1989) *The Caring Relationship; Elderly people and their families* (London: Macmillan).

REID, I. and WORMALD, E. (1982) *Sex Differences in Britain* (London: Grant McIntyre).

REID, M. G. (1934) *Economics of Household Production* (New York: John Wiley).

RENVOIZE, J. (1985) *Going Solo* (London: Routledge & Kegan Paul).

RIMMER, L. (1983) 'Changing family patterns', in A.W. Franklin (ed.), *Family Matters* (Oxford: Pergamon) pp. 11–18.

RIMMER, L. and WICKS, M. (1984) 'The family today', in E. Butterworth and D. Weir (eds), *The New Sociology of Modern Britain* (Glasgow: Fontana) pp. 33–42.

RITCHIE, P. (1989) 'Scottish Young People's Survey, Third Sweep of the 1983–1984 Cohort: Technical Report' (Edinburgh: Centre for Educational Sociology).

ROBERTS, K., DENCH, J. and RICHARDSON, D. (1987) *The Changing Structure of Youth Labour Markets* (London: Department of Employment).

ROEMER, J. E. (1982a) *A General Theory of Exploitation and Class* (Cambridge, Mass: Harvard University Press).

ROEMER, J. E. (1982b) 'Property relations vs. surplus value in Marxian exploitation' *Philosophy and Public Affairs*, vol. 11, no. 4, pp. 281–313.

ROEMER, J. E. (ed.). (1986) *Analytical Marxism* (Cambridge: Cambridge University Press).

ROLL, J. (1991) *The Benefit Family* (London: Family Policy Studies Centre Occasional Paper).

ROSSER, C. and HARRIS, C. (1965) *The Family and Social Change. A study of family and kinship in a South Wales town* (London: Routledge & Kegan Paul).

SAHLINS, M. (1965) 'On the sociology of primitive exchange', in M. Branton (ed.), *The Relevance of Models in Social Anthropology* (London: Tavistock).

SCHMIDT, V. H. (1988) 'Arbeitszeit und neue Technologien II: Regelungsbestand und Regelungsbedarfe' (Bielefeld: AfS-Diskussions- und Arbeitspapiere 88/1) reprinted in Berger *et al.* (1991) Chapter 2.

SCHOFIELD, R. (1970) 'Age specific mobility in an eighteenth century rural English parish', *Annales de demographie historique*, pp. 261–74.

SECCOMBE, W. (1974) 'The housewife and her labour under capitalism', *New Left Review*, vol. 83.

SHANAS, E., TOWNSEND, P., WEDDERBURN, D., FRIIS, H., MILHOF, P. and STEHOUWER, J. (eds.) (1968) *Old People in Three Industrial Societies* (London: Routledge & Kegan Paul).

SHARPE, S. (1984) *Double Identity* (Harmondsworth: Penguin).

SHELDON, J. H. (1948) *The Social Medicine of Old Age. Report of an inquiry in Wolverhampton* (London: Oxford University Press for Nuffield Foundation).

SILVER, C. B. (1982) *Frederic Le Play on Family World and Social Change* (Chicago: University of Chicago Press).

SIXSMITH, A. J. (1986) 'Independence and home in later life', in C. Phillipson, M. Bernard and P. Strang (eds.), *Dependency and Interdependency in Old*

Age – Theoretical Perspectives and Policy Alternatives (London: Croom Helm).

SMART, C. (1984) *The Ties that Bind: Law in Marriage and the Reproduction of Patriarchal Relations* (London: Routledge & Kegan Paul).

SMELSER, N. J. (1967) *Social Change in the Industrial Revolution* (London: Routledge & Kegan Paul).

SMITH, R. (1981) 'Fertility, economy, and household formation in England over three centuries', *Population and Development Review*, vol. 7, no. 4, pp. 595–622.

SMITH, R. (1984) 'The structural dependency of the elderly as a recent development: some sceptical historical thoughts', *Ageing and Society*, vol. 4, pp. 409–28.

SMITHERS, A. and ROBINSON, P. (1989) *Increasing Participation in Higher Education* (London: BP Educational Services).

SOKOLL, T. (1988) 'Household and family among the poor: the case of three Essex communities in the late eighteenth and early nineteenth centuries', Ph.D., Cambridge .

SPIEGEL, Y. (1977) *The Grief Process* (Nashville: Parthenon).

STEINER, H. (1987) 'Capitalism, justice and equal starts', *Social Philosophy and Policy*, vol. 5, pp. 49–71.

STREECK, W. (1987) 'The uncertainties of management in the management of uncertainties: employers, labour relations and industrial adjustment in the 1980s', *Work, Employment and Society*, vol. 1, no. 3, pp. 281–309.

SUSSMAN, M. B. (1959) 'The isolated nuclear family: fact or fiction?', *Social Problems*, vol. 4, pp. 333–40.

SUSSMAN, M. B. (1965) 'Relationships of adult children with their parents in the United States', in E. Shanas and G. Streib (eds.), *Social Structure and the Family: Generational relations* (Englewood Cliffs, New Jersey: Prentice-Hall) pp. 62–92.

SUSSMAN, M. B. and BURCHINAL, L. (1962) 'Kin family network: unheralded structure in current conceptualization of family functioning', *Marriage and Family Living*, vol. 24, pp. 231–40.

TAYLOR, M. (1987) *The Possibility of Cooperation* (Cambridge: Cambridge University Press).

TAYLOR, M. and WARD, H. (1982) 'Chickens, whales and lumpy goods', *Political Studies*, vol. xxx, no. 3, pp. 350–70.

THANE, P. (1988) 'The growing burden of an ageing population?', *Journal of Public Policy*, vol. 7, no. 4, pp. 373–87.

THOMAS, G. (1947) 'The employment of older persons. An enquiry carried out in mid-1945 for the Industrial Health Research Board of the Medical Research Council', *The Social Survey*, NS 60/2, January.

THOMSON, D. (1984) 'The decline of social security: falling State support for the elderly since early Victorian times', *Ageing and Society*, vol. 4, pp. 451–82.

THOMSON, D. (1989) 'The Welfare State and generation conflict: winners and losers', in P. Johnson, C. Conrad and D. Thomson (eds.), *Workers versus Pensioners: Intergenerational justice in an ageing world* (Manchester University Press) pp. 33–56.

TODD, J. (1987) 'Changing the definition of a household', *Survey Methodology Bulletin*, no. 20, January, pp. 34–8.

TOWNSEND, P. (1957) *The Family Life of Old People. An inquiry in East London* (London: Routledge & Kegan Paul).

TOWNSEND, P. (1962) *The Last Refuge: a survey of residential institutions and homes for the aged in England and Wales* (London: Routledge & Kegan Paul).

TOWNSEND, P. (1979) *Poverty in the United Kingdom* (London: Allen Lane).

UNGERSON, C. (1987) *Policy is Personal: Sex, gender and informal care* (London: Tavistock).

UNITED STATES DEPARTMENT OF COMMERCE, BUREAU OF THE CENSUS (1989) *Statistical Abstract of the United States 1989*, 109th edn (Washington, D.C.).

VAUGHAN, D. (1988) *Uncoupling* (London: Methuen).

VERBRUGGE, L. M. (1984a) 'Longer life but worsening health? Trends in health and mortality of middle-aged and older persons', *Milbank Memorial Fund Quarterly/Health and Society*, vol. 62, pp. 475–519.

VERBRUGGE, L. M. (1984b) 'A health profile of older women with comparisons to older men', *Research on Aging*, vol. 6, pp. 291–322.

VERBRUGGE, L. M. (1989a) 'Gender, aging and health', in K. S. Markides (ed.), *Aging and Health* (Beverly Hills: Sage).

VERBRUGGE, L. M. (1989b) 'The dynamics of population aging and health, in S. Lewis (ed.), *Ageing and Health* (Michigan: Lewis Publishers).

WALBY, S. (1989) 'Theorising patriarchy', *Sociology*, vol. 23, no. 2, pp. 213–34.

WALCZAK, Y. (1988) *He and She* (London: Routledge).

WALKER, A. (1981) 'Community care and the elderly in Great Britain: theory and practice', *International Journal of Health Services*, vol. 11, no. 4, pp. 541–57.

WALL, R. (1982) 'Regional and temporal variations in the structure of the British household since 1851', in T. Barker and M. Drake (eds.), *Population and Society in Britain 1850–1980* (London: Batsford) pp. 62–99.

WALL, R. (1983a) 'Introduction', in R. Wall, J. Robin and P. Laslett (eds.), *Family Forms in Historic Europe* (Cambridge: Cambridge University Press) pp. 1–63.

WALL, R. (1983b) 'The household: demographic and economic change in England 1650–1970', in R. Wall, J. Robin and P. Laslett (eds.), *Family Forms in Historic Europe* (Cambridge: Cambridge University Press) pp. 493–512.

WALLACE, C. (1987) 'Between the family and the state: young people in transition', in C. Wallace and M. Cross (eds.), *The Social World of the Young Unemployed* (London: Policy Studies Institute).

WALTERS, P. and DEX, S. (1991) 'Feminisation of the Labour Force in Britain and France' in S. Arber and N. Gilbert (eds.), *Women and Working Lives: Divisions and Change* (London: Macmillan) pp. 89–103.

WATERS, M. (1989) 'Patriarchy and viriarchy: an exploration and reconstruction of concepts of masculine domination', *Sociology*, vol. 23, no. 2, pp. 193–211.

WARD, H. (1987) 'The risks of a reputation for toughness', *British Journal of Political Science*, vol. 17, pp. 23–52.

WARNES, A. M. (1986) 'The residential mobility histories of parents and children, and relationships to present proximity and social integration', *Environment and Planning A*, vol. 18, pp. 1581–94.

WATSON, S. (1989) *Accommodating Inequality: Gender and Housing* (Sydney: Unwin Hyman).

WATSON, S. with AUSTERBERRY, H. (1986) *Housing and Homelessness* (London: Routledge & Kegan Paul).

WENGER, G. C. (1984) *The Supportive Network: Coping with Old Age* (London: Allen & Unwin).

WERNER, B. (1987) 'Fertility statistics from birth registrations in England and Wales, 1837–1987', *Population Trends*, vol. 68, pp. 4–10.

WEST, P. (1984) 'The family, the welfare state and community care: political rhetoric and public attitudes', *Journal of Social Policy*, vol. 13, no. 4, pp. 417–46.

WHITE, M. (1983) *Long-Term Unemployed and Labour Markets* (London: Policy Studies Institute) paper no. 622.

WICKS, M. (1990) 'Child maintenance – lone parent lessons from Australia', *Family Policy Bulletin*, 8, p. 6.

WIESENTHAL, H. (1986) 'Kriterien für eine sozialverträgliche', Arbeitszeitgestaltung, epd. 51/86, pp. 33–8.

WIESENTHAL, H. (1987) *Strategie und Illusion* (Frankfurt: Campus).

WILLIS, P. (1977) *Learning to Labour* (Farnborough: Saxon House).

WILSON, E. (1977) *Women and the Welfare State* (London: Tavistock).

WILSON, W. (1985) *The Truly Disadvantaged* (Chicago University Press).

WINYARD, S. (1987) 'Divided Britain' in A. Walker and C. Walker (eds.), *The Growing Divide: A Social Audit 1979–1987* (London: Child Poverty Action Group).

WOOLF, S. (1986) *The Poor in Western Europe in the Eighteenth and Nineteenth Centuries* (London: Methuen).

WRIGHT, ERIK OLIN (1985) *Classes* (London: Verso).

WRIGHT F. (1983) 'Single carers, employment, housework and caring', in Finch, J. and Groves, D. (eds.), *A Labour of Love: Women, Work and Caring* (London: Routledge & Kegan Paul) pp. 89–105.

WYNN, M. (1964) *Fatherless Families* (London: Michael Joseph).

WYNN, M. (1972) *Family Policy* (Harmondsworth: Penguin).

YANS-MCLAUGHLIN, V. (1972) *Family and Community: Italian Immigrants in Buffalo, 1880–1930* (Ithaca, New York: Cornell University Press).

YEANDLE, S. (1984) *Women's Working Lives* (London: Routledge & Kegan Paul).

YOUNG, M. and WILLMOTT, P. (1957) *Family and Kinship in East London* (London: Routledge & Kegan Paul).

YOUNG, M. and WILLMOTT, P. (1973) *The Symmetrical Family* (Harmondsworth: Penguin).

YUDKIN, S. and HOLME, A. (1963) *Working Mothers and their Children* (London: Michael Joseph).

ZAPF, W., BREUER, S., HAMPEL, J., KRAUSE, P., MOHR, H.-P. and WIEGAND, E. (1987) *Individualisierung und Sicherheit* (München: Beck).

ZIEGLER, R., (1983) 'Die Struktur von Freundes- und Bekannten kreisen', in F. Heckmann, and P. Winter (eds.), 21. *Deutscher-Soziologentag 1982, Beiträge der Sektions- und Ad hoc-Gruppen* (Opladen: Westdeutscher Verlag) pp. 684–8.

Author Index

Subject Index